# ANTHRAX: A HISTORY

ALSO BY RICHARD M. SWIDERSKI

*Multiple Sclerosis Through History
and Human Life* (McFarland, 1998)

# ANTHRAX: A HISTORY

Richard M. Swiderski

McFarland & Company, Inc., Publishers
*Jefferson, North Carolina, and London*

LIBRARY OF CONGRESS CATALOGUING-IN-PUBLICATION DATA

Swiderski, Richard M.
    Anthrax : a history / Richard M. Swiderski.
        p.      cm.
    Includes bibliographical references and index.

    ISBN 0-7864-1891-5 (softcover : 50# alkaline paper)

    1. Anthrax—History.    I. Title.
    RA644.A6S935    2004
    616.9'56—dc22                                            2004013462

British Library cataloguing data are available

Manufactured in the United States of America

*On the cover: Bacillus anthracis* spores (Public Health Image
Library, Centers for Disease Control and Prevention)

*McFarland & Company, Inc., Publishers*
  *Box 611, Jefferson, North Carolina 28640*
    *www.mcfarlandpub.com*

# Contents

v

# Contents

# Preface

In the late nineteenth century some publishers felt obliged to inform their readers that the paper in their books was entirely wood-based. There was a tacit understanding that this meant no anthrax spores from rags used to make the paper would be lurking in the pages. Such fears have waned with the arrival of modernization, only to be replaced with others about new manifestations of anthrax—real, imagined or projected. I wrote this book with this reassurance in mind: I am conveying thoughts and ideas about anthrax but not the spores themselves.

This book and the research on which it is based were inspired by curiosity and a feeling of ignorance about the nature of anthrax as it appeared in the news in late 2001. The word "anthrax" had long been an underground presence I never looked for, using any of the tools available to me.

Prior to October 2001, I had no professional involvement—medical, scientific or military—with bacteria or the measures taken to curtail them. Then the spores began to work on my imagination. Rather than try to collect and observe spores, I began to look for words which name them. I found that they have a history, both the words and the spores.

I am at present an investigator for the state of California of alleged civil rights violations by employers. I never encountered anthrax as an occupational disease in any workplaces I visited or reviewed. The 2001 anthrax mailings (the ones actually containing anthrax spores) made me aware that anthrax was at one time an industrial hazard for woolsorters, ragpickers, tanners and a number of other kinds of workers. Now it had become an occupational disease of mailsorters as well. How could it reemerge, kill some workers and then vanish again? Though the anthrax retreated, that question remained. There was no shortage of expertise and reference material exhibited in public media to help understand it. My work toward an answer became this book.

What passing bells for these who die as cattle?
—Wilfred Owen, Requiem

Do not blame God for creating the tiger.
Thank him for not giving her wings.
—Ethiopian proverb

The survival of spores for 30 seconds at 400°
Centigrade is the highest recorded temperature
for survival of organisms known to us.
—Lamanna and Mallette 1965: 483

# Introduction:
# The Spore in the Machine

Anthrax has evolved to exist in the today's environment of fear—the fear of terrorism, of possible biological attack, of "weapons of mass destruction." A model microbe from its first discovery, it underwent a cultural adaptation primarily under the control of humans. Long before October 2001, when inhalational anthrax killed postal workers and random victims in the U.S., its spores had entered the machinery and buildings of civilization, the skin and lungs of workers and residents and the imagination of all concerned. The disease and the bacteria which cause it are always just that distance away, almost completely a symbol, but a symbol which actually can kill, the ideal terrorist environment. Anthrax is not contagious like smallpox or plague, but its spores can be made to carry either of them, or both.

During the nineteenth century, scientists and doctors discovered that the causative agent of what had long been called anthrax, a malignant pustule afflicting humans, was also a causative agent of murrain, a disease of cows, sheep and camels that could cause them to bleed black blood and die so suddenly that they might be dead standing. People who came into direct contact with the meat, hides and hair of infected animals developed black skin lesions. People who ate the meat of these animals also became sick and died, it was assumed, of the poisons the animals' flesh contained. The human pustules and the blood of animals afflicted with murrain contained particles of the same shape, which multiplied in cultures like a microbe but did not move at all when seen under the microscope.

It was not long before a respiratory infection of workers in textile mills was also found to be caused by the same microbe, *Bacillus anthracis*.

Eventually infections suffered by a great variety of users of animal products (ragpickers, gardeners spreading bone meal, craft workers in imported goat hair, purchasers of bongo drums) were attributed to this bacillus.

These discoveries consolidated a range of disparate effects in the word "anthrax," a substance powerful for its ability to decimate herds of cattle and as a weapon in warfare. As anthrax lost its ability to affect animals and animal product industries, it gained an effect upon humans through its presence in bombs, military production facilities and the mails. What was meant by "anthrax" when it was diagnosed on George Washington's thigh is different from what Mao Zedong meant by "anthrax" when he accused Americans of dropping it on Chinese villages during the Korean War. Washington's doctors were referring to a human skin eruption which might also be called a "carbuncle" while Mao, using a Chinese character pair that is the equivalent of the English word "anthrax," was writing of a germ warfare weapon. The word "anthrax" has not always been the word of power it is today, when written on an envelope it can cause a building to be evacuated and the sender, if identified, to be charged with a crime.

The long list of writers who actually used the word "anthrax"— from Hippocrates to Voltaire to Anton Chekhov and Rudyard Kipling— did not use it as we do today. Prior to the twentieth century and its wars anthrax was a nuisance and a source of economic hardship but not a threat and a terror. Sighting backward from our present sophistication, it is difficult to locate plagues and eruptions we can be sure were caused by the bacillus. There are many histories of anthrax.

Anthrax is a word, a disease, a bacillus, a spore, an explanation and a threat.

As a word in Classical Greek it stood for charcoal burning red on black, a gem with that coloring, a dye, and a skin eruption including all these features.

The charcoal left dust which could affect the skin and create a plague passing between animals and humans. The elements of anthrax are visible in Biblical plague accounts, and it retained these properties together and separately throughout its history. The signs of anthrax in the past develop out of present models. Anthrax history is a number of disparate components that organize and reorganize past pieces into the contemporary act. Yet the relations among the components suggest a single object.

Anthrax only became a disease when there was enough experience on record to notice that the red-to-black carbuncles spread from one afflicted skin to another, and could cause death. The bacillus was discovered, by examination of diseased blood and tissue in the carbuncle as well as in the enlarged spleen, lung bleeding and a cardinal's cap on the brain resulting from systemic infection where no skin eruptions occurred.

The bacillus, fragile in itself, became a spore, and the spore could last and penetrate where no bacillus could survive, producing new germs where the conditions were right. The spore explained the sudden sickness and death of workers in textile plants, papermills and tanneries who usually died slow deaths.

From the spore came a weapon and the threat of its use, which returned to the word, now, associated with other threats, a political device.

Like mice, rats and dogs, the anthrax bacillus would have been a success story without humans. More like mice and rats, the bacillus accompanies humans, afflicts us and has been domesticated for medical and military purposes. With humans and their herds of domesticated animals, anthrax exceeded its localized, earthbound, periodic proliferation, and became an epidemic disease. It may have participated in the epidemics of other diseases.

Humans made it a disease of humans alone, a disease of clothes, buildings and even potentially of cities, no longer requiring the animal substrate. To preserve ourselves against the threat, humans created the logic of vaccines, an immune tug of war between protection and affliction. Out of this conflict a new threat arose, completely independent of the bacillus and the spore, but dependent again upon the word. This book begins with the word.

# 1

# Three Anthraxes

About six weeks after his inauguration as first president of the United States, in the middle of June 1789, George Washington developed "a very large and painful tumor" (as he described it in a letter) on his left thigh. Accompanied by a lingering and incapacitating fever, the tumor reduced Washington's ability to meet the demands of his office.

Dr. Samuel Bard, and his father Dr. John Bard, two of the most prominent physicians in New York City, where the federal government offices were then located, diagnosed Washington's condition as "an anthrax." The doctors Bard recommended surgery, and an anecdote preserved in the biography of Samuel Bard has the elder doctor urging his son to "cut away—deeper and deeper still, don't be afraid, you see how well he bears it." Washington survived both the surgery and the long recovery, and of course lived to serve two terms as president.

Guba and Chase, who published an account of the president's anthrax in the aftermath of the 2001 anthrax attacks and worldwide scares, are skeptical of identifying this carbuncle with the bioterrorism agent. Washington had also lived through a smallpox infection and had made plans to immunize soldiers possibly faced with disease attacks by their British adversaries. It is tempting to see Washington at the very beginning of the American state fighting off the same invisible enemies, anthrax and smallpox, that Americans confront much later.

The contemporary description of Washington's tumor is too limited to conclude that it was caused by *Bacillus anthracis*. The bacillus causes a hideous but not very painful skin eruption, and Washington's own description may disqualify anthrax. Yet Dr. Bard's diagnosis, and his recommendation of extensive surgery, would argue for the bacillus.

In an age of extensive daily skin contact with animals and their products, some of which might contain anthrax spores, physicians knew the tumor and its likely systemic effects. Several decades later Samuel Bard's younger colleague David Hosack would publish an account (1812) of an anthrax successfully treated by a technique used even before Ambroise Paré in the sixteenth century learned it from barber-surgeons: draining and irrigation of the anthrax with clean water. But the Bards evidently thought that the chief executive's anthrax called for firmer, more decisive measures.

During his exile in England, Karl Marx was much troubled by carbuncles. On February 13, 1866, he wrote to Friedrich Engels that he was "lying fallow because a vicious brute of a carbuncle" had grown on his left thigh. In a subsequent letter he described carving away with a knife at this and another boil that had erupted.

On January 11, 1868, Marx wrote a jocular letter to his correspondent, the Berlin doctor Kugelmann, who had questioned the competence of English and French physicians: "If you think they cannot distinguish anthrax (carbuncle) from furuncle, particularly here in England, the land of carbuncles, which is actually a proletarian illness."

The carbuncle he referred to with the ancient word "anthrax" (in the original German) is a bacterial skin infection that could have been precipitated by any of the inflammatory particulates in the coal-smoke polluted urban air, held against skin not frequently washed by clothing itself unlaundered. The "carbo" of "carbuncle" in fact stands for "coal," which is also one of the original meanings of "anthrax." The French *charbon* means both "anthrax eruption" and "coal" as well as "carbon." By Marx's time the coal-black lesion may have been precipitated by the coal that named it. The bacteria needed some abrasion to enter the skin.

Distinguishing carbuncles from furuncles, a different-appearing skin eruption with the same cause, was possible only for those who suffered from both. They were a proletarian discomfort, because the working class in their conditions of labor and manner of life were situated to develop such infections with great frequency.

Carbuncles may have been called "anthrax" but they weren't always caused by anthrax bacteria. Staphylococcus and streptococcus bacteria, which are often able to proliferate in a scratch on the skin, were also a frequent cause of carbuncles, furuncles, boils, ulcers and pustules that afflicted people under the darkening urban sky. The products of these infections are called "anthrax" from their appearance and not from their cause.

If the spores carried by Washington's horse made their way onto Marx's skin it would have been from sitting on horsehair furniture produced at the time. Marx associated horseback riding with the military and the landed gentry, and Washington was a member of both. Sitting for long hours on the transposed hair of horses in the furniture of the

British Museum and London apartments was the work of urban scholars and political organizers like Marx.

Marx sat at one remove from Washington in the address of bacteria to the breached skin. An entire layer of industrial processes separated their two situations, yet they both suffered from anthrax entering the skin through scratches and they both cut it away. They both were like anyone else situated on horses or furniture in their time, vulnerable to anthrax and knowledgable of what to do when it appeared.

On February 28, 2002, a worker at a laboratory in Texas cut a bump on his right jaw while shaving. The cut bled briefly, then became itchy and irritated. The next day the worker helped a co-worker move vials in which the co-worker had placed samples of anthrax bacteria removed from blood agar plates, where it was being grown for tests. The co-worker handed the vials to the worker from storage in a biological safety cabinet. Not wearing gloves, the worker received the vials and placed them in a freezer.

During the next two or three days the worker's facial wound increased in size and developed a scab. He had swelling in his neck and a low-grade fever. A swab was taken from the area of the skin infection, and with a diagnosis of cutaneous anthrax being likely, the worker was placed on a course of antibiotics. When the swab sample tested positive for *B. anthracis,* the man was admitted to the hospital and treated with intravenous ciprofloxacin and doxycycline. A radiograph of his chest showed that the mediastinum, the tissue between the lungs, had expanded as would be expected in anthrax infections, and the sample culture was susceptible to the treating antibiotics. The worker's condition improved under treatment and he was discharged on March 9. No one else in his workplace showed signs of an infection.

An industrial hygienist sampled the work environment and found all surfaces negative for anthrax spores except the tops of the vials the worker had handled without gloves. Usually the workers decontaminated all surfaces of their work area with bleach, known to kill anthrax spores, but the vials were an exception. Workers sprayed them with isopropyl alcohol instead of bleach because bleach dislodged the labels. The path of transmission was clear, from vial top contaminated with active spores to bare hand to nick in the jaw skin. The workers then switched to using a type of label not dislodged by bleach.

Washington and Marx may or may not have harbored anthrax bacilli in their skin eruptions. The unnamed lab worker most likely did, and he did not have them removed by surgery. They were eliminated from his system by antibiotics. Though he was far removed from the world of animals in his twentieth century Laboratory Response Network Level B facility, the anthrax spores still penetrated his skin, germinated and multiplied. The worlds of Washington and Marx were still present.

# 2

# Woolsorters and Ragpickers

Early in his medical career, Nicolas Fournier was called to seek the basis of the *peste de Marseille* (1720–22), which likely was bubonic plague. Back at his hospital in Dijon, and in consultation with other physicians, Fournier recognized other types of skin lesions that resembled the buboes he saw in Marseilles but were not contagious in the same way. Over the course of his career he followed the medical practice of his time and compiled his observed cases into a classification scheme (published in 1769). From his observations in villages around Montpellier, Fournier was able to distinguish clinically different appearances of various types of charbon, related to plague, smallpox, furuncles and scorpion bites. He recorded the desperate reaction of the villagers when they saw a skin condition even slightly evocative of plague: isolation of the victim under guard until he died.

*Charbon spontané* was a black skin lesion peasants working in the fields developed in summer weather as the result of exposure to exhalations from waste matter in the ground. *Charbon contagieux* came in two forms, an external lesion or carbuncle and an internal form that quickly killed the victim.

*Charbon contagieux* was caused by contact with fur, hides and meat. Fournier castigated unscrupulous shepherds and butchers for selling to unsuspecting victims the meat of animals that had died of *charbon*. He also observed that *charbon contagieux* appeared on the arms, hands and faces of the laborers in factories of Montpellier, where domestic wool was woven into profitable blankets. He speculated that the same infectious element resided in both the meat and the fur of the animals, but he did not speculate on why some died of internal *charbon* without showing external lesions, he only distinguished them from each other.

A hundred years later, in Walpole, Massachusetts, Dr. Silas Stone treated a number of patients who had come to him with cutaneous lesions. He described as "malignant pustules," dark red, dark purple, purplish-black and black. He made his diagnosis only from written typologies, not having seen this rare affliction before. Six of the eight patients under his care over a period of fourteen months developed gastrointestinal and chest (mediastinal) symptoms, and two of them went into delirium with apparent meningitis and died.

Tinctures of iodine, iron and quinine applied to the original surface lesions did not reduce them, nor did they prevent fever and other symptoms from emerging. Stone noted in the case report he sent to the *Boston Medical and Surgical Journal* that all the patients had been exposed to animal hair or dirt from a local processing plant. He theorized that the cause of the pustule outbreak was "a specific poison, not simply putrescent animal matter."

Dr. Stone died in 1869, and he was succeeded by his son, also a doctor and named Silas. The "Walpole anthrax epidemic," as local historian Guy J. Ciannavei called it, extended from 1864 to 1872 and, he estimates, may have affected twice as many men as Stone counted. From records of the local Catholic parish, to which all the victims belonged, it appears that the afflicted workers had contact with hides imported from Russia to supply hair to make mattresses and curled hair pieces. Town mortality records list the occupations of several of the victims as "hair puller." The cause of death in six of the seven cases was listed as "charbon" and "malignant pustule," in one case as "internal malignant pustule." There was no word on the condition of those who slept on the mattresses or wore the hair pieces produced in the factory.

The use of the phrase "malignant pustule" in the records of the Walpole deaths may reflect the effort of the English physician and epidemiologist William Budd to make the diagnosis better known. Budd collected descriptions of "numerous fatal instances" for a paper on the malignant pustule he delivered before the British Medical Association's 1862 annual meeting. Most of cases Budd cited came from the European Continent (hence the use of the word *charbon* in his and Stone's account), and he asked why British physicians had so infrequently described the malady.

The Academy of Sciences of Dijon, France, in 1780 set as the subject of investigation for competitors in a prize essay contest the nature and treatment of the *pustule maligne* afflicting both humans and animals. This was motivated by Nicolas Fournier, a member of the academy, and by the rise of the disease in the Burgundy region as well as in French colonies in the Caribbean. The treatises that resulted from this challenge contributed to identifying the malignant pustule as a potentially lethal

form of anthrax, distinct from less virulent pustules. That same year
Jean-Francois Thomassin, a surgeon in the cavalry, compiled and
organized recent references to diseases that might be *charbon*. The
veterinary school administrator Philibert Chabert contributed a definitive
essay, confined to veterinary disease, that associated *fièvre charbonneuse*
with *carbuncle symptomatique* and set apart from both of them *carbuncle
primare* (primary carbuncle), which he believed had a separate cause.
In 1781 M. Chambon de Montaux, a prolific physician best know for
a standard work on diseases of young women, submitted a *Traité de
l'anthrax, ou de la pustule maligne,* and in studies and medical atlases
since then the malignant pustule was classified with the anthrax
carbuncle. Enaux and Chaussier appended their *Precis de la pustule
maligne* to their manual of treatments for animal bites and rabies (1785).
These essays initiated the work of characterizing *pustule maligne* as a
disease of humans and animals, and distinguishing it from other similar
diseases.

It was not that the malignant pustule was rare in Britain, Budd concluded in his 1862 paper, but that the malignant pustule was unlike any
other and had escaped general recognition in Britain because it was
unknown to the public and to diagnosticians. Budd's paper was a step
toward spreading knowledge of the condition. In 1863 the registrar general, the chief statistical officer of England, began recording deaths from
malignant pustule.

Though bacteria had been seen in specimens taken from the pustules, there was no widely accepted explanation of what caused them,
and no treatment apart from topical applications and surgery. Some
patients died and others survived. The Walpole factory had created the
circumstances for cutaneous outbreak by bringing together infected hides
and vigorous workers under the same roof. The hair pulling in Walpole
factory was manual and not mechanized, and the disease entered through
skin in direct contact with the foreign hides.

Information, carried by developing transportation and improving
media, spread the diagnosis of the malignant pustule from the Continent to England and thence to America just as the concurrent increase
in trade and development of industry and markets brought the anthrax
media—hair and hides—to Europe and America. The malignant pustule
Fournier witnessed in the 1720s came from native wool; the American
and English pustules were imports.

In England anthrax as an animal or human disease appeared to be
unknown prior to the importation of hair from Russia and the Near East
and the arrival of medical knowledge from the Continent.

In 1880 James Russell, the medical officer of health for Glasgow,
included in his annual report a set of recommendations designed to pre-

vent further deaths like those suffered by three women workers in 1878 at a specific horsehair mill, Adelphi, on Govan Street. Russell suspected that these and previous deaths classified according to various suspicious causes were due to an infectious agent arriving on horsehair imported from Russia. He asked for a ban on the imports as well as preventive boiling of hair bales, and that protective clothing and respirators be supplied to the workers. None of these recommendations was implemented.

Some English factories, working at a higher level of production, had been importing hair already pulled from the hides overseas and were processing it using machinery. The workers' skin was exposed to the infectious matter they also breathed in the confined air of the factory. Some of the Glasgow workers died of "pleurisy, bronchitis" and one of "malignant vesicle." The same mix of respiratory and cutaneous conditions felled workers in Walpole.

On February 5, 1878, Dr. John Henry Bell stood before the Medico Chirurgical Society of Bradford, England, to read to the assembled physicians and surgeons a paper on "woolsorters' disease." Bell had already been one of those who first identified an optical condition of coal miners (nystagmus). Bell considered theories to explain a symptomatic disease affecting and killing workers in Bradford's mills that processed wool for clothing. He evaluated and dismissed the conjecture that the dust of the factories was causing a lung inflammation, and he likewise set aside the idea that it might be animal disease making a transition into humans through the handling of wool and hair.

Bell favored his own speculation that decomposing animal matter communicated a poison to the lungs of those who breathed the air of the processing rooms, and the resulting septicemia precipitated a suite of symptoms. The audience at the meeting generally supported Bell's views, while rejecting the emergent explanation of germs or microbes, which could not cause people to sicken and die so quickly. Bell thought that his conclusion called for disinfecting the wool and hair used, or at least identifying suspicious lots and not processing them. The society's members went away determined to conduct further studies.

The following year Bell identified *Bacillus anthracis* in the blood of afflicted woolsorters, and at the 1880 meeting of the society he recanted his septicemia explanation and declared his belief that the "germ poison" that caused the disease he and other members of the society had found in woolsorters was the same as that which caused splenic fever and malignant pustule in animals: the bacillus which the Prussian doctor Robert Koch had identified. Bell's conversion was not shared by his colleagues, who were only just beginning to find merit in the germ theory of disease. They wondered how the germs, which had only been seen in blood samples, could get from the animals into human victims, and they still preferred Bell's decomposing animal matter septicemia or some variant thereof.

The society set up a commission to study the matter. The twelve members of the Commission of Woolsorters' Diseases studied the steps of processing wool that might contribute to infections, and they evaluated cases of illness, discovering after two years of examination 9 cases they could agree were woolsorters disease. In their unpublished report of 1882, however, the commissioners did not agree on the cause, some favoring germs and some favoring septicemia. Beyond repeating Bell's earlier suggestion of disinfecting suspect wool, the report had no preventive measures to offer.

One of the cases included in the report was that of Samuel Firth, a woolsorter who died in Bradford in May 1880. On the death certificate, Bell, the attending physician, wrote that Firth's death resulted "from his employer's neglect in not having the mohair he was sorting disinfected beforehand."

For several years Bell had been warning the wool manufacturers that deaths like Firth's could be prevented. Now he used the one facility provided by British law, the physician's responsibility to state the cause of death, to give his warnings force. Bell's words were an accusation of human culpability for what had been dismissed as a natural occurrence, and a coroner's inquiry followed.

The coroner's jury did find the manufacturer negligent, and made a number of recommendations on treating the wool before it was sorted and on ventilating the areas where the sorters worked. But the jury could not enforce its rules and some manufacturers, under public pressure because of the number of publicized deaths of woolsorters, only agreed to treat the wool that came from overseas, not the safer domestic wool.

It had taken Bell and the community of Bradford a long time to reach even this point. Discovering the underlying causes of a sickness, and creating rules to prevent it, enmeshed humans, animals, machinery and bacteria in a complex that meant safer working conditions but ultimately provided a model for germ warfare. Samuel Firth was a victim of a human-bacteria relationship unique to the circumstances under which he worked, but he was the ancestor of other victims under very different circumstances.

Sorters were the first to handle the wool after it was shorn from sheep, and they handled it strongly. Raw wool contains masses of soil, stems, excrement and insect parts that are shaken off before the sorter begins the work of clipping out the tough knots (kemps) and separating the fibers according to length and fineness. John Dyer wrote in his long poem, *The Fleece* (1757):

> In the same fleece diversity of wool
> Grows intermingled, and excites the care
> Of a curious skill to sort the sev'ral kinds.
> Nimbly with habitual speed
> They sever lock from lock, and long and short
> And soft and rigid pile in sev'ral heaps.

Sorted fleece had to be washed and scoured to reduce (but not elim-inate) the waterproofing natural grease (lanolin), then combed or carded, spun and woven into fabric. The considerable investment required to process wool into yarn and fabric made it necessary to establish and ensure grades of quality.

Sorting was the first step in the process of making cloth from wool, but because the sorting had to be hand-to-eye inspection it was the last step mechanized. The constant movement created clouds of dust breathed by the workers. A hundred years after the Bradford outbreak of the 1870s, the first worker to die in an outbreak in a mechanized New Hampshire mill was the man who cleaned the picking machine, which had automated the sorting process.

English cloth had a poor reputation on the Continent in the late Middle Ages because it was believed the English sorted their wool care-lessly, but that changed as the relationship between sorted grades and finished cloth became knowledge to be transmitted from sorter to appren-tice. By 1554 a statute promulgated by the Crown stated, "The perfect and principal ground of cloth-making is the true sorting of wools." Dr. Samuel Johnson referred to clothmaking from wool as "our national industry" in his brief review of Dyer's poem. The poem was a georgic for Britain as Vergil's *Georgics* were for Rome, only Dyer, writing in the eighteenth century, never described anthrax visitations, as Vergil did.

Wool finishing was mostly a cottage industry until the late eighteenth century, with clothiers sending (putting out) wool to family homes where it was sorted, prepared, spun and woven.

> Then to another room came they
> Where children were in poor array
> And everyone sate picking wool
> The finest from the coarse to cull...

This passage from *The Pleasant History of John Winchcombe* by Thomas Deloney marks a moment in the long developing transition from cottage to factory in the processing of wool.

As congregate factories were formed and the steps of manu-facture were centralized and finally mechanized, sorting remained a manual process, but was increasingly the province of men. Women and children operated the middle phases of spinning and weaving before men once again took over in the clothing manufacture. Sorting was a practice included in the broader acts of carding or weaving rather than a trade in itself.

The quickening pace of industrialization brought numbers of people to work in the cities, where the native wool was shipped to be sorted as the preamble to the other steps of the process. They were both lured to the cities and driven there as the centuries long destruction of the common lands, deprived them of rural livelihood. The reference to the children "in poor array" in Deloney's poem also reflects another development in the wool industry. As formerly independent workers became the employees of crowded factories, the miseries of their condition became noticeable.

Bradford was well situated for the development of the wool industry, but it lacked the water power resources that drove the cotton mills. In 1794, when manufacturers attempted to build a factory in Bradford, Yorkshire, based on the steam-powered spinning device called the water frame, the town residents objected to the "smoky nuisance" and threatened legal proceedings. In 1825 the union of woolcombers in Bradford worsted mills declared a general strike demanding better wages and working conditions. Around twenty thousand workers were affected. The owners locked them out, and when workers in other towns supported the strikers with cash donations, they were threatened with loss of their jobs. The strike went on for five months in a "peaceable and orderly manner," and did not accomplish its aims. The smoky nuisance prevailed.

The Bradford strike was only one event in the labor movement that included all types and classes of workers reacting to the conditions resulting from mechanization, rapid urbanization and immigration of unskilled workers. Friedrich Engels' descriptions of workers' misery in *The Condition of the Working Classes of England* (1844) applied mainly to the cotton industry, but they represented the mingled health and economic problems of an entire class of laborers. Engels concentrated on conditions in the suffocating interiors of the factories.

The wool industries had their own descriptions of misery. The combers often sorted the wool in their own homes before bringing it through the later processes. A journalist in 1830 described the combing:

> The wool-combers assort the wool chiefly in an apartment of their own dwelling. The work is done over a fire of charcoal which sends forth volumes of carbonic acid gas, and the workpeople are obliged to keep their windows open in all weathers to prevent or to mitigate the evil effects of the gas. They are roasted to perspiration on one side, and have often a current of cold air rushing upon them from the win-

dow. They look pale and cadaverous and are short-lived, few reaching fifty years of age.

The atmosphere of wool processing was unhealthy to breathe even without the introduction of anthrax spores.

And to eat. On May 18, 1832, Michael Sadler, a member of the House of Commons investigating factory conditions, was told by Matthew Crabtree, a mill-boy, that the "flues of wool" accumulated on any food he tried to eat during work and had to be picked or blown off.

The workers expressed their discontent with these conditions through strikes, protests, and taking advantage of any opportunity to gather more benefit from their production, which the manufacturers defined as theft. There already had been legislation, irregularly enforced, setting a minimum age for child textile workers. In 1833 an older system of factory "visitors" was replaced by factory inspectors, who eventually were empowered to enforce legislation regulating first the safety (protection from machinery) then the conditions (temperature, humidity, particulates) of the workplace. English workers were ahead of their Continental counterparts in winning legislation in 1847 that set the work day at ten hours for women and children, but men continued to labor and be exposed to hazards for long periods of time. There was a struggle over definitions and descriptions that extended into the legal, medical and journalistic writing by middle class professionals who had some reason to be involved with the wool industry.

In 1832 Charles Turner Thackrah, "presumably inspired by the experience of practicing medicine within a rapidly expanding industrial town," published *The Effects of the Principal Arts, Trades and Professions ... with Suggestions for the Removal of Agents which Produce Disease and Shorten the Duration of Life.* The success of the book caused Thackrah, in spite of his own pulmonary tuberculosis, to expand its scope and include the diseases of 120 occupations beyond his home city of Leeds. He does write of workers in the wool industry, but nowhere does he make suggestions to reduce the occurrence of malignant pustule or pulmonary anthrax. Yet Thackrah's book was the signpost of a reform movement that reached into the factories and into the halls of government.

The manufacturers could argue through their own surrogates that the ill health of those who sorted and combed wool at home called for the introduction of machines. The workers' advocates countered that if the manufacturers demanded that level of production, they would need to guarantee healthful factory conditions. In the context of this struggle those who sorted the wool developed their own peculiar disease, and circumstances in Bradford and the surrounding area fashioned a medical and political response.

It is difficult to recover from the woolsorters themselves when and how they came to distinguish this disease from any other affliction. According to contemporary journalistic accounts and to Dr. Bell, writing years later, they associated it with the introduction of foreign materials. It was Bell who identified the disease, defined it as a historical event associated with changes in the materials woolsorters were given to sort, and sought a cause and a way to prevent the disease.

Bell had received his training at the University of Edinburgh, where he learned French pathological anatomy and German cellular pathology, and the use of the microscope to detect evidence not readily visible in the surface appearances of a disease. His education emphasized proceeding from evidence to theory. All of these came into play in his conclusions. It also helped that another Edinburgh graduate, John Burdon Sanderson, was the head of the Brown Sanatory Institution in London.

The disease itself and Bell's care of the woolsorters came about in the environment of industrialization and labor agitation that eventually made it possible to take steps against the condition. It was not simply workers demanding better conditions from profit-motivated capitalists. As the factories grew so did the manufacturers' paternalism. Middle-class professionals like Bell were actively mediating between the workers and the owners. They were professionally concerned for workers' health as an expression of the owners' need to provide for laborers.

Initially Bell believed that the woolsorters disease, with its own distinctive set of symptoms, was caused by a poison that entered through the foreign mohair and alpaca. His views were in keeping with the scientific understanding of infection in the mid–nineteenth century. The fibers were imported from Persia and Afghanistan into the worsted industry of Bradford in 1837 to make up for the inability of domestic production to supply sufficient wool of a quality to meet the demand for fine textiles.

There did not seem to be a specific disease connected with the domestic sheep's wool that had been processed for centuries. Bell wrote that the woolsorters who handled the imported fibers became so conscious of their association with a deadly disease that they drew lots to decide who would work with the most suspicious batches.

The phrase "Bradford disease" was used in the newspapers for woolsorters disease because of the concentration of cases reported from the town. A letter published in *The Bradford Observer* on February 27, 1878, contained all the accumulating components that identified it as a unique disease:

> Dear Sir: Within a month, three woolsorters have died from blood poisoning contracted in the same shed of the same factory on Man-

chester Road. Occasional deaths from blood poisoning through the handling of some foreign wools, may perhaps be inevitable, but the recurrence in so short a time seems to suggest either that the wool itself, or the method in which it was sorted, is especially unwholesome. May I hope for your help. To induce manufacturers to remedy all that be remediable in this deadly trade. No doubt, the death of a woolsorter means to the manufacturer the loss of an easily replaceable hand, but to others it means the loss, never to be replaced, of son, husband or father. That I have just come from one such desolate home may be my excuse for troubling you with this letter.

The statement that some blood poisoning may be inevitable in handling foreign wools is more the result of the belief that contamination comes from overseas rather than from handling wool. Otherwise, the letter's focus is on a problem that the manufacturers can do something about if only a prominent authority like the newspaper would urge them to change the procedures.

Bell's study of woolsorters disease started from these premises and moved toward finding a way to pressure the factory owners to act. As Bell observed woolsorters do their work and come down with the blood condition, he initially believed that it was some putrefaction product of the animal that had entered the fibers. The foreign goat hair differed from domestic wool in that it was sometimes pulled from dead animals rather than sheared from living ones, and it had clots of blood amid the other matter woolsorters shook out when they graded the batches. Easily pulled mohair brought with it parts of the decomposed flesh of the animals and the poisons produced by decay.

Bell was unable to identify this poison, but then he received word from Dr. Eddison of Leeds, who had visited bacteriology labs on the Continent, that Robert Koch had elucidated the life cycle of the anthrax bacillus. It was well known that anthrax infection spread from the bodies of dead animals to other animals and sometimes to humans. The possibility that woolsorters disease was caused by anthrax agents was compatible with Bell's belief that the disease came from putrefaction products of the dead animal supplying the fiber.

As part of therapeutic procedure Bell bled a patient who was dying of woolsorters disease, but this time he reserved some of the blood and examined it under the microscope. He found great numbers of the filiform bodies already associated with anthrax symptoms. Following an established diagnostic technique, Bell used the blood to infect mice and rabbits with anthrax.

Bell did not culture anthrax bacteria and use the cultures to infect a variety of animals in sequence, as Koch did. He was determined to demonstrate publicly a direct relationship between substances in imported mohair, the illness and deaths of woolsorters and the presence of bacilli in their blood. Each woolsorter who came down with symptoms of the disease provided one more public association between imported goat hair, disease and bacteria.

Bell did not identify the bacterial spores Koch described in the infectious mohair. The goat hair was apparently dirtier than normally rather dirty wool and it would have been difficult to make out the spores. Bell could only address the causes of the disease by urging the manufacturers to institute a practice of washing the apparently dangerous fibers before they were handled by the sorters. Other physicians practicing in Bradford and neighboring wool towns could agree there was an infective principle contained in the wool, even though, as the report of the Commission on Woolsorters Diseases proved, they did not all accept that bacteria were the cause.

By making a connection between the visible condition of the mohair and disease, Bell convinced some factory owners to add a step to the processing. It was not difficult to convince the woolsorters and their families of this, but he had to resort to his ability to inscribe death certificates with cause of death to make the scientific findings compelling.

When dirt and the bacteria within it became the basis of a coroner's verdict, the manufacturers were placed in the position of not acting in the face of evidence of their negligence. Bell's science became advocacy for workers' rights to healthful conditions in the face of the owners' indifference. The happy order of wool processing as portrayed in earlier poetry had not become the paternal order of the factory. The idyllic past could not be recovered.

By identifying the cause of sudden death as woolsorters disease peculiar to the factories where imported hair was processed, Bell was shifting responsibility for the condition to the factory owners. The context of a victim's disease now made early diagnosis possible, but there was no effective treatment, only prevention. This would remain the central problem of inhalational anthrax: the appearance of recognizable symptoms so closely precedes death that even effective treatments may not save a victim. As with plague and cholera, prevention was best.

The coroner's jury in Samuel Firth's death made a series of recommendations for the decontamination of foreign goat hair and the ventilation and cleaning of the rooms where it was sorted. These became known as the Bradford Rules. There also was a provision for reporting and compiling information on instances of the disease.

In 1857 a barrister named Thomas Brown endowed at the University of London an institution for the study and healing of animal diseases, and after years of wrangling the Brown Animal Sanatory Institution was established in 1871. Veterinary schools had been opened in Europe and in England, but the Brown Institution was the first animal disease research organization with special interests in experimental comparative studies. Under the first Professor Superintendent John Burdon Sanderson, the Brown Institution proceeded to study cattle diseases of economic concern, bovine pleuropneumonia and foot-and-mouth disease.

In England animal anthrax had been dismissed as a condition confined to certain areas of the Continent. In the 1870s, however, the upheavals of war and increased trade of breeding stock spread anthrax into English farms and the veterinarians associated with the Brown Institution saw an opportunity for active experimentation. This wave of anthrax in the 1870s was also the medium of the definitive work of Robert Koch in Germany and Louis Pasteur in France.

During 1878, his last year at the Brown Institution, Sanderson experimentally established that anthrax "poison" could be transmitted through food of any sort that originated in infected animals, not just their meat. Sanderson, who had witnessed Koch's demonstration of the infectiousness of anthrax, also showed that if blood from anthrax-infected cattle was injected into small rodents (guinea pigs) and after the rodents die their blood is injected into uncontaminated cattle, the cattle recover. This was only a short step away from the anthrax vaccine tested between September 1879 and early 1880, by W.S. Greenfield, Sanderson's successor as professor superintendent, at the same time and independent of the vaccine tests of Toussaint and Pasteur in France.

In May 1880, the same month the commission was formed and Samuel Firth died, Greenfield accompanied John Spear, a local government board inspector, on a tour of Bradford mills, to seek ways to reduce contamination by foreign infectious agents. In his report Spear recommended measures to detect and disinfect the fleeces and hair taken from animals that had died ("fallen fleeces") which were included in bales shipped from abroad. Inspection of arriving shipments by port officials created the prospect of officials being infected before the factory workers. The existing disinfection procedures, boiling the hair or treating it with carbolic acid, which was used as a disinfectant following the work of Joseph Lister, were either ineffectual or destroyed the valuable material. And it was difficult to enforce inspections and decontaminations.

Spear was called on to investigate the deaths of woolsorters in a Leicester factory. After the London and Southwark coroner wrote to the local government expressing concern about cases of malignant pustule among tanners and hide workers in Bermondsey, Spear traced the infection to "fallen" hides imported from China and processed in a specific tannery. See Appendix D for a contemporary account of the Chinese source of the spores. Those unpacking the hides at the wharves, tanning them and working them were all subjected to sometimes lethal skin infections. Spear was able to compile a list of geographical sources of these hides, but lacking any official precedent for regulation of imports that created occupational health problems, he was unable to institute changes at the point of entry.

Tanneries were even more likely than textile mills to be an entry point for anthrax because tanning solution made contact with the skin of workers, which might be open to infection. Also, the use of animal organs and human and animal wastes in the tanning process, to cultivate the bacteria that promoted tanning, could encourage the culture of anthrax and other pathogens. And the effluents of tanneries could carry infectious matter into ground water and surface flows, where cattle graze.

Bell was a little more successful at the factories in Bradford. The publicity around the death of the woolsorter Isaac Saville in 1884 led to a public health conference held in Bradford that recommended additions to the Bradford Rules. As these rules were adopted by manufacturers, the number of deaths of woolsorters declined. But workers farther along the line of wool processing still succumbed to the identifiable symptoms of the disease. And there were always unreported cutaneous infections, the proletarian carbuncles that also were considered the lot of workers. It was known that the bacteria caused the infection, but how it was transmitted via the wool still was not clear.

Britain did not have the kind of anthrax surveillance established by customary law in parts of Continental Europe and Russia, where it had become endemic. The state authorities only began to show regulatory interest when anthrax seemed to be arriving with imported livestock and when it affected factory production.

The Cattle Disease Prevention Act of 1866 established compulsory destruction of stock infected with rinderpest, but it was not until 1886, after the ravages of the 1870s, that the act was amended to include anthrax and its frequent associate, rabies. Britain then formalized and legislated surveillance procedures that had long been community responsibilities where anthrax was endemic on the Continent. The 1896 and 1898 Diseases of Animals acts established import and transport controls and powers of seizure and extirpation to prevent a list of diseases that could become epidemic in livestock if introduced from the outside. Around the same time the industrial diseases of humans were placed within the legal framework.

The 1891 Factory and Workshop Act gave the home secretary, under whose authority the factory inspectorate fell, the power to draw up special rules for industries using materials and processes that threatened the lives and health of workers. Anthrax was not specifically included. A report made by the London County Council's assistant medical officer of health in 1894 spurred the formation of an investigating committee that made a thorough review of anthrax in industry throughout the country, identified those industries most susceptible and articulated a set of rules similar to those already voluntarily observed by factory owners in Bradford.

The 1895 Factory and Workshop Act made anthrax a notifiable disease together with workplace lead, arsenic and phosphorus poisoning. Anthrax was the only acute, organic disease included among the slower, devastating poisonings caused by the inorganic substances. A physician diagnosing a notifiable disease had to alert public health authorities to its presence. The first medical inspector of factories, Thomas M. Legge, was appointed to his post in 1898 and set about defining the medical tasks of attending physicians at factories. These tasks were spelled out further in the 1901 amendment of the 1895 act, stipulating that the physician at a factory where an anthrax infection occurs must notify the chief inspector of factories at the Home Office. But anthrax was not made "generally notifiable" (all occurrences to be reported) until 1960.

National regulations for preventing anthrax infections from skins and hides, based on Spear's work, were published in 1899, augmented in 1900 by regulations derived from the Bradford Rules for the wool industry, with further extensions in 1905 and 1908 for types of wool and hair. Anthrax was keeping pace with the regulatory environment created by a growing body of specialists amid the increasing political power of labor.

Only property owners were able to vote in general elections (to Parliament) until reform legislation in 1867 extended the vote to all native males over the age of 21. Organized labor began to acquire a political voice, and the quickening pace of legislation related to all aspects of workers' well-being reflected this. Workers' compensation for on-the-job injuries and work-related illnesses became law in 1897, and anthrax was one of the compensable diseases listed by special legislation in 1905. Where the establishment of rules and regulations did not succeed in preventing infections, afflicted workers did not always face destitution for time lost.

In 1905 Bell co-authored with Legge a section on industrial anthrax in volume 2 of Allbutt and Rolleston's *The System of Medicine,* and after placing his claim to the clinical entity "woolsorters disease," he died the following year. The volume was dedicated to tropical and exotic diseases. By then the work Bell had begun of urging on a coalition of medical practitioners, manufacturers and workers' representatives had passed to successors. The manufacturers' refusal or inability to adopt global disinfection measures could only be answered by finding the exact source of the infection in the goat hair.

The task of identifying this source of infection was taken up by the next generation of Bradford physicians, specifically by Fritz W. Eurich.

Eurich's family had fled political persecution by the German state and settled in Bradford, where as in Manchester there was a community of liberal German refugees. Eurich went to school and grew up in the community beset by woolsorters disease. He studied medicine at Edinburgh University, as had Bell, and after clinical training in a national sanatorium he set up a practice in Bradford in 1896.

When the Bradford Chamber of Commerce and trade unions, which were growing in influence locally and nationally, determined in 1905 to set up an Anthrax Investigation Board to engage in a continual examination of the problem, they were able to obtain funding from the Home Office as well as donations from individual manufacturing enterprises. This constitution created a potential for balancing conflicting interests and seeking ways to address the problems affecting both workers and employers. The election of Labour members of Parliament for the first time in the general election of 1906 underlined the need for compromise.

Acceptance of the bacterial source of the contagion had advanced to the point that it was obvious the board must have a consulting bacteriologist. Eurich was asked to serve as the first district bacteriologist and director of the Anthrax Investigation Board. He soon began research into the vexed issue of how to eliminate anthrax spores from imported wool and hair without destroying the materials, insuring that workers would not be harmed by the contagion while protecting the assets of the manufacturers.

Eurich had the advantage of Robert Koch's research on disinfection and sterilization procedures. Koch had used anthrax spores as a test case in determining which treatments would work best on different materials containing them. He did not address the concerns of specific industries, but he did make the important observation that materials that are not themselves bacterial culture media might still harbor viable spores after seemingly effective application of disinfectants. The worth of a disinfectant could be deceiving if—when treating a sample with a chemical then trying to culture bacteria from the sample—some of the chemical carried over into the culture. The object was to find a substance and a method that killed all the spores at first, and show that no bacteria could be cultured from the material after it was washed clean of disinfectant. To find an effective method of disinfection by these standards required painstaking trial and error.

In the following years Eurich determined that immersing infected wool in water heated to 160 degrees Fahrenheit for 15 to 20 minutes destroyed bacteria but not spores. Boiling the wool killed more spores but not all of them, and it damaged the wool. If a disinfectant such as formaldehyde was used to eliminate viable spores, Eurich found, it was necessary to treat the wool in narrow vessels under pressure to ensure that all the fibers were reached.

After painstaking microscopic examination of wool and hair samples, Eurich made the important discovery that it was blood adhering to the strands and not the strands themselves that bore the spores. This meant that the infected fiber must have been harvested by pulling it from recently dead animals and that disinfection must address the adhesive mass of spores. These discoveries did not lead to a practical treatment or suggestions for anthrax abatement. By 1910 the labor representatives on the Anthrax Investigation Board declared their dissatisfaction with the board's efforts and resigned. Despite the measures taken in the factories, woolsorters were still getting sick and dying at about the same rates as they did when reporting began in 1896.

It was only in 1914 that Eurich, working with Elmhirst Duckering, a factory inspector who joined the Anthrax Investigation Board that year, described the Duckering process. By bathing wool successively in troughs filled with solutions of sodium carbonate and of sodium hydroxide (lye) then immersing it in hot (100 degrees Fahrenheit) formaldehyde, "duckering" reduced the spores in wool below the critical infectious level without destroying the wool.

The outbreak of the First World War made it difficult to implement this system in any concerted way. Wartime demands on industrial production, the departure of skilled workers for the battlefront and the breakdown of existing inspection and abatement procedures led to an upsurge in anthrax cases of woolsorters and other workers. The number of cases of occupational anthrax reported to the factory inspectorate in 1916 was 100, more than double the previous year, with 12 deaths, and in 1917 it was 93, with 8 deaths.

The war years saw the greatest number of reported cases, but not the greatest number of deaths, which had peaked at 17 in 1906 and had fallen steadily as a percentage of the total number of cases. In other words, though there was an upswing in anthrax morbidity, anthrax mortality as a percentage of morbidity declined steadily from the beginning of notification. This may have been due to the relative success of factory-based measures in controlling inhalational anthrax, and because the less lethal cutaneous anthrax accounted for a greater proportion of cases. The decrease in lethal cases may also have been due to the decline in imports during the war. There simply was not so much spore-bearing wool and hair entering the country.

The Anthrax Abatement Act of 1919 finally gave the government the power to ban the import of raw materials and processed goods likely to be infected with anthrax. These items could only be brought through ports equipped to disinfect them by duckering. In 1921 Liverpool became the first port and for a long time the only port equipped with such a station. Reported anthrax cases declined to the point that woolsorters disease became a medical curiosity by the late 1920s.

Anthrax did not cause the same degree of occupational death and disability as the inorganic pathogens (lead, arsenic and phosphorus) that joined it as the subject of the 1896 legislation. That legislation served as a template for other countries which received British industry and with it occupational illness. The 1955 Accidents and Occupational Diseases Act of Guyana includes the same four "poisons," though Guyana did not have industries that exposed workers to them.

The gradual reduction of anthrax as an industrial pathogen may have been due to the heroic efforts of Bell, Spear, Eurich and Elmhirst Duckering, or it may have diminished as part of a general improvement in living conditions (despite wars) and in working conditions in Western Europe from the 1890s onward. Other occupational diseases also were reduced or vanished during this period (but new ones were being created).

Anthrax rose to notice over other conditions that caused greater morbidity and mortality. Unlike, for instance, particulate respiratory diseases of workers, it was not a normal part of the workplace atmosphere. It was accepted as the lot of workers in the wool industry, as "phosphor jaw" was accepted as the lot of matchmakers. Anthrax was acute, the black lesions developed suddenly, and fever and death came rapidly to the heads of families who supported large numbers of people. In this way anthrax became the subject of medical attention, newspaper commentary, labor agitation, voluntary regulation and enforced legislation. When it was discovered that the infectious agent entered from abroad in materials imported from unknown and unfriendly countries and stole into the bodies of unsuspecting workers, the basis of a vague but persistent popular image was formed. Anthrax was the alien invader permeating the atmosphere and swiftly seizing the livelihood of families. The government and even the manufacturers who brought it into the country could collaborate with physicians and scientists to reduce the invader's destructiveness.

One element almost entirely missing from woolsorters disease as it matured in public attention was the bodies of the woolsorters. Their social condition was the subject of debate and regulation to which the medical establishment contributed, but among the evidence they presented, there was no description of the internal course of the disease. The identification of the bacterial cause was an opportunity to avoid the image of the anatomized woolsorter. In a Britain where social pressures had greatly restricted the use of cadavers for medical study, the results of any thorough post-mortem were not widely publicized.

In 1890, in the midst of the struggle to make woolsorters disease a subject of occupational health policy, an otherwise obscure writer who identified himself as Samuel Lodge, *fils* (the younger), published in a new French journal on experimental medicine and pathological anatomy an article on the medical case histories of woolsorter deaths in Bradford. The article translated information that would be the subject of coroner's reports in Britain into the idiom of pathological anatomy.

While accepting the bacterial basis of the changes in tissue observed in the remains, Lodge made a careful examination of the progress of the disease through the internal organs. The object of pathological anatomy was to identify the visible variations of organs and tissues that constituted disease, not to seek causes, and Lodge's work is an episode in the assimilation of bacteriology into this way of looking at illness. The article did not receive much attention in Britain or in France, where the chemical bacteriology of Pasteur and his followers was opposed by anatomists, but it did have an audience in the Austro-Hungarian Empire.

Between February 19 and March 14, 1870, 16 female ragpickers (*Hadernsorterinnen*) working at a papermill in Schlöglmuhl, Austria, fell ill with a respiratory illness, and within days nine of them died. The workers were employed to sort by hand scrap cloth, clothing, blankets and sheets, cotton, wool and linen, and to eliminate burned and damaged cloth that would foul the papermaking process. The sorting was fast and vigorous; the workers were paid based on production, not time.

The factory doctor recalled later that two to three of these infections occurred per year, and they were usually attributed to diet and sexual excess. The women were young immigrants from the eastern Austro-Hungarian Empire, mostly from Hungary; they were unskilled, not fluent German speakers and they were inured to tedious labor. To have nine die within a month's period was unusual, and it attracted the attention of physicians. No one noticed it at the time, but between 1868 and 1870, concurrently in American, British and Austrian factories, there were surges of deaths from respiratory disease of workers in industries handling dusty animal products.

There was no further cluster of deaths as large as this one, but a steady stream of single deaths of female ragpickers and of ragmen (*Hadernfaktoren*), who collected the rags, provided a basis for speculation on the source of the precipitate infections. Several papers were already published on *die Hadernkrankheit*, "the rag disease," by the time Hans Eppinger took up the matter in 1878.

Eppinger was professor of pathological anatomy at the University of Graz in Austria. Graz was also the location of one of the larger paper mills, where the factory doctor had witnessed periodic deaths of ragpickers and other laborers. Eppinger had doctors at several factories alert him by telegraph to these deaths when they occurred and he gathered a growing volume of case histories. In some cases he was able to collect information on post-mortem examinations, and he performed a number of them himself.

In 1894 Eppinger published a monograph, *Die Hadernkrankheit, eine typische Inhalations-Milzbrandinfection beim Menschen (The Rag Disease, a Typical Inhalational Anthrax Infection in Humans).* The book was subtitled, " with special emphasis on its pathological anatomy and pathogenesis." It features case by case tabulations (anticipating in their parameters the tabulations of cases during the 2001 American anthrax attacks), summaries of the course of infection in individual cases, and a single book-width lithograph illustrating the cellular anatomy of infection in tissue samples.

Eppinger devotes a separate section to bacteriological research on anthrax infections, and he compares inhalational infection with other types of human anthrax and with animal infections. In a stark reminder that most of his cases were young women, he devotes a chapter to the transmission of maternal anthrax to the fetus, and the development of anthrax endocarditis in the infant. Anthrax was passing to the next generation, like syphilis and tuberculosis.

Eppinger's book was the culmination of a German case history approach to anthrax that had first appeared with Schwab's publication on animal and human anthrax poisoning in 1844 and would continue into the next century in Germany (Meyer) and in America (Gold), where German medicine had a strong influence. The individual anthrax cases that accumulated in the American medical literature and eventually as anecdotes in popular literature are a continuation of case study in the absence of a single industrial setting. Eppinger produced the only comprehensive case studies of a type of industrial anthrax prior to the American textile mill studies of the 1950s. He identified *Hadernkrankheit* as a "typical infection," a description which establishes its status in a typology of disease. He drew comparisons with the English factory studies and made special reference to Lodge's paper, which was uniquely concerned with pathological anatomy.

Eppinger did devote a final section to prophylaxis, to the "modern and exact" measures taken from 1878 onward at the Steiermark papermill by Professor Schauenstein that reduced the number of deaths. Schauenstein examined the procedures of rag sorting to determine which motions caused spores to enter the lungs. As many as 111 workers might be stationed in the same cramped, overheated room.

Each worker stands at a kind of work table beside several movable wooden receptacles; on the table itself is fixed standing vertically an almost scythe-shaped sweep knife. Cloths held tight with both hands are pulled back and forth across the blade of the knife, causing dust to swirl up, even more as the cloth is shredded. The pieces are, if necessary, shredded once more at the knife and, finally, once they have reached the necessary degree of separation and dust removal, are thrown at once into the waiting receptacle. Then the torn pieces reach the "ragwolf" [*Lumpenwolf*], a machine positioned under the floorboards where another shredding takes place and more dust rises up to reach the workers. For our concerns, no need to continue to further processing.

The workers "dwell in waves of dust," he wrote. Schauenstein, however, made the distinction between lung conditions caused by breathing the dust and rapid onset infections. He determined that the infections occurred when the sorters were processing "footscraps" (*Fussfetzen)* from Hungary, especially after the pieces had been stored a few months before being brought to the factory.

A range of hygienic measures were introduced, including washing the most infectious pieces, treating them with a disinfectant and reducing the dust mass by improving the ventilation of the work room. The sources of the material were also "refined." The net result was a reduction of lethal infections between 1880 and 1894, when Eppinger was able to report the result in his book. As in England, this was the result of physicians and factory inspectors applying the findings of contemporary science to a specific problem. Unlike England, however, the ragsorters did not become a cause in a national labor movement.

Ragpickers disease joined woolsorters disease as a form of occupational anthrax that had been addressed and to some extent controlled, through scientific measures brought down to just a few cases. It was the first anthrax entirely created by humans for humans with only the spores provided by the bacteria. It was a model for the control of anthrax and for its use.

# 3

# Models

Nicolas Fournier had commented on workplace anthrax and its causes in the late eighteenth century, but the importance of the British textile industry and the workers rights movement had created woolsorters disease and the preventive regulatory response. The British experience served as model for other countries and for the international workers' movement in general.

Ragpickers disease remained a medical sidelight, rather than a major clinical entity with political implications. It was one of many types of anthrax infection that flashed into being at some juncture in the processing of animal materials, and either came to medical notice or remained unobserved by inspectors and suffered by workers. States, or at least the rising public health and industrial medicine professions, attempted to control this type of occupational anthrax by introducing sanitation measures.

The International Labour Office, which was formed in 1901 to monitor workers' issues and legislation, in its 1908 bulletin included extracts of British and French laws pertaining to the decontamination of the products of animals likely to be infected by anthrax.

> In establishments where skins, hides, hair, silk, wool, horns, bones or other products of animals capable of being attacked by anthrax are handled, employers and managers are recommended ... to take the especial measures of sanitation and protection set forth in the following paragraphs....

This *circulaire* of February 18, 1908, addressed by the French minister of labor to divisional inspectors, then recommends that the materials be disinfected prior to use, the workers be supplied with gloves, the operations be carried out under dry conditions and if there has been a case of anthrax within the previous six months, the floors and walls of the workplaces should be given an impervious covering and cleaned in the damp state. Any "wool, hair, pigs' bristles or hides, coming from non–European countries" should be treated in closed receptacles. Any worker with a pimple, cut, scratch or open wound should inform the employer or doctor attached to the works, and the wound should be covered and the worker withdrawn. The document ends with the language of a warning sign to be posted for all workers to see (see Appendix B).

This is not legislation or regulation but recommendations to factory inspectors to spread knowledge on how to prevent anthrax outbreaks wherever imported materials are used. Disinfection is the first defense but it is not certain to be practiced, nor to be effective if it is, and so the workrooms and the skin of the workers have to be fortified against entry of the spores. By requiring that the workers have notice, the inspectors can create another level of pressure on the factory owners to provide health care.

Recommendations like these were a way of disseminating practical knowledge of anthrax to permit owners, managers and workers to pursue their own interests in preventing it. Not every economy with workers suffering occupational anthrax was as centered around textile industries as Britain, and a centralized duckering station was not feasible elsewhere. Even that intense disinfection, once implemented, was not completely successful in removing anthrax from the manufacturing and commodity stream. In most shops the prevention of human infections was a matter of surveillance and reaction to individual cases. Anthrax was expected to be in the environment of certain industries; the degree to which cases appeared depended upon the ability of the potential victims, the workers, to reduce the odds against them.

The International Labour Organisation, which assumed many of the responsibilities of the International Labour Office, was created as part of the peace treaty ending hostilities at the end of the First World War. Their general conference, convened on October 29, 1919, in Washington, D.C.,

> having decided upon the adoption of certain proposals with regard to women's employment: unhealthy processes ... adopts the following Recommendation ... to the Members of the International Labour Organisation ... that arrangements should be made for the disinfection of wool infected with anthrax spores, either in the country exporting such wool or if that is not practicable at the port of entry in the country importing such wool.

This Anthrax Prevention Recommendation was the first effort to suggest an international model for curbing anthrax among workers. Advising disinfection in the source countries included the explicit recognition that those countries, or the European and American enterprises operating there, might not be able to set up disinfection procedures. Even more significant is attaching anthrax prevention to women's health in the workplace. The first victims of workplace anthrax described at the Glasgow horsehair mill by Russell in 1878 and by Eppinger from 1870 to 1894 were women, and they were forgotten as medical professionals and workers' movements turned to address the social calamity of male workplace anthrax. Yet the aggregate number of women victims of inhalational anthrax exceeded the number of male victims in the available tabulations, and the international labor movement seemed at least to acknowledge this.

Anthrax abatement procedures became part of the industrial processing of fibers from overseas, and succeeded in further reducing deaths of woolsorters and other wool industry workers. "Woolsorters disease" entered medical textbooks as a synonym for inhalational anthrax. The campaign to identify the causes and reduce the instances of the disease became a fundamental case of industrial medicine. In the American translation (1910) of Salinger's *Deutsche Klinik,* for instance, both woolsorters and ragpickers disease are mentioned as examples of industrial anthrax infection.

The other industries with a potential load of anthrax spores, tanning and leathermaking, did not receive enough official attention to give a name to a type of anthrax. Smaller scale and persistently artisanal in nature, the hide industries were subject to sporadic regulation by local authorities, but they did not have the number of workers to push industrial reform movements. At first professional bodies, like the leathermakers' guild of London, published regulations for preventing anthrax. Soon insurance companies also began to advise the small enterprises they covered on how to reduce liability for worker illness due to threats peculiar to that industry.

The workers compensation system, developed first in Britain and then in the United States, became another secondary defense against anthrax in peripheral industries. Tannery workers sought to have anthrax infection included among compensable work-related injuries. In the United States, where no national industrial anthrax authority ever developed to control anthrax in textile mills, a court of the State of New York ruled that an employee who handled dirty and diseased hides while wearing gloves, and contracted cutaneous anthrax through abrasions in his skin, had experienced an unusual, extraordinary and therefore compensable disease (*Heirs v. Co* 178 App. Div. 350,164 N.Y.S. 767 [N.Y. App Div. 1917]. The workers compensation system to some extent made up for shortcomings in the public health system.

Anthrax in a range of industries and in agriculture had become such an occasion for national and state legislation in the United States that in 1898 the Delaware College Agricultural Experiment Station could devote an issue of their bulletin to a study of these laws.

Woolsorters disease itself was replicated in the United States and elsewhere, but the preventive and regulatory environment was not. In 1916 the Massachusetts Board of Labor and Industries published Rules and Regulations Suggested for the Prevention of Anthrax.

Textile workers in Europe and America, then in Asia and Latin America, continued to work under miserable conditions. Bissinosis ("brown lung") and other respiratory diseases caused by breathing particles suspended in the air as the result of the heat and the workings of machines had far more impact on the health of workers than anthrax ever did. But these conditions acted over the lifetime of the worker and the workers' struggle was to escape having to accept them as their lot.

The abrupt onset of woolsorters disease, its frequent fatality, and the ability to control the source and ultimately to treat or immunize the victims made woolsorters disease a model condition despite the relatively small number of workers who actually died from it. The labor movement could use it to dramatize the need for government regulation of working conditions, and it was not infrequently mentioned in early twentieth century studies of labor movements and workers' health benefits.

Establishing the political and technical means of reducing the risk of woolsorters disease in European and then in American factories did not keep it from being exported to other countries where corporations set up factories because local governments did not have such stringent labor standards. As an occupational hazard, woolsorters disease returned to obscurity again, a disease of working women and children in factories far away from regulatory authorities.

In English and American factories, the Bradford Rules and factory inspections did not eliminate anthrax spores from workshop atmospheres. Rather than ceasing to use the inexpensive imported wool and mohair, the factory owners acted pragmatically to reduce the number of infections and deaths among workers. Vaccines and antibiotics were one further step in keeping the workers from coming down with apparent disease without clearing away its source. By the 1950s the anthrax atmospheres maintained by a few factories attracted the interest of experimenters.

Woolsorters disease was a historical moment of human-bacteria interaction. Its social and industrial context, the conditions of those affected and its control by an intersection of science and politics formed an arena which could be reproduced and modulated for a purpose. Once begun, a complex like woolsorters disease perpetuates itself.

Arms Textile Mills in Manchester, New Hampshire, in 1957 employed

632 workers in a cluster of chestnut-beamed brick factories on the banks of the Merrimack River, which formerly provided water power for the mills' engines. Like other American manufacturers during the 1950s, Arms Mills imported goat hair from Pakistan, Iraq and Iran to make the warm, waterproof lining of men's coats.

The goat hair was not disinfected, and between January 1, 1941, and June 30, 1957, there were 136 cases of cutaneous anthrax at the mill, only one of which was fatal. Sixty percent of the anthrax infections occurred within two weeks of a previous one, which suggested that particular batches of goat hair were more contaminated (or contaminated with more virulent spores) than others. Some years there were no infections and some as many as 16. Cutaneous woolsorters disease was established at the mills. There were no cases of inhalational anthrax until 1957. Then, during a ten-week period from August to November, nine employees had anthrax infections: five inhalational and four cutaneous. Four of the inhalational cases were fatal; one of those who died was a 65-year-old woman who had worked at the mills for nearly 12 years without previously coming down with anthrax.

From May 1957 the mills were being used as a test site for an anthrax vaccine, developed by Dr. George G. Wright of the Biological Warfare Laboratories of the U.S. Chemical Corps at Fort Detrick, Maryland. The military interest in anthrax was the result of competition with the Soviet Union to provide security against possible biological attacks. More specifically, the Soviets had developed an anthrax vaccine for humans, and the United States needed to do likewise. One of the founders of the Fort Detrick biological warfare program was George Merck, who headed the pharmaceutical firm that was attempting to commercialize the vaccine.

Arms Mills was one of four mills in New Hampshire, Pennsylvania and North Carolina used in the study. The 313 Arms Mills employees who joined the study were divided into a group that received the vaccine and a group that received a placebo. None of the five who developed inhalational anthrax had been inoculated with the vaccine, though two of them had elected to join the study and were in the placebo group. The other three, including the one who did not die, were not included in the vaccine trial, one because he refused and the other two because they started working after the trials began.

The outbreak was an opportunity for the doctors conducting the vaccine trials to study "an epidemic of inhalational anthrax: the first in the twentieth century," as their papers were titled. Autopsies of three of the workers established that they had suffered from systemic anthrax infections; bacterial cultures and tests performed on blood samples from others showed positive for the anthrax bacilli. At the end of the trials the vaccine was offered to all employees, and was credited with forestalling further inhalational infections and reducing cutaneous occurrences.

According to health records kept by a resident nurse, none of the people infected in 1957 had previously come down with anthrax. In the sequence of processes that led from unbaling the goat hair to scouring, drying, carding, combing, drawing and weaving it, the researchers found that anthrax cases were concentrated in the dusty work of carding (4), combing (2), weaving (2) and cleaning the weaving bobbins (1). The first worker to develop inhalational anthrax was Antonio Jette, who encountered the spores in the greatest concentration because he cleaned the machines that picked and sorted the unbaled hair.

The authors of the paper, knowing the susceptibility of the anthrax bacilli to chemical modification, suspected that a detergent the plant began to use in 1957 may have released the virulence of the spores. However, the first inhalational case preceded the first use of the detergent. A single bale of black goat hair from Pakistan possibly was the source of the unusually toxic spores: samples caused test animals, guinea pigs and a monkey, to develop anthrax and die. But the lethal dose of these spores calculated from the animal studies was over six times what was in the atmosphere of even the dustiest work situations.

The authors could only speculate that a singularly virulent anthrax strain had caused five cases of inhalational anthrax during the period of the study where none had previously occurred during the entire history of the mills. Neither John Spear nor John Henry Bell, astute observers of the only other inhalational anthrax epidemic described in the medical literature (nineteenth century Bradford—the others were not mentioned), had been able to ascertain why some of those exposed to the same spores in the same concentrations sickened and died, and others didn't. There was no visible thread connecting the cases. The conclusion of the study was that better ventilation was needed in shop rooms and the goat hair might be disinfected before processing, as it was in England. The authors mentioned the "civil defense" implications of anthrax at the very end of the article.

In 1966 a worker in a metal fabricating shop adjacent to the Arms Mills building died of inhalational anthrax, but he had a "smoker's cough" and was already suffering from diabetes and alcoholism. Other people regularly working in the area were unaffected. Yet a woman living at some distance from the factories in that same year developed cutaneous anthrax on her hands. The best guess was that she picked up the spores from knitting yarn, which tested positive for their presence. But this did not explain why only she and not others using the yarn showed the skin lesions.

When the Arms Mills business failed in 1968 the owners wanted to adapt the buildings to a more current urban use, but the "Lethal Spores," as the *Manchester Union-Leader* put it in a 1970 headline, "Could Menace All Manchester." The buildings were closed and their interiors were treated with hot vaporized formaldehyde. When tests revealed that the spores persisted, an incinerator was built on site and the wooden structural beams were burned. The ashes were buried in the mill lot, which became a public park where the city's annual Riverfest is held. No traces of anthrax were found in the soil, and no more anthrax cases of any kind were reported from the area.

The treated bricks were trucked to another location and buried close together (to keep the rats from entering) beneath what became another park. The mills were a major employer and the cases of cutaneous anthrax and even the inhalational epidemic went without comment in the newspaper while the mills were operating. Afterwards, during the Cold War, the threat of foreign spores infiltrating the city from the factory remains required forcible measures. The threat was attacked with chemicals and buried beneath a park.

The families of the people who died in the 1957 epidemic said they did not learn that anthrax had been the agent until 2001, when news media contacted them in the wake of the October mail-borne outbreak. As the news of the first inhalational anthrax case in Florida became known, a reporter for the *Manchester Union-Leader* asked Antonio Jette's wife and for her reaction. Mrs. Jette said that she feared the Florida death was due to terrorism, and was not caused by the "natural anthrax" that killed her husband.

Local hospitals and physicians likewise said they were unaware of the nature of the epidemic during its occurrence. This may have been the result of deliberate concealment by company officials and government agents, or it may be a reflection of mill towns' tendency to overlook maladies resulting from the factories in their midst. Men had been dying in Bradford for years before the cause was studied. It was a hazard of working in the mills, which is why it was called woolsorters disease. Cutaneous anthrax was familiar, and an accepted risk; inhalational anthrax was outside the experience of everyone except specialists. When it occurred it was passed over as it had been in Bradford.

One investigative journalist obtained a document dated summer 1958 detailing a meeting attended by Fort Detrick officials, a representative of Britain's Porton Down Biological Warfare Center, and Drs. Philip Brachman and Stanley Plotkin, the lead authors of the 1957 epidemic study. The purpose of the meeting was to continue giving "maximum support to the BWL (Biological Weapons Laboratories) program of follow-up investigation on "N" (the code letter for weapons-grade anthrax, which was being produced in quantity by Fort Detrick at that time).

At the meeting Brachman presented a rough version of the clinical observations and epidemiology which were to appear in the 1960 papers on the Manchester epidemic. Interest by the biological warfare elite in the Arms Mills deaths seemed to go beyond the ostensible testing of an anthrax vaccine. In 1958 a young military volunteer at Fort Detrick had died of inhalational anthrax after receiving injections of live and killed anthrax bacteria. He could not have died from the vaccine alone.

In 1995 the National Committee on Human Radiation Experimentation requested from the Department of Defense documents related to human experimentation. Neither Arms Mills nor any other anthrax vaccine test site was mentioned in the final report, which can suggest a conspiracy of silence or just that the investigators did not find human experimentation had taken place. Looking backward from 2001, some commentators saw the military testing not only the vaccine but the agent N, another example of human experimentation by germ warriors without a regard for human life.

Whether Arms Mills was an example of the U.S. Army's germ warfare testing, both attack and defense, or an occasion when experienced medical observers happened to be present when an inhalational anthrax epidemic took place, its entire history is viewed through the model of woolsorters disease.

Untreated foreign fibers are unleashed in an enclosed space agitated by machines and people die suddenly. Now the attack-defense duality is included in the model: the deaths may be the result of deliberate introduction of the lethal component or the result of a failure to defend against its natural occurrence. That actual wool (or hair) sorters were afflicted creates a historical basis. Woolsorters disease was replicated at Arms Mills by a combination of factors, including the presence of reporting observers. But the model had evidently become something both to be used as a framework to describe and imagine events, and to plan them.

In 1959 Drs. W.S. Albrink and R.J. Goodlow reported inducing inhalational anthrax in a chimpanzee by exposing the ape to the atmosphere of a textile mill where goat hair was processed.

In 1971 Dr. Frederic Dalldorf of the U.S. Army Biological Center at Fort Detrick, Maryland, in collaboration with Dr. Arnold Kaufmann, a veterinarian, and Dr. Philip Brachman, a physician and part of the epidemiology program of the Centers for Disease Control, collectively published a research paper entitled "Woolsorters' Disease: An Experimental Model."

The scientists had housed a collection of ninety-one monkeys, two to a cage, in a trailer beside a North Carolina textile mill where goat hair, "known to contain anthrax spores," was regularly processed.

The dust drawn into a hood over the picking machine that raked the dry clumps of goat hair was passed through the trailer and out through the factory exhaust. It was the same environment in which Antonio Jette had worked at Arms Mills.

The purpose of the experiment was to study the pathogenesis and pathophysiology of anthrax, "but also demonstrate a common mechanism of tissue injury and death caused by many bacteria."

The monkeys were exposed to the dust for a maximum of thirty-two days, in five distinct groups subjected to five exposure periods over eighteen months. Twenty-three of them contracted anthrax infections; twenty died of the disease and it was considered a contributing cause in the deaths of three others. Eight monkeys died of other causes.

"The anthrax mortality rates were directly related to the amount of exposure," which meant not only the amount of time exposed but also the density of spores in the dust. Through autopsies and histological examination the experimenters analyzed how the bacterial infections proceeded among the cells of the lymph nodes and lungs. Photographs of infected tissue samples were reproduced in the report.

Since the 1930s it was known that the bacterial capsule of anthrax itself caused antibodies to form, and since 1955 it was known that anthrax has its effects due to a toxin produced by the bacteria, and not by the bacteria alone. The toxin's action upon living tissue caused vascular injury with edema, hemorrhage and thrombosis.

The experiment used woolsorters disease as a model, but it was not dedicated to reducing the disease among the workers in the mill. The only mention of workers in the article is at the beginning under the Methods and Materials heading: "all employees in the plant had been immunized with Wright anthrax antigen." The field evaluation of the vaccine in which Brachman participated nine years earlier is footnoted.

The physicians had observed their Hippocratic oath even before beginning the 1971 study and made sure that workers exposed to the spore-laden dust were not in danger of infection. The ability to channel the dust from the factory through the trailer was the result of the application of a form of the Bradford Rules to the workplace: updraft venting of the sorting area, and the innovation of mechanized sorting.

The experiment also was possible because this factory, like the factories in Bradford, was processing anthrax-laden goat hair from overseas. That this fiber carried and transmitted anthrax to those who handled it was known even before woolsorters disease was defined as a clinical entity. But the experiment results offered no arguments for discontinuing the processing of goat hair, or stopping the venting of the dust into the outside through exhaust. That's not what the experiment was about.

The conditions that caused woolsorters disease, against which the workers were protected by a vaccine, were a resource to be exploited for knowledge of the pathology of bacterial infection. If that was the aim then why not just infect experimental animals with any of the virulent strains of anthrax that had been collected since the 1930s? Eppinger and many others since him had studied the cellular pathology of the disease. Why did further knowledge need to be gathered through this experiment?

It clearly wasn't to protect the workers or explore how the infection might be affecting people down and up the commodity stream, the ones who pulled the goat hair or the users of the mills' products.

The experiment was an investigation of the pathology of inhalational anthrax, not of cutaneous anthrax (skin infections), the only form that still occurred among textile workers, or of ingestional anthrax (from eating tainted meat), which didn't occur at all among textile workers. And it was not only an investigation of the cellular effects of the toxin, but of the susceptibility of monkeys to the disease at different exposure levels.

Unprotected by vaccines and subjected to the full force of machine-driven spore-laden dust flow, the monkeys were like woolsorters before there had been any medical or civic attention to their working health. Even without consulting the complex history of the North Carolina textile industry, its technology, raw material sources and workers, it is obvious that the conditions that produced woolsorters disease were replicated there so well that an experiment like this one could be undertaken. The replication was not deliberate: the factory was not set up to cause the disease. But it wasn't designed to avoid it either.

The material circumstances—anthrax spores communicated to humans through the air from imported goat hair—were secondary to the model of woolsorters disease that had been reproduced, could be experimentally manipulated and could even be extracted from the factory setting. Arms Mills was the discovery and the North Carolina mill was a reproduction. Possibly the North Carolina mill was Arel Mills, one of the four sites at which the Wright vaccine was tested in 1957.

Woolsorters disease had become a model for the interpretation of disease outbreaks in textile mills, and a model for staging such outbreaks, for vaccine testing and for military attack-defense studies. The model had become separated from its own circumstances and even its own history because it had become imaginatively assimilated to another model.

On 25 November 1969 President Richard Nixon announced that the United States was unilaterally renouncing the use, research and development of all biological agents and weapons. To reassure the public and the military, Nixon added that research would continue into immunization and safety measures.

Nixon's public statement was the most prominent expression of a policy movement in the military and the administration to end the U.S. Army's forty-three-year-old germ warfare program. Pentagon officials were willing to accept termination of the program because they had greater faith in the tactical and deterrent effectiveness of fission and fusion bombs, and they were aware of the public relations value of renouncing insidious biological weapons while the Soviet Union was aggressively pursuing the development of these weapons. It was also the beginning of an ultimately successful strategy of forcing the Soviets to move away from cheap biological and chemical weapons and concentrate on ruinously expensive nuclear weapons.

Over the course of a year the army gathered and openly incinerated all their stocks of biological warfare agents. That incineration, mostly at Dugway proving ground in Nevada, would itself have implications for the health of workers in the vicinity. The army continued to produce small quantities of anthrax and other agents at Dugway, to be used for testing in bioweapons laboratories at Fort Detrick, Maryland.

Taking as their basis an earlier British proposal, administration officials began the diplomatic work of forming a worldwide Biological and Toxic Weapons Convention banning both germ and chemical weapons of mass destruction. Seventy-eight nations, including the United States and the Soviet Union, signed the convention in April 1972, and most of these nations' legislatures had ratified it by the time President Gerald Ford signed it for the United States in 1975. The list of signatories has grown over the years.

The woolsorters disease study was taking place in an environment of international rapprochement over the possible use of biological and chemical weapons during the Cold War. The motives for this emergent agreement among the major combatants parallel the motives for the woolsorters model study.

In the germ warfare and Cold War context, woolsorters disease is a model of an attack of suffused anthrax spores deliberately deployed to disable and kill civilians. A key connection between the woolsorters and germ warfare models is the knowledge on the part of the scientists that anthrax spores can be prepared and distributed in the air as a military assault. The spores are delivered on foreign goat hair (not domestic sheep fleece) or they are sent by a hostile power into the air we breathe.

The monkeys stand for civilians captive in some setting where the air can be affected and the factory stands for any source of airborne anthrax spores. The infection rate and pathology exhibited by the monkeys tells us what to expect from an attack, but they also tell us the concentration needed to make the attack effective. The knowledge gained is simultaneously useful for defense and offense.

The implementation of the woolsorters model in the context of germ warfare was not just a cynical attempt to mask military planning with medical research. The complex of the disease was more fully replicated than that.

In the mid–1950s there was a series of cutaneous anthrax outbreaks at the Arel Mills textile plant near Charlotte, North Carolina.

Within months of the plant opening in 1953, and again in 1955, there were individual instances of anthrax-caused skin infection. In 1956, six workers in the spinning rooms blending imported goat hair with cotton to make the lining fabric of coats developed the blackened skin lesions of anthrax within days of each other. No one came down with the inhalational form. Arel Mills was one of the test sites for the Wright vaccine in 1957, though it wasn't named as such in the publications on the Arms Mills outbreak of inhalational anthrax.

North Carolina public health authorities, sensitive to workers' health issues at textile plants, adopted preventive rules. They attempted to keep the contaminated goat hair from entering the state or, failing that, they tried to encourage the plant owners to disinfect the goat hair before workers handled it.

Like the manufacturers John Henry Bell addressed in Bradford during the 1880s, the North Carolina plant owners dismissed procedures for washing the goat hair and hides with formaldehyde as too expensive, and likely to create another set of health problems from chemical exposure.

In 1952 Brachman had published the results of a field evaluation of the Wright vaccine in textile plants. With the most recent outbreak, he offered the plant owners and the workers vaccination as an alternative to treating the raw material.

The effectiveness of the vaccine did not prove sufficient to maintain the Arel Mills plant, which closed soon after the vaccine was tested. Plant owners did not want to pay for the repeated administration of the vaccine after workers realized that it could prevent the hideous skin infections. The history of the woolsorters model at Arel Mills was different from that at Arms Mills. It was another set of mills in North Carolina which provided the spore-laden air to expose the monkeys in the late 1960s experiment.

Woolsorters disease does not exist simply as a result of goat hair brought into contact with workers in enclosed factories. The possibility of treating the goat hair to eliminate the spores, known since Bradford, and, later, the possibility of vaccinating the workers to make them resistant to the proliferation of the bacteria should they be exposed, are both components of woolsorters disease.

The factory owners and the workers themselves can decide if either of these measures is implemented. And of course the bacteriologists and physicians can provide both the means and the advice to remove the spores from the environment or immunize those exposed to the disease. Entering further into this motive is the defensive or offensive use of anthrax in germ warfare.

Each reported instance of woolsorters disease is an instance of all these factors, and where the disease is deliberately or accidentally reproduced all of these factors are present. The 1971 study was a report of another instance of woolsorters disease and can be described in the same terms as any other outbreak of the disease.

In 1988 the United States Centers for Disease Control and Prevention publication *Epidemiologic Notes and Reports* described the first case of human anthrax in the United States since 1984. A 42-year-old male maintenance worker at a North Carolina textile mill developed a lesion on his right forearm which did not respond to topical treatment. Hospitalized with pain, fever, chills and edema, he was diagnosed with cutaneous anthrax, and treated intravenously with antibiotics. His condition improved and he was released to return to work a little over a month after he came down with the infection.

Blood and wound cultures did not reveal any presence of anthrax bacilli, but another assay demonstrated the presence of antigens against anthrax bacterial capsules and the presence of an anthrax toxin. The man had not come into contact with anything outside the plant which would have caused his infection (no travel, contact with animal or agricultural products likely to carry spores). The plant where the afflicted man worked had never had a case of anthrax during its twenty-five years of operation, and there was no vaccination program.

The plant did use cashmere goat hair from China, Afghanistan and Iran, which was washed at a plant in Texas before being shipped to North Carolina. The team of doctors, nurses, veterinarians and bacteriologists who reported the study found that eight of twelve cashmere samples examined contained anthrax spores. They recommended a vaccination program for both the Texas and North Carolina sites. There was no word on whether this suggestion was implemented.

Despite glaring differences, the environment of woolsorters disease remains constant between the death of Samuel Firth in 1878 and the survival of the worker at the North Carolina plant in 1987. The North Carolina worker developed a cutaneous infection which treatment prevented from becoming systemic. The substrate of skin lesions, or carbuncles, that had always occurred among workers, and which they apparently had resisted, and which were not included in woolsorters disease, now became foregrounded as a sign of anthrax infection.

Samuel Firth, the afflicted woolsorter, did not survive but his demise created the opportunity for medical authorities to give their urgings to the manufacturer's legal and finally political force.

The afflicted maintenance man did survive, and the investigation of his infection galvanized a team of public health practitioners to examine its cause and potential for further damage. The investigative institutions were in place; the scientific and clinical means for treatment and prevention were available. One successfully treated skin lesion was the occasion for a thorough investigation and suggestions for preventive measures, which, as in 1878, did not have to be implemented.

In 1987 the goat hair was being washed (as it was not in 1878 and 1956), but that did not remove all the infectious material; the vaccine works but only is recommended, as were the Bradford Rules at first. The conditions for woolsorters disease remain in the equilibrium reached between the opposing and mutually accommodating interests of regulatory knowledge and political economy, which includes germ warfare.

On August 18, 2000, the BBC World Service reported that a worker in Bradford, England, was diagnosed with an anthrax lesion on his skin. The article mentioned that anthrax was once a common illness among workers in the woolen trade, that it is sometimes referred to as woolsorters disease, and described anthrax as a biological weapon of mass destruction, but did not give specifics about where or how the man might have picked up the infection, only that his colleagues had been contacted. Only the woolsorters model was on exhibit in this article.

One other factor continues. J.W. Ezzell, the bacteriologist among those reporting the 1987 case, was stationed at the U.S. Army Medical Research Institute of Infectious Diseases, Fort Detrick, Maryland. Dr. Ezzell was a specialist in the infectiousness of airborne anthrax, an expertise difficult to obtain under normal circumstances. He was a consultant in the investigation of the 2001 cases of inhalational anthrax at American post offices and media centers. Dr. Brachman was publicly consulted about these outbreaks as well.

# 4

# Mailsorters

When in October 2001 American agents entered Kabul, Afghanistan, they were not seeking one of the sources of contaminated goat hair that had been spreading spores into the air of European and American factories for over one hundred and fifty years. In the office of an organization headed by Bashiruddin Mehmood, a Pakistani nuclear scientist, among other objects they found sketches and some components for a bomb designed to shower anthrax spores on a large public gathering from a balloon disguised as a weather balloon. There were disassembled parts of a Russian rocket, a canister labeled "helium" and copies of documents on anthrax downloaded from the Internet. The discovery was widely reported in Western newspapers, often with photos of the sketches.

Anthrax in the period before the mailings of October 2001 was publicly imagined in terms of a woolsorters' model aerosol environment created by terrorists.

In the July–August 2000 issue of a United States Centers for Disease Control periodical, *Emerging Infectious Diseases*, Thomas Inglesby of the Johns Hopkins School of Medicine describes the scenario of a possible bioterrorist attack on an American city: FBI offices in five U.S. cities receive threats that a "shower of anthrax would rain on U.S. cities," if certain demands are not met. Shortly afterward an unmarked truck traveling upwind of a large outdoor stadium where a football game is going on releases an aerosol of spores which travels undetected over the stadium and environs. As the driver of the truck and his associates escape, hundreds of people develop symptoms of inhalational anthrax.

Jeanne Guillemin's book, *Anthrax: The Investigation of a Deadly Outbreak*, published in 1999, was a careful study of the 1979–80 deaths of civilians in the vicinity of a (then) Soviet biowarfare facility. Guillemin described the painstaking but thwarted pinpointing of the locations of

44

individuals at the time of the accidental release of spores from the facility. The human map traced the shape of an anthrax plume spreading over the city. This representation of aerial anthrax linked the sudden onset of disease with a political system. It was anything but fiction, but it fit into the current imagining of an anthrax environment.

In his 1999 novel *Vector,* the prolific writer of medical thrillers Robin Cook imagines a disgruntled Russian technician aiding American domestic terrorists in their attempt to introduce anthrax spores into the ventilation system of a large office building.

The bacteriologist John Tierno, admitting that he doesn't write thrillers, includes a piece in his book on germs about a disgruntled USARMIID (U.S. Army Research Medical Institute in Infectious Diseases) lab technician using a crop duster to spread anthrax spores over Manhattan on New Year's Eve.

In the wake of the 2001 attacks, the independent researcher Martin Furmanski suggested that the prevailing winds at the time may have carried spores to the people whose infections were difficult to explain by contact with a known source. But in 1997, before the woolsorters model took hold in public discourse, an obscure medical researcher named Steven Hatfill was cited in a *Washington Times* article reflecting on fake threats of anthrax placed in food, and speculating that "some guy might spray plague bacteria around the men's room in the World Trade Center."

A newspaper article on San Francisco's bio-warfare sentries (April 3, 2003) began with the scenario "something as innocuous as an advertising airplane dragging a banner over Pacific Bell Park—as it secretly sprays anthrax on the crowd." Anthrax remains in the air.

There was only one known deliberate attempt to create an anthrax aerosol environment in a populated space. In 1993 the Japanese cult Aum Shinri Kyo dispersed anthrax spores in a liquid medium into the air of Tokyo, first from their building and then from trucks traveling the center of the city. There were no anthrax infections reported. No one even knew they made the attempt until cult members later confessed.

When the actual attack occurred, it was not engineered by foreign terrorists, and it was not a mass release of spores in an aerosol sprayer or a bomb. It came from an envelope.

He opened letters all day long, the wife of the first victim of inhalational anthrax, Bob Stevens, told an investigating doctor. Stevens was an editor for American Media, Inc., a publisher of tabloid newspapers (*The Sun*) located in Boca Raton, Florida. His job was to sort through the many pieces of mail proclaiming the advent of flying saucers, offering photographs of monstrous births or revealing the scandalous activities of celebrities, in search of striking pictures. He was an expert photo retoucher, having rendered lifelike an image of Elvis Presley in his coffin and a giraffe-necked human, among many other displays.

Stevens was of British origin, an outdoorsman with a good medical history even though he had needed a cardiac stent. While on a family trip to North Carolina, where he visited Charlotte and several other cities, he felt some nausea and respiratory difficulty, but it reached a crisis only after he returned home five days later. No other cases of anthrax appeared in North Carolina and attention moved elsewhere. After Stevens' death the American Media website contritely announced that they would concentrate on news stories with stronger evidence and verifiable rumors about celebrities. They were also relocating their operations, and the building was decontaminated. Sales of American Media's tabloids briefly declined as their readers feared the papers themselves might carry anthrax.

Stevens' colleagues recalled that he opened a letter addressed to pop star Jennifer Lopez and a strange-smelling beige powder he considered suspicious drifted out. The powder entered Stevens' lungs and turned into a fulminant anthrax infection.

The results of a culture drawn from a spinal tap led physicians to suspect anthrax soon after Stevens was admitted to the hospital, and they initiated aggressive treatment. But Stevens had come to the hospital after the latent period of the infection was over and the bacilli had spread into critical areas of his body. An autopsy confirmed the cause of death, and the anthrax finding was only then released to the media.

The federal authorities on alert for deaths from any unusual infections at first thought Stevens must have drunk water from a contaminated stream while hiking, or been in a shop selling goods made from imported hides, but they could find no evidence of this. Then Stevens' colleagues recalled the envelope, which had been destroyed, and another employee in the building was hospitalized with an anthrax infection.

The spores lingered in the air of the building even after a thorough decontamination, yet no one else who worked there came down with any form of anthrax though several tested positive for the presence of spores.

*The Wall Street Journal* on October 19, 2001, reported that workers in the building were being shunned by others, as if they could spread anthrax by contact.

Shortly after Stevens died employees of two television networks in Manhattan, and a seven-month-old child who had been visiting the offices of another network, developed lesions of cutaneous anthrax, which was identified and treated. A letter carrier and a sorter for two post offices in New Jersey then were diagnosed with skin infections.

Over the next seven days, from October 21 to October 28, 2001, four workers at the Brentwood mail center in Washington, D.C., one at a State Department mail facility and another the Hamilton Township mail center in New Jersey, all came down with inhalational anthrax. Two of the Brentwood employees died, but the others recovered. Another worker at the Hamilton Township center also developed an internal anthrax infection on October 30. He was the last postal worker to show any signs of anthrax infection.

Other workers at the affected facilities were tested for anthrax spores and all were offered both oral antibiotics and vaccine. Kathie Nguyen and Ottilie Lundgren, the two remaining people who died of anthrax in late October and early November, did not work for the post office, or open mail as part of their jobs. It became a work of epidemiological detection to try to determine how they were exposed to the spores.

The measures taken to protect individuals who may have been exposed and to eliminate the spores from the buildings seem to have been effective at least by the measure of no further anthrax instances. Tests of the buildings still showed a few lingering spores and the buildings remained closed as studies and decontamination proceeded.

The outbreak was over. Unsorted mail that had arrived at Brentwood during that period was stored in sealed drums and examined as potentially infectious material, and as evidence of a crime. No new sources were allowed to enter the system. The Brentwood facility remained closed for further decontamination, and postal workers were offered anthrax vaccine, which many refused. All the while hoax letters labeled "anthrax" containing a white powder continued to be sent through the mails.

In all twenty-two people were listed as having anthrax-related illness, eleven with cutaneous infections and eleven inhalational, of whom five died. All of these cases together were taken as an anthrax outbreak deliberately caused by a human agent, the first time in American history that anthrax had been spread that way. The letters resembled hoax letters, but this was the first time they contained a substance that actually caused harm.

Bob Stevens was reputedly the first person to suffer from inhalational anthrax in the United States since 1978, when the victims were the unvaccinated Arms Mills workers.

Between 1978 and 2001 there were other, isolated cases in the United States of inhalational anthrax. Some of them were unvaccinated employees of textile mills who breathed the environment, a maintenance man who entered the plant to change a light bulb or a secretary who left the office to find someone in the machine room. There were also individuals who developed anthrax infections without ever having entered a known anthrax environment, but they were not part of the prevailing woolsorters model and remained as obscure as the numbers of people in parts of Africa and India who suffered anthrax infections for reasons unrelated to terrorism.

Though all those affected did not work or live together, their illness was treated as happening within the same large social and political structure. During October 2001 people hoarded supplies of Ciprofloxacin, the antibiotic of choice for anthrax infections. Masks, respirators and devices signaling the presence of spores were all available for sale over the Internet.

The mails, which reach everyone, had become the factory in which anthrax spreads. Even the two victims who were not associated with the mail system were connected to anthrax through the sorting and delivery of mail in their vicinity. Single spores traveled from an imbued envelope and entered the respiratory systems of Kathie Nguyen and Ottilie Lundgren.

The means of transmission was letters, not an animal or animal product. The letter that released the spores that killed the tabloid editor was simply addressed to the news organization he worked for. The letters that released spores in Washington were addressed to two of the leading senators of the Democratic Party, Tom Daschle and Joe Lieberman, and to an Independent, Patrick Leahy, who had dropped his Republican affiliation. In New York letters were addressed to network news anchors, and to a *New York Times* reporter who had written on bioterrorism.

None of the politicians and celebrities to whom the letters were addressed actually came into contact with anthrax. A single spore recovered from the nose of California Senator Dianne Feinstein made the newspapers. Some of the people who opened mail sent to celebrities developed anthrax lesions, but the cluster of illness and deaths from inhalational anthrax was confined to people who worked in the vicinity of high-powered sorting machinery.

Like the machinery in textile mills, the rapid postal processors aerosolized the spores packaged in the letters and for a brief moment, in a confined space, created mailsorters disease parallel to the woolsorters disease that was produced in Bradford one hundred and seventy five years earlier. The affinity of the machine for the spores (and of the spores for the machines) was so great that spores were still being found on the rollers of the main mail chute in Brentwood weeks after several decontaminations and sequestration of mail to prevent further infected letters from entering the stream. And spores were detected in air samples as well.

The differences between woolsorters disease of European and American textile workers and the mailsorters disease that briefly appeared in October–November 2001 are differences in sources and intent. But on examination, these differences become absorbed into the same general pattern. An extraneous infectious agent enters into an established mechanical process that distributes the agent to the operators.

The discovery of anthrax bomb plans among papers in Kabul confirmed the potential for anthrax to be used destructively as an atmosphere. Despite a few coincidences—such as the residence of the terrorist Mohammed Atta being located not far from the American Media building in the months before the September 2001 attacks on the Pentagon and World Trade Center—there was no clear evidence connecting the anthrax mailings to al-Qaeda. Terrorists were connected only to the wish to create anthrax atmospheres.

It was not the intention of the factory owners to make the woolsorters sick, but once the cause of the particular sickness was identified the factory owners only reluctantly took steps to reduce it. It was the intention of whoever put anthrax spores into envelopes addressed to individuals to cause illness, as it was the intention of those who designed the spores that they become widely distributed once they entered the air.

While individuals might be targeted by a name on the envelope, they are not the ones who get anthrax unless they actually handle the envelope. The woolsorters disease model has its limits.

In the days after the mailsorters' deaths from anthrax, Dr. Philip Brachman, then a professor at the Emory University School of Public Health, was interviewed by reporters as an expert on anthrax infections. Brachman's career had spanned the investigation of anthrax in North Carolina mills, the testing of vaccines and the implementation of the woolsorters model for studying infection. Through figures like him, the intellectual coordinates of woolsorters disease were maintained. The persistence of the model is not due to any one of its aspects but to their continuing and repeated coherence.

Bacteria, transmission, workers, and interiors all converge to cause the disease to recur. Woolsorters disease is not the only environment of anthrax among humans, and anthrax is by no means the most serious condition suffered by the workers who also are exposed to it.

Woolsorters disease is given as an example in microbiology textbooks and in industrial medicine textbooks. It doesn't usually appear in lists of respiratory diseases suffered by workers in mines, sugar cane factories, pepper mills and potteries. When work conditions in mills are shown from the worker's point of view, "brown lung" that results from the long-term breathing of the dust of manufactures is the main concern and anthrax isn't even mentioned.

The U.S. Department of Public Health issued a series of reports on "the health of workers in the dusty trades" in the 1930s. The trades they referred to were granite quarrying and cotton cloth manufacturing. Wool and anthrax were not included at all. Woolsorters disease is a specialized involvement of bacteria with humans under the guidance of experts.

In mid–January 2002 authorities halted the reopening of the Hart Senate Office Building in Washington when a plastic bag containing equipment and suiting that had been used in the decontamination fell out of the ceiling as workers removed tiles. The material tested negative for bacteria and the building was reopened.

The means of decontamination had become the potential source of contamination. The history of woolsorters disease had come full circle and was compacted into the objects used by experts that were supposed to prevent it, and which actually weren't infectious.

Within the current matrix of industry and office space anthrax only breaks out occasionally, somewhere on the border between deliberation and negligence, between dust and bacteria. The remarkable ability of anthrax spores to be carried by human activity into both humans and animals is enhanced by developments in technology that do not relate to spores at all.

Human awareness of and intentions toward the bacteria have matured and become more practiced over the last few hundred years, and the ability to protect against infections has increased with the ability to cause infections in test subjects and enemies. The woolsorters disease model contains this fluctuating mixture of abatement and attack, including another, apparently older model that only some die.

In the American attacks of late 2001, a stream of specially designed anthrax spores coursed through the mail system in one section of the country. The woolsorters model seemed to motivate the design of the spores as much as the design of the attack. The spores must have reached a great many people but they germinated in only a few.

# 5

# Only Some Die

A twenty-year survey conducted by the American Public Health Association, Industrial Hygiene Section between 1919 and 1938 found 1,683 cases of human anthrax with a mortality of 21 percent. Of 640 cases analyzed, 629 were external (cutaneous) and 11 internal (pulmonary and ingestive, though no ingestive cases were reported). All 11 of the internal cases were fatal but hundreds of the cutaneous cases were as well.

The disease was enough of a threat for governments, insurers, and individual companies to create warning signs, often in several different languages, exhibiting photographs of the characteristic skin lesions, and advising the workers to bring any blister resembling the image to the attention of the company medical staff. The United States Department of Labor issued posters with photographs of anthrax lesions and warnings to bring any blister of that appearance to the attention of a supervisor or medical staff (see Appendix B).

The survey authors observed that anthrax among tannery workers, who accounted for the majority of cases, occurs during "prosperous periods" when the demand for hides is high and the pressure to process the quickly excludes time-consuming tests for the presence of bacteria during inspection. During less prosperous periods, the demand for leather declines and so do the reported anthrax cases.

The incidence of tannery-related anthrax fell as the economic depression of the 1930s set in: more time for testing and less demand for hides. At the same time the incidence of wool-industry anthrax rose as the demand for cheaper wool clothing increased. The high cost of applying the Bradford Rules and disinfecting imported wool in England caused it to be diverted to the United States, where textile workers handled it raw.

Like woolsorters disease, tanners' anthrax and American workers

51

getting anthrax because they worked with untreated wool were the result of an intersection of economic, social and technical factors.

The survey also mentions occasional cases of cutaneous anthrax from shaving brushes, hair brushes and agricultural activities. As the century progressed the clusters of cases became more specialized with more specialized uses for animal products that might be a medium for spores.

Any industrial or consumer practice that regularly caused cuts or scrapes in the skin exposed to spore-bearing animal products could lead to an anthrax infection. Men shaving their faces with straight razors could receive small cuts then vulnerable to spores carried by shaving brushes made from horsehair and used to spread lather. During the First World War, the United States Quartermaster's office refused to allocate horsehair shaving brushes to the troops because they might spread anthrax.

Shaving brush anthrax was one of the fears of the period. Instances are sometimes identified in personal reminiscences. Laura Anne Harrison, an assistant in the genealogy room of the Hickory, North Carolina, library, recalls the 1921 death of her grandfather from anthrax because a horsehair shaving brush touched an open pimple on his face. On Easter Sunday morning 1921 Fred Littlejohn, a supervisor for an Ohio colliery company, nicked his face while shaving, and later that day complained of feeling ill. By the next day he developed a high fever and several days later he died of "blood poisoning, a type called Anthrax, common to horses."

At the beginning of *The Mottled Lizard* (1962), the second volume of her autobiographical novel that began with *The Flame Trees of Thika*, Elspeth Huxley describes her father's request made of her mother, returning to Kenya from England after the First World War. Robin asks Tilly to bring him a windmill and a shaving brush. The windmill she can't manage and the shaving brush, she explains, would carry anthrax.

Later, as they travel over the countryside in a balky vehicle on the way to their remote property, Tilly hatches another of her entrepreneurial schemes.

> "Surely badgers don't get anthrax," she inquired. "I'm thinking of the shaving brush."
>
> "It was only a rumour. They're hideously expensive in Nairobi anyway."
>
> "Badgers are indigenous," Tilly reflected. "I'm sure I've seen them about."
>
> "I'm afraid it may be the piston rings...."
>
> "If they have the right hair for shaving brushes we might start a local industry. You could get an awful lot of brushes out of one badger, I should think."

As with most of their schemes this comes to naught. It does reflect contemporary beliefs about brushes and badgers.

In 1927 W.D. Stovall, the director of the Wisconsin State Laboratory of Hygiene, authored a paper published in the *Wisconsin Medical Journal* on a case of human anthrax among the many cases of animal anthrax in the state, acquired from a badger hair shaving brush. Japanese badger-hair brushes imported during the period were blamed for instances of facial anthrax. A newspaper clipping from 1931 preserved in the National Archive of Australia recounts the death of G.M. Murphy of Pino Pirie, South Australia, "supposedly from infection by the use of a shaving brush."

The consumer anthrax of shaving materials was reported in magazines as late as 1939, and was probably diminished only by a switch in shaving habits that all but eliminated brushes. A British company selling badger hair brushes today carries on its website a paragraph mentioning the horsehair shaving brush anthrax of the First World War as something their badger-hair brushes are certain not to repeat.

Accidental shaving brush infection turned Cold War plot merges with the terrorism threat. An unnamed Texas laboratory worker who contracted anthrax from a shaving nick didn't get it from his shaving brush, but from a container of samples from the 2001 bioterrorist attacks.

Shaving brush anthrax was a rare instance of consumer anthrax reported and reflected in the literature. It emerged at a convergence of materials from overseas with safety razors, home shaving and consumer habits. For the most part anthrax was industrial and occupational, more an inconvenience of the work than a lethal property of the materials.

Clusters of anthrax skin infections were identified in the Belgian and American gelatin industry where the slaughterhouse byproducts used to make the gelatin arrived with anthrax spores. Cutaneous anthrax was almost routine among ranch workers and craft handlers of imported animal hides and hair.

A mink breeder developed anthrax lesions after he skinned mink fed with scrap meat from an infected horse. The rancher was treated with serum and an antibiotic and made a full recovery. After a series of anthrax outbreaks on mink farms in England, skin workers were warned of the dangers they faced handling the mink furs.

Cutaneous anthrax was characteristic of certain industries in which the workers' abraded skin made direct contact with animal products that could carry the spores (hair, gelatin, bone meal).

Inhalational anthrax was woolsorters disease because it was historically confined to the textile industry. After abatement procedures, inhalational anthrax gave way to cutaneous anthrax, which recurred whenever raw material arrived from parts of the world where animal anthrax was endemic. Industrial hygiene measures kept anthrax spores out of the lungs more successfully than off the skin.

When inhalational anthrax cases did continue to occur in America and Europe, they were isolated and idiosyncratic instances in which an unknowing individual encountered a channel of spores. These anthrax infections did not characterize an occupation but rather were instances of spores reaching unprotected individuals unknowingly working with or amid raw animal materials.

In his 1999 novel *Vector*, Robin Cook has the renegade Soviet technician who supplies the right wing plotters (firefighters!) with anthrax spores test his creation by sending an envelope of spores to a carpet importer. The technician assumed that a carpet seller coming down with anthrax would not lead to further inquiry. Cook imagined a typical post-woolsorters urban anthrax infection: isolated, occupational and remarkable until the sources are considered.

Story-like non-industrial cases of anthrax were collected in the medical literature and are repeatedly cited in later studies. Anthrax anecdotes describe peculiar entrances of the spores into urban life. Where plague and cholera made novels and syphilis and AIDS made poetry, anthrax, not spread from person to person directly, only produced stories. The stories were generated by its ability to fatally infect one person before treatment can be administered and then show up elsewhere under unrelated conditions, but perhaps connected to the same supply of spores through a shipment of goat hair or hides. The circumstances that prevailed when and where people picked up anthrax directly from animals were telegraphed to susceptible individuals further along the commodity stream through imported fibers.

Hermann Gold, who conducted a medical survey of anthrax cases and potential treatments in the United States between the 1930s and late 1950s, in his first study reported on two children who showed anthrax lesions on their bodies. It turned out not to be difficult for a local physician to explain. The children had been playing in a lot adjoining a textile mill where imported goat hair was processed, and where one worker had died of woolsorters disease.

Donald Hoffman, a construction worker helping to remodel a hospital in Oxford, Ohio, in 1964 fell ill from a neck abscess which his doctor first diagnosed as cellulitis. Treatment with antibiotics relieved the patient, but the doctors observed a worsening infection and increased the dosage. Suffering constricted breathing and fluctuating blood pressure over the following night, the patient went into shock and died. An autopsy gave ambiguous indications but blood samples taken on admission yielded a growth that was identified as anthrax bacteria.

The ensuing epidemiological detective work, conducted by Dr.

Philip Brachman and an assistant, then of the United States Public Health Service Communicable Disease Center, determined that insulating felt Hoffman had been placing around pipes in the hospital kitchen and nursery contained anthrax spores. Brachman traced the felt to a batch that was in part composed of imported goat hair. The public health officials located and had destroyed the remaining felt, and they alerted other users of the material. It only became clear later how Hoffman had contracted anthrax from the felt: he wore a sweatshirt to work and probably carried a roll of felt over his shoulder, putting it in direct contact with his neck.

On December 28, 1973, a 22-year-old woman, a United States Navy journalist-photographer stationed in Jacksonville, Florida, took shore leave at Port-au-Prince, Haiti, when the hospital ship she was assigned to docked at that city. Medics on the ship treated 30 Haitians for anthrax during the visit. The woman returned to the ship with six bongo drums and one large conga drum with handmade goatskin drumheads. She soon developed an infection in her left eye which was diagnosed as anthrax.

This incident spurred the Centers for Disease Control and Prevention to undertake a review of the records on human anthrax occurring in the District Sanitaire de Cayes, where the woman had done her sightseeing. They found recorded a total of 387 cases (all cutaneous) during 1973 and another 74 during the first four months of 1974. The investigators were unable to trace the source of these infections since cases of animal anthrax were rarely reported. Though anthrax had been endemic in Haiti for some time, producing as many as 500 recorded human cases per year from the 1970s onward, it took one American case to bring about a study. It was speculated that the infections were caused by people using the carcasses of infected animals rather than letting them go to waste. For at least two hundred years they had been taking their chances, ever since the 1770 earthquake made people so desperate for food they consumed the meat of infected cattle.

Between 1963 and 1974, 194 cases of anthrax, cutaneous and inhalational, were identified among Haitians working to produce goatskin crafts for export. The Centers for Disease Control and Prevention team tested 368 goatskin handicraft objects and found 96 contained concentrations of anthrax spores. The Consumer Products Safety Commission tested 287 of these craft objects, including voodoo balancing dolls, mosaic pictures, whole skins and rugs, purses and drums, and found that samples from 72 of them cultured positive for anthrax.

After the 2001 anthrax attacks in the Eastern United States, Haitian news media expressed concern that Haitians would be branded as the originators of anthrax, as they had been associated with AIDS. Haiti was only one country with endemic anthrax producing goods that could carry anthrax spores directly to personal users overseas.

Only American craftspeople working with imported raw materials accounted for the occasional domestic case of anthrax. In the home of a 32-year-old male home handweaver who died of inhalational anthrax in 1976 investigators found yarn which tested positive for anthrax spores. The yarn was obtained from Creative Handweavers, a supply house in Los Angeles which had imported it from Safraz Brothers, Lahore, Pakistan. It contained various mixes of goat and camel hair, and skeins to the amount of about 15,000 pounds had been distributed nationwide. Creative Handweavers cooperated with the Consumer Products Safety Commission to issue a nationwide alert to users of the yarn, warning them to seal the yarn in double plastic bags and call their local or state health department for disposal instructions. Consumers were warned not to attempt to decontaminate or incinerate the yarn. No further anthrax cases came to the national health authorities' attention.

The idiosyncratic non-industrial incidents of anthrax are the result of susceptible individuals entering or recreating the woolsorters' environment out of the same raw materials that produced disease in the factory. The accidental precision of such an encounter is the result of an incursion of spores into space usually free of them, or of individual action that creates such an exposure.

An office secretary in a Philadelphia textile mill in 1971 died of inhalational anthrax while workers in the mill were unaffected, because she left her office and entered the plant on one occasion. A Philadelphia factory worker who died of inhalational anthrax in 1957 seemed to have received his dose of spores not at his workplace but during his daily walks past a plant that processed goat and other animal products to make glue. The man already had sarcoidosis, a condition of tubercle-like growths on the skin and lungs, which seemed to have disposed him to anthrax while others who worked in the plant or merely walked by did not come down with the disease.

An environment of endemic anthrax reaches into the factory through shipments of goat hair, and the factory environment reaches outside or is recreated in an isolated case from raw materials. The anthrax environment known to exist in mills and tanneries is extended to reach people outside their walls.

In October 2002 Philip Brachman was part of team that published a compendium of 49 field investigations of anthrax occurrences, mostly within the United States, involving animals and humans. Only two investigations involved epidemics of inhalational anthrax among humans, Arel Mills and the October 2001 outbreak, and 15 investigations were focused on animal anthrax with no human cases. If humans were involved in the animal outbreaks (only three investigations), it was veterinarians who examined animals afflicted with anthrax or ranch workers who handled the animals' remains. The remaining cases were individual instances.

The occasional odd case of anthrax observed locally but not investigated by a national body gives a few more instances that confirm the nature of the idiosyncratic cases. Nursery workers who spread bone meal made from the bones of cattle dead of anthrax became infected; dock workers who unloaded the bones used to make the bone meal became infected; a football player picked up the disease probably from the stirred up soil of a playing field where diseased cattle had once been buried; a carpet salesman came down with what seemed to be pneumonia after reviewing newly imported stock.

Anthrax was listed as a hazard of historic preservation workers when laborers removing plaster from the walls of King's Cross Station in London developed skin lesions. The horsehair that had been used in the late nineteenth century to bind the plaster was found to carry anthrax spores. Horsehair had been an agent of anthrax transmission through horsehair furniture at the time the station was built in the late nineteenth century. Using horsehair in plaster preserved the spores long after such furniture ceased to be common.

Advertisers of early twentieth century soundproofing panels, Keystone Hair Insulation, informed the buying public that their product was made of "thoroughly disinfected animal hair." Prior to the development of plastics, animal hair was one of the best materials to stifle reverberation in buildings, but the producers of the insulation did not want their buyers to think that infectious matter, anthrax spores, would be released into the insulated building.

In each of these cases conditions that could have caused the deaths of many people caused only the anecdotal or medical case history deaths of individuals. They were index cases for a greatly dispersed population. These individuals encountered anthrax spores from sources like those that have sickened unprotected textile workers and before them farmers and pastoralists for centuries, but not within an environment dense with anthrax.

Even where there was an environment saturated with anthrax spores, only certain individuals sickened and even fewer died. There was a largely forgotten background of people who must have been exposed at the source—the producers of the goat skins for the bongo drums, the original processors of the bone meal—but if they suffered anthrax infections it is not known. The infections came to the attention of those who watch for odd disease occurrences as individual cases, caused by sources that might infect others.

The death of Kathie Nguyen on October 31, 2001, and of Ottilie Lundgren on November 11 under any other conditions would have been classed with these isolated instances. Nguyen worked in the basement of the Manhattan Eye, Ear and Throat Hospital, and Lundgren, long since retired, lived by herself in central Connecticut. They were both isolated individuals, but the source of the spores that reached them was not discernible as it was in other cases. The pathology reports published by a team of investigators in the *Journal of the American Medical Association* in February 2002 concluded that each of the women had indeed died of anthrax but the source of the infection was still unknown.

Both women worked and lived far from the mail processing and media sites of the other October 2001 envelope-borne infections. The timing of their deaths and absence of immediate sources of anthrax in their workplaces and homes caused Nguyen and Lundgren to be associated with the concerted postal attack. It strained the investigation to apply the woolsorters' model of airborne spores to their deaths. Investigators could not find spores in the environments of their everyday lives or at points of recent travel. No one else in the vicinity was stricken by anthrax.

The two women were both over 60 years of age (Nguyen was 61 and Lundgren was 94), and their ages seemed to associate them with others who had died (Bob Stevens was 63; the Brentwood postal workers were 47 and 55). That did not reveal why other people over 45 years of age in their vicinity were not sickened by anthrax. If there was a cloud of anthrax spores that reached individuals some distance from the points of release—the letters—why didn't it affect anyone else? Their deaths seemed to be like the many other idiosyncratic anthrax infections that were recorded over the years. Investigators considered the possibility that plant potting soil, for instance, might have carried a spore or two from bone meal, thus making either or both victims another instance of spores reaching vulnerable individuals through a commodity. But there were no concentrations of anthrax spores in the soil either woman used. They were individual cases somehow connected to the other infections and deaths of late 2001. But why only these two at this time far from each other with no other victims in between?

Calvin Schwabe asked a Maasai "cattle expert" why the Maasai eat the meat of cattle that have died of anthrax. The elder replied that not everyone who eats the meat gets anthrax and not everyone who gets anthrax dies. "Why waste good meat?"

By eating the infected cows, the Maasai recover some of their great investment in the animals, satisfy an immediate need for food and expose themselves in the most direct way to the pathogen. Those who survive ingestive anthrax will probably also survive other exposures; those who don't survive would not be able to continue living where sometimes to have food is to eat infected meat. Schwabe's survey of veterinary practices among other African pastoralists further supported the prevalence of this attitude. The disease cannot be prevented or cured in animals or humans, but why let it take the food?

Change in pastoral societies exposes this attitude as well. While she was a Peace Corps volunteer in Ethiopia, the author's wife Sandi transported to the mission clinic three deathly ill members of a family who had eaten a cow dead of anthrax. The husband, wife and their young son were starving when they came upon the animal. Because they were refugees from another part of the country and not herders, they did not have the local contacts or the knowledge of animal diseases that might have given them pause before eating. Perhaps they did know what eating a dead animal with congealed black blood about the mouth and eyes would lead to, and their hunger overcame usual precautions. Sandi never learned what became of the people, but knowing the missionaries did not have antibiotics, she assumed the worst. The Danakil people, pastoralists who lived in the area, were more direct: they were sure the family died. Only some die, but some do die.

These anecdotes illustrate what ethnographic research has confirmed more generally. People who depend upon livestock for their livelihood, and who live among the animals and their products, have ways of recognizing diseases and avoiding them. They codify their pragmatism in beliefs about sickness which may not coincide with categories of disease and prevention current in European and American urban society but which express the same need to preserve the animals and their human dependents.

Veterinarians who have studied the traditional knowledge of Oromo pastoralists in central Ethiopia found that they recognize anthrax as a contagious condition spread from one animal to another. The name of the disease, *abbaa sangaa*, "father of the ox," is the name of a bird whose urine is thought to initiate new cases of anthrax. The name must not be uttered in the presence of cattle lest it precipitate infection. Possibly the belief codified the observation that the bird appears during those seasons when anthrax spores proliferate. A number of diseases, both human and animal, are explained by bird urine. *Abbaa sangaa* can be used for diseases other than anthrax, and anthrax can have other names or no name at all.

The Oromo diagnose anthrax (and other diseases) in animals by clinical manifestations which they closely monitor (temperature, coat condition, breathing, activity), but these can be similar for a number of diseases. Not satisfied with the black blood flow that suggests to Western veterinarians that an animal has died of anthrax, the Oromo dismember dead animals and roast their muscle. "Respondents claimed that on roasting the size and length of beef, a strand from an animal afflicted with anthrax would remain the same while that from negative ones was reduced to about half the original size."

Roasting the meat of a dead animal would seem to be taking a lot of trouble to determine whether the animal died of anthrax or not. And the roasters would have exposed themselves to anthrax spores and spread them into the soil by draining the animal's blood and butchering its carcass. A pragmatic measure like this helps determine what will be done with each part of a dead animal and the roasting reduces the likelihood the disease will take hold whether the animal is consumed or buried.

The Oromo said that they "usually" avoided eating the meat of animals with the disease but, as Wirtu and colleagues noted, the skinning and carcass manipulation to determine the cause of death and the use of the skin in carpet-making "has serious public health implications."

While these beliefs are locally distinctive in Ethiopia, the practices they encode seem to reflect a general accommodation of anthrax among herders. Anthrax infestations are too infrequent and difficult to ascertain for the herders to have considerable specific knowledge about the cause and healing of the disease. The pragmatic approach to dead animals becomes the source of exported skins and hair that introduces anthrax spores into industrial machinery.

The people who live with the animals are subject to fluctuating visitations of anthrax and they play their own immunity against the investment the animals represent. The number of people actually affected by products taken from diseased animals is so small that it hardly becomes the subject of local lore and the information about the disease agent remains minimal. The isolated cases of anthrax in Western medical literature follow the same pattern.

Ethnographies of herding people known for their cultural embrace of the animals do not mention anthrax or anthrax-like infections. "With regard to the stock it may, however, be said that it suffers from many different diseases and that Nuer usually have some treatment for them, though it may be doubted whether it has much, if any, therapeutic value," is E.E. Evans-Pritchard's dismissal of Nuer veterinary practice and related human health concerns. By contrast, Jacob Black-Michaud, noting that internal parasites kill or maim a great many of the sheep on which the population of Luristan depend, explains that [Western] veterinary medicine has found so many adepts because "the Lurs had few, if any, folk remedies of their own which could keep the sheep from dying or wasting away." Passivity before the "will of God and quiescence to ecological dictates" characterizes the Lurs' entire attitude toward animal husbandry. This frame of mind is very similar to that which is described for Roman Catholic Mexico prior to the introduction of scientific veterinary medicine and especially vaccination practice from Europe at the end of the 19th century.

Anthrax of animals and of humans are not connected, and are part of a much larger realm of affliction which may or may not be broken down into distinct types. Anthrax alone occurs so infrequently that it is not distinguished from similar conditions. Whether the ethnographer is sensitive to the life of the people or is just an outside observer, whether there is an apparent preventive and curative system or not, chance and the will of God prevail before and after Western medicine arrives.

This combination of scientific knowledge and giving in to chance (only some die) was recreated in the textile factories of Europe and America. As knowledge of contagion and specifically preventive measures grew, the regime of chance was replaced by the factory owners and the state.

In August 2000 six members of a Roseau County, Minnesota, family were treated with antibiotics on the assumption that they had become infected from eating the meat of a cow later found to have died of anthrax. One teenager and an adult developed gastrointestinal symptoms, but recovered before it was learned that it was anthrax, and the others who ate the meat did not seem to be affected by the time they were being treated.

Minnesota state health authorities were alerted on August 25 when a veterinarian diagnosed anthrax in a cow that had fallen and died. The farmer then mentioned that another cow had fallen in July, and a veterinarian had approved it for slaughter. A private slaughterhouse had cut the cow and produced steaks and ground beef which the family consumed after cooking.

The anthrax bacteria found in the second cow, and the reported illness of the family members, caused the state epidemiologist to prescribe antibiotics and to administer vaccine from the U.S. Army bioterrorism unit. Though the outward illness had passed, the bacteria might have ridden out the antibiotic regimen in the family members' lymph nodes, and could begin to produce toxins again later. The vaccine would reassure everyone that the authorities had done what is possible.

There was no suspicion of bioterrorism in this outbreak. Anthrax had been reported in a number of other Minnesota herds in 2000, as well as in South Dakota and Manitoba, Canada. But the transition of the disease to humans through eating infected meat was unusual, even unique in American history.

In early 2001 there were a number of outbreaks of anthrax among cattle near Kimberly, South Africa. As a result of eating the carcass of one such animal, 26 people were infected and hospitalized. Antibiotics were not readily available and the hospital had to send for emergency supplies. The journalist Adriana Stuijt, reporting these events, wondered what would happen if the anthrax made its way into the enormous impoverished squatter communities in South Africa, already afflicted with a high rate of HIV-AIDS.

Infected meat had escaped the safeguards of inspection and entered the earlier model in which only some die, which didn't include any of those affected in Minnesota and South Africa. Only a few got sick. The Minnesota family didn't need to know or believe that they could tell whether that it was anthrax that killed the cow by the size of the meat on the shank after roasting. They trusted the veterinarian, and the slaughtering and cooking processes to give them safe food. And this wasn't the only meat available to them. They didn't know they were engaging any anthrax model at all. As Stuijt suggested, however, a South African epidemic could be driven by hunger and preexisting disease.

That first unreported case of anthrax in the Minnesota cow did not raise cautionary alarms and bring into play preventive measures to keep the infection from spreading to other cattle and possibly to humans. Neither farmers nor the veterinarian recognized the presence of the bacteria. The older, vaguer chance model of anthrax, which apparently prevailed in South Africa, reasserted itself in Minnesota before the antibiotics and vaccines were rushed in. Health authorities can't allow that older model to assert itself. The state has a monopoly on anthrax.

When the Sverdlovsk (Soviet Union) anthrax deaths became known to the outside world in 1980, Soviet health authorities explained them as the result of people eating infected meat purchased on the black market. Around the same time, but of less interest to the Western media, were the deaths of 137 people in Rhodesia from eating anthrax-infected cattle.

The earliest forms of germ warfare using anthrax attempted to kill cattle which people would then have to eat. Anthrax was imagined, and implemented, in terms of the chance ingestional model, but the model was now imposed through an act of aggression.

The deaths of Kathie Nguyen and Ottilie Lundgren after the infections and deaths of mailsorters and others threatened to introduce the chance model of infection, death and survival into an urban population.

Government measures were rapidly engaged to safeguard the population against contagion, but the population already had survived. The deaths were explained as the ultimate result of state control of anthrax, where the state had produced the anthrax able to infect people not living with animals and no longer subject to the chance model. State control of anthrax was the capacity to initiate the chance model. Industrial anthrax and all the anecdotal instances of spores making their way into commodities were reassertions of the chance model which authorities both restricted and managed.

Only some died even with the authorities in control, because the authorities were in control.

# 6

# Ancient Anthraxes

Articles about anthrax often allude to its long history, drawing from the Bible, classical sources and medieval chronicles. The articles concentrate on Western plagues and usually leave out references to what may be anthrax in Russian, Chinese, Sanskrit, Persian and Arabic sources. The nineteenth century identification of anthrax bacteria and their association with human and animal diseases has led to a retrospective interpretation of reports of "ancient plagues" among humans and animals as anthrax visitations. The anthrax in these reports is elusive and imagistic. Like the spores themselves, the possibility of anthrax lurks in many places undetected for a long time undetected until there's an outbreak.

The sixth and seventh plagues visited upon Egypt in the Old Testament Book of Exodus have been naturalistically interpreted as anthrax since the early twentieth century.

Scholars treating the Bible as history have attempted to link all ten plagues together in a sequence of natural disasters emerging from the annual Nile floods. Anthrax is a helpful link in the ecological chain.

Literature scholar Greta Hort in 1957 proposed that the Nile flood in the time of the plagues carried an algal bloom permeated with anthrax bacteria. According to Hort's scenario the blood-red tide washed ashore fish dying of anthrax, which in turn infected the frogs and forced them ashore, where they carried anthrax to domestic animals. The flies multiplying in the shore plants decaying in the floods then fed upon the dying animals and carried anthrax to live animals and humans, precipitating the boils of the sixth and seventh plagues. The severe weather that caused the unusual flooding also accounts for the hail and locusts. The plague of darkness and the death of the firstborn are also worked into the sequence.

The role assigned to anthrax in this sequence doesn't accord with its

observed place. For one, it doesn't infect fish or frogs in nature, only in
the laboratory. It can be carried by carrion flies between animals and
humans. It does not spread directly from one animal to another as readily as an epidemic disease, but it does spread from some common source
to a number of animals. In fact, anthrax in this account is acting more like
cholera, which can persist in algae and be carried ashore to humans in fish.
Other writers have eliminated anthrax entirely from the naturalized Biblical plague sequence, and replaced it with other pathogens, for instance
*Pfisteria piscicida*, a microorganism responsible for severe fish kills.

The attempts to connect the plagues together do represent a wish
to see them as part of the actual ecology of ancient Egypt and not isolated supernatural events. Without venturing into epic constructions, it
is possible to tease a peculiar anthrax plague from the words of the Bible.
Seeing anthrax as a plague disease does begin with linking anthrax knowledge to Biblical wording.

The "murrain," the seventh plague visited upon Egypt in Exodus 9
of the Bible, is a word the King James translators took directly from the
Anglo-Saxon. Derived from the Latin "morire," "to die," it simply meant
"death in numbers."

"Murrain" is only used once in the King James Bible, at the end of
Exodus 9:3 to denote a disease of horses, asses, camels, oxen and sheep,
and that has remained its definition in English. It has been used to name
a number of diseases with generally similar symptoms and outcomes.

"Murrain" in this one instance translates the Hebrew word *dbr*, which
is translated 46 other times as "pestilence," and once as "plague." All three
separate English translations of *dbr* occur in Exodus 9, and nowhere else
in the King James Version.

After the murrain has ravaged the livestock of the Egyptians, the
Lord gives instructions to Moses and Aaron:

> Exodus
> 9:8
> And the Lord said unto Moses and unto Aaron, Take to you hand-
> fuls of ashes of the furnace, and let Moses sprinkle it toward the
> heaven in the sight of Pharaoh.
> 9:9
> And they took ashes of the furnace, and stood before Pharaoh; and
> Moses sprinkled it up toward heaven; and it became a boil breaking
> forth with blains upon man, and upon beast.

It is easy to read a great deal into the translated Bible that would not be
supported by the wording of the original text, while not quite grasping
the original text. It is best to center anthrax suppositions by linking the
words of the text to characteristics of anthrax spread.

The ancient Egyptians did describe in their own writings on, and had a hieroglyph for, what probably was anthrax, and a number of other diseases.

If animals died of anthrax and their corpses were incinerated, then the ashes of the furnaces might contain some viable spores and Moses and Aaron may have been engaging in an early version of biological warfare when they cast spore-containing crematory dust into the air. Unlike later germ warriors, Moses didn't have the woolsorters disease model to inspire ambitions of mass inhalational anthrax. The boils and blains were themselves signs of God's wrath, often expressed through pestilence, and the specific causative agent doesn't matter.

The Biblical imagery of anthrax pestilence created by humans spreading ash resurfaces occasionally in imaginative literature, for instance in Richard Hoyt's 1995 novel *Snake Eyes* in which his series detective John Denson tries to undo the work of an itinerant preacher who is using anthrax infections to dramatize his road show. The preacher refers to Moses casting the ash into the air as he begins to move among the people gathered in the revival tent himself infected with anthrax ready to spread.

Moses' *dbr* had two features long associated with anthrax. It caused a skin affliction which looks like coals fallen on bare flesh, caused it to "boil," and it was shared by humans and animals. The crematory dust and the spread through the air suggests the atmosphere that produces inhalational anthrax, and the Hebrew word translated as "blain" or "boil" suggests boiling water, as if the ash had some heated essence that burned the skin. In later periods the smoke of cremated animals dead of anthrax was known to cause disease in those who breathed it.

None of the other evocations of *dbr* translated as "pestilence" in the King James Bible includes either cattle or dust. The late prophetic book of Habakkuk 3:5 reads: "Before him went the pestilence, and burning coals went forth at his feet."

There is no evidence in the rest of the book that this refers to anthrax. The juxtaposition of pestilence with burning coals is, however, prophetic.

At the beginning of Homer's *Iliad* the Achaeans refuse to return the captured daughter of the priest of Apollo and they insult the old man when he comes to plead for her release. Apollo avenges them by descending from Olympus and shooting the arrows of pestilence through the Achaeans' camp. First the dogs, then the asses and finally the men fall to the "miasma," the fierce atmosphere of divine displeasure.

The miasma that spreads from Ethiopia and Egypt into Athens at the beginning of the Peloponnesian War also strikes down both humans and animals. Thucydides, himself an observant survivor of the plague, notes in his *History of the Peloponnesian War* that its fever passed from one person to another, and no amount of sacrifice or prayer could stop it.

A legend grew that Hippocrates himself showed the Athenians how to dispel the miasma by building fires which warmed and dried the city's cold humidity, in keeping with Hippocratic theory. Thucydides recorded, however, that the doctors were the most likely to die because they visited the sick to apply their useless remedies.

There is nothing really to suggest that Homer's or Thucydides' miasma actually was anthrax, but their words contributed to a vision of plague that has included anthrax. Even after the nature of its infection became known, the spread of anthrax was still envisioned to be a miasma and it was even deliberately engineered to act like a miasma covering a city or an arena. If anthrax were a miasma it could extend from Florida to Connecticut and kill both Bob Stevens and Ottilie Lundgren. The *dbr* of Egypt becomes the miasma of Greece in some twentieth century imaginations.

While these Biblical and miasmatic visions of disease were always available for anthrax, there was also an accumulation of other themes associated with the word and the traits of the affliction.

Hippocrates, or one of the physicians writing under his name, lists *anthrakes* with erysipelas and other skin diseases that accompany the prevailing cold of early spring, in *The Epidemics*, Book 3:7 and again in 3:9. One translator into English just uses "anthrax" for this *anthrakes*, while another uses the word "carbuncle," derived from "carbo," the Latin word for what the Greek *anthrax* usually stood for, "charcoal." French *charbon* preserves this matrix of meanings.

Merely by listing *anthrakes* together with other epidemic eruptions Hippocrates established a tradition which continued over the ensuing centuries. Because Hippocrates associated the conditions with each other, later writers assumed they must have the same cause and be susceptible to the same treatment, and they must be related to seasonal and weather conditions.

The late 17th century priest Jean-Baptiste du Hamel wrote that breathing the corrupt air (*miasme*) during a plague goes to the blood and causes both *bubos* and *anthrakes*. The pain is diminished by applying a poultice of dried powdered toad soaked in water. The toad draws out the cold and restores balance to the body. In the *Grande Chirurgerie* (1363) of the physician to Avignon popes, Guy de Chauliac, plague *bubos* are distinguished in appearance from *anthraces*. The book was an influential surgical textbook that went through numerous editions over the following centuries. Surgeons made a distinction between the appearance of plague and the appearance of anthrax when called upon to excise the blackened flesh. Hippocratic physicians, treating the humoral causes of all such appearances, preferred to use poultices.

Carbuncles also were distinguished from malignant pustules in surgical treatises and anatomical atlases.

The word was usually used in the plural, *anthrakes,* and in classical Greek literature it meant "charcoal" or "coals," but always in the sense of burning charcoal. Aristophanes and Aristotle, separated in time, medium and usage, both have burning *anthrakes* in their texts. Aristotle also uses the word for a ruby, a garnet, or the kind of semiprecious gem also called a carbuncle in English, a deep black stone with red highlights, like a burning coal, and endowed with healing properties. A reference to *anthrax* in the *Historia Naturalis* of the Roman author Pliny is to the precious stone and not to the infection.

Henry Liddell and Robert Scott, in their *Greek-English Lexicon,* infer that Hippocrates and his commentator Galen were using *anthrax* by extension from its basic meaning of "charcoal," for a malignant pustule that resembled burning coals on the skin. The red-burning-in-black color quality was shared by coals and pustule. The word might equally well have meant "smallpox," which can look and feel on the skin black-red-burning, and can be as consuming. The herb woad was *anthrakisatis* because it gave that appearance when used to dye cloth or the skin.

The word *anthrax* denoted an imaginative state shared by a burning coal, a color composition, a gem and a pustule, and the word suggested that one element could cause, or at least represent, the other. The Greek *anthrakes* is not, however, associated with an animal disease, because animals do not show this distinctive appearance on their skin. The pestilence shared by humans and animals only was associated with *anthrakes* when the skin eruptions were associated with miasma, as in du Hamel's example. The progressive observation of contagion between animals and humans, and the use of the microscope, distinguished infections caused by *Bacillus anthracis* from other *anthrakes.*

The sole use of the word *anthrakes* in the Greek New Testament is in Romans 12:20, a passage that has become proverbial in the King James translation:

"Therefore, if thine enemy hunger, feed him; if he thirst, give him drink; For in so doing thou shalt heap coals of fire [*anthrakes*] on his head."

No disease is mentioned, but comforting an enemy is as good as making him suffer an affliction.

The texts of the Greek story of the end of Herakles do not employ the word, but can be taken to refer to the malignancy often named anthrax. From far away, Herakles shoots the centaur Nessus as he attempts to rape Herakles' wife Deineira, whom the centaur was ferrying across a stream on his back. Removing the arrow, the dying centaur tells Deineira that a shirt soaked in his blood will bind Herakles to her.

Later, made jealous by Herakles taking yet another mistress, Deineira treats with the centaur's blood a ceremonial wool shirt she has woven and sends it to Herakles, who removes the lion skin he has always worn and puts on the shirt. The shirt of Nessus (ironically) attaches itself, burning to Herakles' skin and in agony he tears at it, ripping out his own flesh. Apollo orders Herakles' corpse cremated and Herakles rises to heaven a god, the human part having been burnt off.

Positivistic medical interpretations of events with symbols of their own can easily become embarrassing. Anthrax spores might have arrived in Nessus' blood or been resident in the woven wool. The spilling of blood in ancient Greece always called for expiation, and might bring plague to the entire community of the murderer, so the blood did not have to contain spores to make Herakles into a sacrifice. The artificial, woman-made, infectious shirt replaces the natural, manly lion's skin.

Medea, the foreign bride Jason brought back from his Argonaut adventure, was infuriated when Jason installed himself in the local elite by marrying Glauke, the daughter of the tyrant Creon. Medea's response, referred to in Euripides' play *Medea*, was to give Glauke a cloak which, when she placed it over her shoulders, burned and incinerated her. Like the Nessus shirt, Glauke's cloak became a theme in art. A Roman sarcophagus has a bas-relief of Glauke enmeshed in flames while a horrified Creon rushes to her aid.

The one element shared by both the Herakles and Glauke stories is skin inflamed by contact with poisoned cloth. Any number of organic or inorganic poisons may have been responsible. Anthrax pustules are notable in not being painful, but painful skin infections caused by other bacteria and by toxins don't need to be transmitted by spores from animal products. Anthrax is an explanation of the death by cloth contact episodes, however, because it might actually have been an element in cloth made from animal fibers.

There is, unfortunately, little record of how the cloth produced from the mills where the woolsorters worked affected its wearers, and only a limited record of how it ultimately affected the ragpickers. The history of anthrax the suspected disease diverges from the history of anthrax the word. Where the dust, animals and carbuncles are present the word is not, and vice versa. When the word "anthrax" is actually used, it is always the skin eruption and sometimes the clothing and animals, but not until the nineteenth century is it the plague and the mill dust.

Anthrax by name is included in the list of diseases visited upon pagans and other sinners in early Christian writings; for instance in Augustine's *City of God*, and Saint Jerome's *Letters*. The ancient Greek word is included in the suite of Christian execrations which merely locate the disfigurement of the damned and cursed on the surface of the skin. It is not even seen as spreading from a specific source, dust or clothing; it is a figure of visible moral decay.

Palladius, a seventh century C.E. Christian writer in Latin, tells the cautionary tale of a young desert monk who "being on fire" left his retreat and went to Alexandria and the embrace of a prostitute. "An anthraks grew on one of his testicles...." Palladius continued, "and he was so ill for six months that gangrene set into his testicles which finally fell off." This may have been a venereal disease, or it may have been the result of the passion-driven monk exposing his privates to bedding or skins, luxuries of the city, that carried bacteria and spores. This does not add syphilis to plague and smallpox as the anthrax of black skin eruptions. Syphilis does not progress as Palladius describes.

Some later authors link animal skins to transmission of a fatal infection among animals, and this sometimes is called anthrax even without reference to black ulcers. Fitzherbert's *Boke of Husbandry* (1523), after a description of a *murrain* that at least one commentator believes to be anthrax, enjoins readers not to bring home skins of cows dead of *murrain* because it will spread to healthy animals.

Blancou cites the story, published in 1758, of a bear in Finland that died after unearthing and eating an animal dead of *anthrax*. A peasant who skinned the bear died, as did the parish priest who received the bear's skin as the price of reading the interment service for the peasant. Three other villagers who helped the priest prepare the skin all died. This was only the preparation; no one actually wore the skin.

As the mediators between dead animals and hungry humans, butchers both suffer from anthrax and spread it by distributing diseased meat. In 1769 the French physician Fournier observed that *charbon* pustules developed on skin in contact with meat or soiled linens, and he condemned unscrupulous butchers who sold innocent peasants meat of animals dead of the malignant pustule.

The English physiologist Gamjee (1854) told of a man who unearthed the corpse of a cow to butcher it and sell it on the black market. He carried the bloody pieces in a cloth sack slung over his back. Several days later his back erupted in *charbon* pustules and he soon died. Contact with animal flesh, malignant pustules and death were all associated with each other, but the word *anthrax* was not part of the collection as national languages developed their own versions.

After anthrax came into focus as an individual bacillus causing a variety of diseases in animals and humans, and the spores were identified as the agent of spread, the association between the word *anthrax* and diseases caused by clothing continued to be diffuse. There was only scattered information about the effect of the cloth produced in the factories that sickened the woolsorters, upon tailors, wearers and other consumers.

In mid–1945 Jean Cocteau began preparations for *La Belle et La Bete* (*Beauty and the Beast*), his film version of a classic fairy tale. At the beginning of the journal he kept during the making of the film, and which he later published, Cocteau wrote, "I had to add to marshalling the decors, costumes, hunting for exteriors daily visits to doctors and nurses. I came back from vacation with two *anthrax* [word in the original French] on my chest, the result of sunburn and mosquito bites."

Over the ensuing months, as Cocteau and his crew struggled with the technical details of making a film in a war-ravaged country, a story set in other times and remote, enchanted places, they were themselves ravaged by anthrax infections. Jean Marais, who played Avenant, the male lead, developed an anthrax on his leg, and Jeannot, the man within the dense costume of the Beast, was temporarily immobilized by a developing infection on his back. Cocteau himself was attacked on the face and hands, which he saw covered with scabs and fissures. At one point he grumbled that the doctors cost a fortune. The victims were treated with regular irrigation of the lesions, fumigations of the skin, injections with bacteriophage and applications of salve.

> [Doctor Vial] sprays Marais' leg and lances the anthrax. Marais who is very brave and strong suffers terribly. I leave him at the clinic. Tomorrow morning we'll take it in stride. I'll avoid horse scenes and turn to relaxed scenes. The doctor will keep him still for twenty-four hours while the anthrax is ripe.

Cocteau declared that the microbes were one more obstacle to surmount in completing the film.

Marais and Jeannot had to wear the large mask of the Beast during filming. Cocteau doesn't comment on this, but from a viewing of the film it appears to have been made of animal hair, which could have been a source of anthrax spores. Cocteau's early anthrax of the chest and later more serious eruptions on the face and hands could have had the same source. Other performers who did not come into direct contact with the mask of the Beast, the actress who played Beauty, for instance, were not described suffering from anthrax. Instead, she fell from the horse early in the filming and had to be hospitalized.

At the 1958 Fort Detrick meeting at which Philip Brachman presented the results of his Arms Mills studies one of the attendees asked whether viable anthrax spores ever got through the fabric produced by the mills to infect customers. It was a touchy question. Some products, the answer went, did test positive for anthrax, but then tested negative after disinfection. The example was mentioned of an unidentified grocery clerk in Philadelphia who came down with cutaneous anthrax after purchasing a new coat four weeks before his illness. The coat was a rough woolen mackinaw the clerk wore over a short-sleeved shirt. His wife had accidentally scratched him on the arm where the lesion later developed. Samples taken from the coat cultured positive for anthrax.

The Consumer Products Safety Commission in 1974 warned consumers, "particularly horse owners," that 5,000 to 10,000 Alaskan hair saddle pads sold by the Perforated Pad Company of Woonsocket, Rhode Island, could be contaminated with anthrax spores. "The saddle pads are about three-quarters to one inch thick with cotton duck quilt on one side and exposed short coarse grayish-black colored animal hair on the other," the commission reported. The exposed hair was not from Alaska but from Pakistan and Afghanistan.

The commission was alerted to the spore content of the pads by the Washington State Department of Social and Health Services. A horse which had been saddled with the pad had died, its meat was fed to cougars and other large felines in a private game park in Sequim, Washington, and 42 of the animals had died of anthrax in quick succession.

In 1991 the sole case of human anthrax reported to the World Health Organization from Canada was a woman who contracted a cutaneous infection from a sweater she bought at a used clothing store.

Butchery, tanning and other treatment of flesh, hair and hides may have eliminated possibility of infection for the ultimate user, but there was still exposure to blood and skin during processing and there still was the concealment of the infected source, which processing could also accomplish. Preparation techniques draw a line between moderate exposure of the end user and serious infection of the preparer, or the relative immunity of the preparer and the susceptibility of the consumer. These stories from Moses and Herakles to Cocteau and the Canadian sweater trace that division, and the words used to name it.

A certain amount of information about human contact with anthrax would come from the history of animal product treatment before industrialization, and those who performed these treatments had some traditional knowledge of what they faced. Louis Pasteur, who devised a vaccine against anthrax, was the son of a tanner.

Epidemic disease can be anthrax or any other disease affecting humans and animals; what is named anthrax stays closer to the skin and only travels by discernible contact. The epidemic and individual skin contact themes are intermingled in the word *anthrax*.

# 7

# Morbus et Pestis

In the latter part of the Third Book of the *Georgics*, the Roman poet Vergil declares that he will instruct the listener in the sources and signs of diseases (*morborum*). He has already warned the shepherd to take up stones and drive away the snake, the plague (*pestis*) of cattle that shoots his venom (*virus*) at the flock.

The *morbus* that he describes causing copious bleeding and death among sheltered cattle during the rainy winter is probably anthrax.

> ...sin in processu coepit crudescere morbus, tum vero ardentes oculi atque attractus ab alto spiritus, interdum gemitu gravis, imaque longo ilia singultu tendunt, it naribus ater sanguis et obsessas fauces premit aspera lingua.
>
> As the sickness [*morbus*] begins to advance and gather violence, then indeed their eyes burn and their breath is fetched deep, heavy with broken moans, their flanks heave with long-drawn sobs, black blood [*ater sanguis*] oozes from their nostrils, and their throat is blocked by their rough and swollen tongue.

That is a good account of how an infection appears to a cattle keeper. At this level of observation, however, Vergil could also be describing babesosis or rinderpest.

At the end of the book the description turns to the effects of the livestock sickness upon humans. Evoking the general dying of animals as the winter flood waters recede, Vergil identifies the Fury Tisiphone raising her head ever higher and driving Morbus (Disease) and Metum (Panic) before her.

> Iamque catervatim dat stragem atque aggerat ipsis in stabulis turpi dilapsa cadavera tabo donec humo tegere ac foveis abscondere discunt.

Nam neque erat coriis usus nec viscera quisquam aut undis abolere
potest aut vincere flamma; ne tondere quidem morbo inluvieque peresa
vellera nec telas possunt attingere putris; verum etiam invisos si quis
temptarat amictus, ardentes papulae atque immundus olentia sudor
membra sequ batur nec longo deinde moranti tempore contactos artus
sacer ignis edebat.

And now she deals destruction in battalions, and heaps the very
folds with carcasses rotting in foul decay, til men learn to cover them
with earth and hide them out of sight in pits. For neither might the
hides be used nor can any one dissolve or consume the flesh in water
or flame: not even can they shear the fleeces, eaten through by corrup-
tion of the pestilence [*morbo*], nor set hand to the rotten web: nay, even
if any had braved so abhorred a garment burning pustules [*papulae*]
and foul-smelling sweat overran his limbs, and in no long space of
delay thereafter the fatal fire devoured his infected frame.

Vergil wrote in a poetic tradition that described rural life evocatively
while being specific about agricultural practice and animal husbandry.
One translation into a modern language differs widely from another
depending on how the translator interprets individual Latin words naming tools and techniques.

Even in his own time what Vergil describes may have been obscure
and half-forgotten. He wrote the poem to celebrate the peace and prosperity the Emperor Augustus had brought to the land after years of civil
war, and to encourage people to take up skills they had abandoned. It is
a city dweller's view of the remembered countryside, but in a didactic
and not a pastoral mode. The shepherd Corydon burns for his fair Alexis
in Vergil's *Ecologues* and its many imitations and descendants; in the *Georgics* anonymous farm folk reap the abundance of the land.

Into the managed abundance of the *Georgics* comes the illness, which
also has to be managed to avoid human injury. Vergil refers not to a historic outbreak but a seasonally recurrent loss of animal life which both
affects and infects humans; in other words an endemic disease which
goes through cycles and not an epidemic one that appears, wreaks its
devastation and vanishes.

In Vergil's account the disease spreads among animals not as the
result of divine displeasure but because of seasonal changes in temperature and humidity: the Hippocratic view rather than the Homeric. Once
the disease has spontaneously begun, human action can control it. The
Romans made gods of every object and gesture, and in Vergil's evoca-
tion Tisiphone, one of the three Furies who relentlessly pursue humans
guilty of violating divine law, personifies the inescapable death that takes
place after the winter floods. Drying after protracted wet weather is also
the seasonal-climatic condition most promoting of anthrax infections
among animals.

Pit burials and incineration of corpses eliminate the spread of the infection, but they also destroy the valuable parts of the animals. Vergil cautions those handling the animals not to be tempted by the meat, hides or fleece. Both the ingestive and the cutaneous disease are evoked in these warnings. Herakles accompanies Hippocrates in Vergil.

Vergil does not use the Greek word *anthrax*, nor does he mention the coal-like skin lesions, but he does refer in one passage to oozing black blood (*ater sanguis*, gloomy blood) and in another passage to contagion spreading to humans through animal flesh and skins. If he is referring to the same disease in both passages, then a diagnosis of anthrax is a strong likelihood.

Several of the elements that alone caused writers to suspect anthrax in earlier texts are present together in the Vergilian *morbus*, the disease of animals spreading to humans through physical contact with dead animals. In Vergil's countryside, however, humans have ways of controlling transmission.

Vergil passed into Latin tradition imagery for the word *morbus*, which other writers in Latin may have recalled and used to structure their own descriptions of endemic and epidemic diseases of humans and animals. Roman literature and the Latin Bible formed intellectual and stylistic standards for early Christian and medieval European writers, who framed their observations and descriptions accordingly.

What appears to later periods as a historic epidemic related to a distinct cause may actually be an upswing in the virulence of an endemic disease reported because of a war, a famine or other devastating events. The epidemics in turn resulted from and caused social and political chaos which seemed to end a world. The environment that associated extreme weather with animal and human disease and death in the Bible and in georgics came to characterize the conditions for a type of *morbus*. Many diseases might arise in that environment, and there are occasional suggestions of what we learned to call anthrax.

Vergil's instructions are at least some indication that anthrax was recognized and controlled by the same means used for centuries, burial or cremation of afflicted animals, refraining from contact with their products.

The Christian Church Father Eusebius gives what may be the first description of an anthrax outbreak among humans in the ninth volume of his *Ecclesiastical History* (written in Greek, 311–24 C.E). Eusebius describes the persecution of Christians by a tyrant amid other troubles.

> The customary rains, indeed, and showers of the then prevailing winter season were withholding their usual downpour upon the earth, and we were visited with an unexpected famine, and on top of this a

plague, and an outbreak of another kind of disease. This latter was an ulcer, which on account of its fiery character was called an anthrax. Spreading as it did over the entire body, it used to endanger greatly its victims; but it was the eyes that it marked out for special attack, and so it was the means of blinding numbers of men as well as women and children.

Eusebius is the first classical author to use the word *anthrax* for a condition that may actually have been caused by *Bacillus anthracis*. It spreads over the entire body, which is more like the pox or plague, and it spreads during a drought, both the Hippocratic condition of climate and the likelihood of dust, which carries anthrax spores to the eyes.

Disfigurement about the eyes was a serious condition for people whose judgment of another's nature centered on the eyes, and that made it stand out for Eusebius.

People living in areas where anthrax is endemic develop carbuncles about the eyes; it is one of the most frequently illustrated anthrax lesions, and one familiar to the staff of clinics serving the rural poor. One of the few Americans to contract an anthrax infection in the late twentieth century was a military photographer who suffered an eye infection after visiting Haiti. Eusebius doesn't enumerate livestock deaths, but he does write of famine, which may have carried the same meaning for him. The first description of zoonotic anthrax after Vergil is of a *peste* in the French colony of Saint-Domingue during a famine after an earthquake, a combination of the Vergilian and Eusebian conditions.

A word that Vergil used only to refer to annoying animals, *pestis*, which also meant a plague or a curse, by the Middle Ages was being used to denote visitations of threatening animals such as mice, rats and fleas, and the diseases spread among people when these animals multiply out of hand.

The *pestis* that devastated Europe in the fourteenth century, and left islands of infected suffering long afterward, is an object of speculation and probing analysis based on very limited material evidence and ambiguous records. The equivalent of the English phrase "The Black Death" (Latin *mors negra*) was first used in Danish and Swedish chronicles of the fourteenth century to connote the dire nature of *pestis* visitations without referring to physical appearances of black blood or black skin lesions. The Black Death in its own time was not usually called the Black Death.

*Anthrax* (the word) is associated with the skin condition of the *pestis* by some contemporary writers. Guy de Chauliac (1348) contrasted *anthraces* with *bubos* by physical appearance because he had the opportunity to observe both of them on the same plague victims. John of Trevisa (1398), a translator of Latin texts into Middle English, equates *anthrax* with *carbunculus*, translating the Greek into Latin, and Henry de Mondeville in his *Chirurgia* (1306–20) offers five traditional liniments for treating *anthrax* ulcers in humans. The liniments were applied after the black pustules were drained and irrigated, a treatment of serious skin eruptions that has continued to the present day.

Medieval chroniclers did refer to the pustules and boils on victims' bodies, sometimes using the language of *anthrax* and *carbunculi* to describe types of darkened blisters. As later writers pointed out, however, fourteenth century chronicles did not mention mass deaths of rats and mice that came to be identified with infection by *Yersenia pestis*, the bacterium recognized in the late nineteenth century as the cause of *pestis*. The chroniclers sometimes recorded deaths of domestic livestock, especially ungulates, and the crusted black blood, concurrent with human *pestis* or not, and they recorded the other disruptions in society and commerce that accompanied outbreaks. One writer may or may not have drawn upon classical or Biblical examples, or fashioned the account after another writer's.

For anthrax, strictly a description of a skin appearance, to be distinguished from the skin appearances of smallpox and plague, it had to occur along with the epidemic diseases. It is quite likely that outbreaks of what we call anthrax accompanied outbreaks of epidemic disease. Under conditions of epidemic spread the cautionary measures described by Vergil may have broken down and people took the risk of handling and eating the meat of any animal available, thus spreading anthrax to humans. This gave the impression that the separate skin appearance of anthrax was epidemic like the others. Humoral and climatic ideas of disease further encouraged this belief: it seemed that anthrax, which looked much like plague and smallpox, arose under weather conditions that also favored them. As knowledge accumulated and was communicated, *morbus* became *pestis*.

By the end of the 16th century medical treatises and treatment manuals begin to appear that separate pestilential anthrax from the plague while using the same language for both. Giorgio Rivetti's 1592 *Trattato sopra il mal delle pettechie, peste e giandussa.... Treatise on the disease of pustules, plagues and disorders...*) offers a method for curing pestilential fevers in humans and animals that depends on the use of humorally balancing herbs. This is probably the first Western European medical advice writing that separates anthrax contagion from plague contagion while associating both with black pustules.

Athanasius Kircher, the learned Jesuit, commented on a *pestis* that in 1631 spread from cattle to humans in central Europe. An inaugural dissertation, the lecture delivered in Latin by a professor on assuming his post at a German university, was delivered on the subject of pestilential anthrax (*Anthrax pestilens*) in 1681 by three professors at Jena University. The plague-like contagion of anthrax was coming under closer scrutiny.

In 1832 a Berlin academic doctor and historian of medicine, Justus Friedrich Karl Hecker, published *Das Schwartze Tod*, which was translated into English as *The Black Death* the following year by Benjamin Guy Babington, a physician who had recently witnessed the cholera epidemic in London. Hecker begins his book evoking the Omnipotence who reveals himself in great pestilences, but quickly cites "the sultry dryness of the atmosphere" and "the mist of overflowing waters" as harbingers of destruction. A historical sketch of these mighty events "after the manner of the historians of wars and battles, and the migrations of nations" would give a clear view of the mental development of the human race and ways of Providence.

Hecker's subject is the great pestilence of the fourteenth century:

> It was an oriental plague, marked by inflammatory boils and tumours of the glands, such as break out in no other febrile disease. On account of these inflammatory boils, and from the black spots, indicatory of a putrid decomposition, which appeared upon the skin, it was called in Germany and in the northern kingdoms of Europe the Black Death, and in Italy, la mortelega grande, the Great Mortality.

Hecker cites a Byzantine writer's mention of the great imposthumes on the thighs and arms of those affected, distinct from smaller boils on the arms and in the face, as well as on other parts of the body: "In many cases black spots broke out all over the body, either single, or united and confluent." Hecker's one use of the word *anthrax* in his original German refers to the form the plague took in Western Europe where the "buboes and inflammatory boils" were preceded by the disease "in the form of carbuncular (*anthrax-artigen*) affection of the lungs" which destroyed the life through an ardent fever and evacuation of blood before the other symptoms developed. Babington saw fit to retain Hecker's coinage *anthrax-artigen*, "anthrax-like things," in his translation. It refers to the black blood expectorated by the victims before they die, before they are even able to break out in black spots or buboes.

The divine and climatic causes of the plague remained the chief force in Hecker's work, but he also gave a fermentative emphasis to the blackness of the Black Death. The theory of the chemist Justus Liebig that disease is a manifestation of ferments, bodily decay which can be spread, found its historical exponent in Hecker. The black skin and blood were outward signs of putrefaction brought about by extremes of weather. General conditions had general effects, and the remedies were varied, but often those applied suppress decay: fumigation, bathing, excision of the corrupt parts.

Hecker's book through Babington's and other translations into European languages was influential in establishing the idea of the fourteenth century *pestis* as an occurrence of black blood, and black boils, buboes, imposthumes, anthraxes and carbuncles, as the Black Death. The discovery of the rat and flea vectors of plague and finally of the plague bacterium itself in 1895 confirmed the Black Death image of the plague, associated with grand cataclysmic events Biblical in scope and Hippocratic in environment. The anthrax carbuncle, fever and hemorrhage of black blood were mingled in the vision of floods and droughts, rat infestations, deaths of animals and boils erupting on humans even as anthrax was itself defined as a disease distinct from plague and the plague bacterium was considered the sole active agent of the Black Death.

Anthrax boils were named after and likened to coal, as were the black buboes of the plague. Coal itself, long a semi-precious gemstone, was coming into use as fuel, primarily for blacksmiths and other metalworkers, and more in Britain and Belgium, where there were great deposits. The sulfurous coal smoke stained the clothes and skin of everyone who lived in its environment and gave them a wheezing cough, filling the air of London even before industry and the railroads added to the blanket. It was an industrial plague after the plague had ceased its cycles in Europe. In coal the ancient anthrax made a new Black Death. As late as 1902, William Futhey Gibbons was using the word "anthrax" to refer to coal exclusively, in his novel of a strike in the Pennsylvania coalfields, *Those Black Diamond Men: A Tale of the Anthrax Valley.*

By the late twentieth century historians looking carefully at the records of physical symptoms and the geography of mortality of fourteenth century *pestis* discovered that the distribution of lesions on the body, and the progress of the disease, were not entirely compatible with the symptomatology and epidemiology of the plague bacterium. "Plague" in the sense of "high mortality" had become identified with the "true Oriental or bubonic plague," which in turn was given as the cause of many epidemics. But bubonic plague could not be the cause of all the epidemic disease deaths recorded, for instance, in the registers of London parishes between 1348 and 1665. The historian Graham Twigg observed that bubonic plague is a tropical disease that needs several weeks of temperatures of at least 21 degrees Centigrade (70 degrees Fahrenheit), and coexistence of the black rat and its flea, both warm-adapted species. These conditions were not met in London every time a plague outbreak occurred. The known logistics of plague diffusion do match the spatial and temporal spread of recorded mortality.

Twigg, David Herlihy, Norman Cantor and other historians suggested that diseases besides bubonic and pneumonic plague brought about the sickness and death of the Black Death. The murrains of animals in the early fourteenth century could not have been caused by *Yersinia pestis*, the plague bacteria killing humans. Cantor took the concurrent murrains as evidence that another pathogen that caused skin lesions in humans resembling plague buboes could be involved.

This revision of the Black Death to include a more pluralistic disease profile in a way returns to Hecker's dark imagery with a more detailed account of the medical background. The scientific incompleteness of the written sources and the inability to examine and diagnose patients will always permit—even require—an ambiguity. Discovering anthrax spores in a hospital burial ground in Soutra, Scotland, does not prove that anthrax was the cause of bubonic plague, but it does not rule it out entirely. Plague sufferers had anthraxes on their bodies; they may also, some of them, have had anthrax bacilli in their blood.

The *pestis* tradition of anthrax continues to enter interpretations of epidemic disease in approximately the same way anthrax itself enters the life of communities. The English village of Eyam became a test case for students of the Black Death because it was and remained isolated from the main trade routes. The introduction of plague-bearing fleas was traced to a shipment of cloth a local tailor received from plague-stricken London in 1665. When the first black skin eruptions appeared the village was quarantined, left in isolation while those who had contact with contagion either died or survived. Mortality records revealed that a number of people did survive, and their descendants, many of whom remained in the village, carried stories of those times down the centuries.

The survivorship in Eyam was much greater than would be expected of plague and for a time a less deadly black death, anthrax, was suspected. Examination of property records showed that there were no mass deaths of animals which would have to precede human anthrax deaths on any scale. Once the anthrax *pestis* was ruled out, the way was open to examine the genetics of resistance to *Yersinia pestis* infection. The Eyam population was shown to carry greater than usual concentration of the Delta-32 gene, which blocks the entry of the invading bacillus into phagocytes that gather at the infection site. This gene was also concentrated along the main route of the plague on Continental Europe and among descendants in America: survivors' descendants were more likely to carry the gene.

And it also was compatible with concentrations of the gene among people who resisted infection by the most recent plague, Human Immunovirus (HIV) that causes AIDS. HIV, a virus very different from the plague bacillus, has the same mode of attack upon phagocytes, and is resisted by the same Delta-32 variation in the surface of the cell.

Perceiving all this depended upon rejecting the anthrax *pestis* explanation of survivorship.

The seasonal disruption described by Vergil in which humans and animals are included in a round of morbidity becomes a historical disruption in retrospective visions of the Black Death. That in turn becomes the basis for the ecological interpretation of the plagues of Egypt and all other plagues. These anthrax interpretations of *pestis* are not evocations of woolsorters disease because animals are immediately present in *pestis*. In the anthrax *pestis* the mass deaths of animals anticipates and surrounds the human epidemic, and there is a sense of transmission of the causative agent from animals to humans rather than a global affliction reaching both from the outside.

Anthrax is an element in *pestis* assimilated to the properties of other epidemic diseases of humans such as plague, smallpox and cholera. We cannot help but look backward from our own present state of mind, but looking we can see how anthrax became what it is for us, and why we have such extraordinary expectations of it. It probably did participate in complexes of other diseases capable of person to person transmission through the air, and it is easily projected into those other diseases and ascribed their communicability. Anthrax is anticipated to act like plague and smallpox, and even designed to be that way.

When anthrax epidemics did occur they spread in Vergilian terms, that is, as the result of direct contact between diseased animals and humans. *Pestis* was actually *morbus*. There always was a tendency to gloss over the lack of direct spread and to treat anthrax as another plague. As with other epidemics, anthrax epidemics were preceded by natural cataclysms. This contributed to the sense of their being a state of divinely ordered epidemic, but the were actually precipitated by conditions specifically favoring anthrax—the abandonment of existing safeguards in the treatment of sick animals and the handling and consumption of their products.

In the 1770s there were a series of anthrax epizootics described in the French colonies of Guadeloupe and Saint-Domingue. Henri Bertin in 1775 published by the *Imprimerie Royale* in Paris, an account of the *maladie epizootique* in the colony of Guadeloupe. Bertin dissected both humans and animals and found similarities in the pathology of internal organs, yet he also discovered that the disease did not spread directly from one person to another, but only came as the result of physical contact with the flesh of dead animals or from eating their meat. He also called it a *maladie putride y pestilentielle*, spread from the decay of victims but also as a plague.

On June 3, 1770, an earthquake devastated Port-au-Prince and settlements in the surrounding area in the French colony of Saint-Domingue (contemporary Haiti). In the aftermath many people died of what historian Michel-Placide Justin, writing in the next century, called *charbon*.

The colony had a large population of slaves brought from Africa to work on the sugar plantations. The destruction of port facilities disrupted the supply of the large quantities of codfish which were used to feed the slaves. Unscrupulous Spanish cattle ranchers stepped into the breach with quantities of smoked and salted beef, which they prepared from cattle that had died in numbers because of a terrible epizootic (Justin uses the word *epizootie*). An epidemic disease (*peste*) called *charbon* spread among those who consumed the infected (*infectees*) meats because the meats contained a germ (*germe*), an agent of infection. Over six weeks, fifteen thousand colonists, white and black, died, and it only stopped when colonial administrators and the inhabitants themselves halted the meat distribution. That cut off the only significant food source, and the resulting famine killed another fifteen thousand, most of them slaves. The mass escape of slaves desperately seeking food and seeing opportunities for freedom contributed to the collapse of the social (colonial) order.

At the time the colonial authorities asked the newly opened veterinary school in Alfort, France, for suggestions on controlling the epizootic. Philibert Chabert answered the request with a report (1774) based on what little information he could gather, giving general advice on how to halt the spread of the disease among the animals, but not among the slaves.

The colonial setting with its large, heavily worked population dependent upon an imported food supply magnified the conditions that existed in many cities, and made it possible for anthrax to pass from epizootic, affecting animals, to epidemic, affecting people.

D.M. Morens includes Chabert's report among the efforts to characterize a "new" disease with distinct animal and human phases made possible by colonial circumstances.

Michel-Placide Justin was writing his history (1826) at the time, after escaped slaves had effectively revolted and established the independent nation of Haiti (1804), which resisted attempts by Napoleonic France to reassert control and became the first nation to abolish the practice of slavery in the Americas.

A contemporary anti–Spanish bias colors Justin's account of ranchers deceitfully selling infected meat. Two hundred years later, despite vaccination programs and other public health measures, anthrax remains endemic in Haiti because of the consumption of tainted animals by desperate people. And Haiti developed industrial anthrax as well, in the goat skin industry. Eva de Hart, the head of the service organization To Haiti with Love, told an interviewer for the online serial *CounterPunch* that an entire family living downwind of a tannery had died of pulmonary anthrax.

The everyday details of anthrax (*maladi chabon*) in Haiti have not been observed. The surface information suggests a Vergilian cyclical endemic state occasionally breaking into epidemic. In January 2001 *Haiti Progres* reported an outbreak of anthrax on the Isla de la Tortue, with three people and 60 animals dead. A vaccination campaign was announced, but people in the shore towns near the island were warned not to purchase the meat of animals killed by the disease.

Haiti today is closest to the anthrax environment that existed in Europe before anthrax bacilli were observed and associated with the disease of animals and humans through spores. This may also be what anthrax was like in Iran, Pakistan, and Afghanistan, the sources of the wool that made woolsorters disease. An anthrax epidemic took place in Rhodesia during the revolution that created Zimbabwe when the disease surveillance system broke down and anthrax was deliberately introduced to cripple the cattle-based economy in the tribal trust lands and sicken the revolutionaries. One proposed British campaign against Germany during the Second World War was the dropping of anthrax-imbued feed cakes onto pasturage, with the intention of precipitating a Vergilian cattle and human epidemic. In Haiti anthrax is endemic because it is not prevented; elsewhere the epidemic arrives with the breakdown of surveillance and prevention.

By the middle of the nineteenth century people still aware of the rural world described in the *Georgics,* and of the *Georgics* themselves, were able to make new observations bringing older and previously unassociated traditions together in the word "anthrax." Virgilian *morbus* and Biblical *dbr* found their microbes. In Bradford, England, during 1870s, as there was a search to explain the mysterious deaths of woolworkers, the newspapers speculated that it might be bubonic plague.

A 225-meter Egyptian vessel was placed under a 1,000-meter exclusion zone when it arrived near the mouth of the Halifax (Nova Scotia, Canada) harbor on Friday, April 25, 2003. The ship was originally headed toward a smelter in Quebec but it was diverted to Nova Scotia after it was discovered that an Egyptian crew member had died shortly after the ship left port in Brazil. A Health Canada official told reporters at a news conference on Tuesday, April 29, that test swab samples taken from the ship showed no sign of anthrax. The "potential plague ship," as news reports called it, was allowed to go on its way.

The beginning of the Black Death in fourteenth century Europe is often fixed with the entry of a ship with dying sailors and rats into the port of Genoa in 1347. The nineteenth century Barbary Plague in San Francisco, California, which eventually spread the plague bacterium to rodent reservoirs all over the American West, started with a ship with ailing passengers and crew, and rats with infected fleas, entering the port.

The Health Canada officials in 2003 were responding to precedents like these, far more powerful than the mundane facts. Over a hundred years of scientific discovery cannot keep anthrax from being the plague when an afflicted ship enters the harbor.

# Charbon, Milzbrand, Koch and Pasteur

In 1745 the members of the medical society of Geneva wrote about the malignant skin tumor "called 'charbon' by the peasants, an area of decay about the size of a nut that hangs from the flank and grows without the animal knowing...."

From the writings of Aristotle onward, there were explanations of and treatments for surface infections of animals that may have included anthrax. The infected area was excised, bathed, treated with balms, and kept from contact with healthy skin of humans and animals. In the practice of husbandry there was evidence that the *charbon* could spread to other animals and to humans through direct contact with the weeping ulcer or cloth it had touched.

An early student of anthrax epidemiology, Johann Heuschinger, recounts the treatment of tongue lesions in cattle in late 17th century Germany, France and Switzerland by removing them with a silver blade. A man who used the blade to cut food was stricken with a fever and died.

Where anthrax was endemic, surveillance was maintained by linking mandatory actions to signs of the disease. Local laws restricted contagion by requiring the isolation and destruction of animals diseased with, as a series of 16th century Castilian laws called it, *sangijuelo*. These were the forerunners of laws requiring that animals dead with black blood running from apertures and with blackened tongues not be opened for examination, and requiring that their corpses be burned rather than buried. During the following centuries many local governments adopted rules requiring those noticing the signs of the disease to report to an official, and the official to see to the removal of the animals.

Such laws faced opposition throughout history: it was difficult for

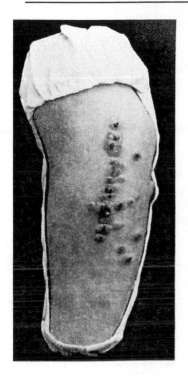
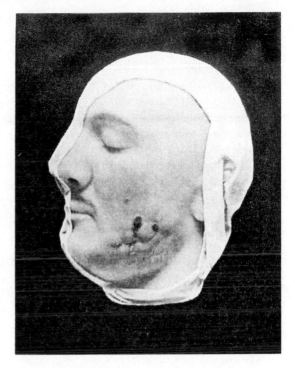

Anthrax (pustula maligna) left side, actinomycosis, right side. (Jacobi [Pringle] 1904: vol. 2, figure 38. Wax models in the Neisser clinic at Breslau reproduced in color [in the original] by the Citochrome process.)

cattle owners, who had often invested a great deal in a small number of animals, to destroy their investment to halt the spread of an invisible contagion. What Henry Washburn wrote of the American context in 1911 had been true for centuries.

One of the most common obstacles to sanitary police control of outbreaks of anthrax is the opposition of the owners of the affected animals to any regulation which requires them to dispose in a safe and satisfactory manner the cadavers of animals dying from the disease.

Most localities have failed to secure legal enactments demanding suitable destruction of infectious carcasses, and others which have laws upon their statute books have an opposing public opinion that nullifies the real intent and purpose of the law....

European principalities began adopting policies of mass destruction of livestock to prevent the spread of disease through animals and the human users of their products. A rigid exercise of coercive state power made these practices effective. Giovanni Maria Lancisi, the personal physician to a succession of Popes in the late 17th to early 18th centuries, after considerable effort and initial failure, succeeded in controlling cattle plague (rinderpest) in the Papal States by quarantine, isolation and slaughter. These methods, applied locally and sporadically to control other diseases as well, culminated in the construction and operation of centralized but isolated animal crematories.

Friedrich Brauell, a professor of pathological anatomy at the Dorpat Veterinary Institute (Tartu, Estonia) relates (1857) the death of a worker in a crematory where cattle dead of *Milzbrand* infections were burned. Microscopic examination showed non-motile rod-shaped particles in the worker's blood similar to those the German physician Pollender had reported in a medical journal shortly before. This was the first microscopically verified observation of a human death from *Milzbrand* communicated through the air from animal remains.

Brauell also witnessed the death of one of his own assistants, Carl Shuppe, an anatomy *Diener* (assistant) who had performed the autopsy of three animals dead of *Milzbrand*. Brauell examined Shuppe's blood 33 hours after his death and found the same particles in the man's and animals' blood. He also observed them in the blood of a sheep injected with Shuppe's blood. The particles could not be the result of postmortem decay but must be an active agent in the disease. The link between human and animal disease was presenting itself, and so was the nature of the hazard to anyone working with the blood or flesh of diseased animals.

Konrad Ludwig Schwab, a veterinarian at the Munich *Tierenarzne Schule*, in 1844 published a number of cases of "anthrax poisoning" in animals and humans, including animal handlers.

It was already embedded in the medical literature that shepherds, butchers, tanners, and woolworkers suffered from *charbon*. Now new categories of workers were added. During the Guadeloupe epizootic of 1774, the slaves who tended to animals, gave them enemas and examined their entrails after they died developed black lesions on their arms and hands. In his list of those who contracted *typhus charbonneux* (charbonic infection) from animal innards, Hurtel d'Arboval, author of an early medical encyclopedia (1839), lists two veterinarians. The survey of anthrax investigations between 1950 and 2001 conducted by a United States Centers for Disease Control and Prevention team includes a crematory worker who died and a number of veterinary workers who performed autopsies of animals infected with anthrax (they survived with the help of antibiotics). The professionalization of animal medicine created opportunities to study the transfer of disease between animals and humans and enhanced the risk of humans contracting the disease.

With increased probing into the bodies of dead animals in search of causes of disease, and with increased experimentation using infected animals' body fluids, more humans were exposed to the principle of the disease, leading to more infections and death, and more chance to collect specimens and view them. It was learned definitively that glanders, a bacterial disease primarily of horses, could be contracted by humans who allowed the pus of glandered horses to make contact with their bodies. Honoré Fragonard's museum of preserved medical specimens, opened in 1766 at the École Nationale Vétérinaire d'Alfort, had on exhibit a model of a man's face covered with the pustules of rampant glanders. Its disfiguring transmissibility gave glanders a place alongside anthrax on its journey to twentieth century germ weaponry.

Professionalization of veterinary medicine, increasing the likelihood of contact with anthrax and other diseases of animals, is a historic trend, but changes in the practice of an individual animal handler, or an increase in anthrax infections, also place the individual at greater risk of contracting a skin infection. The first case of indigenous human anthrax in Texas in over twenty years (reported in 1993) was in a 63-year-old sheep shearer who had begun to dissect sheep that died suddenly. His necrotic lesion was resolved with oral and intravenous penicillin treatment. Pre-antibiotic herders, farriers and shearers, searching for the causes of livestock mortality, or the assistants of physicians and scientists studying animal diseases, were not as well protected.

The first veterinary school in Europe opened in Lyons, France, in 1762; the second at Alfort in 1766. Honoré Fragonard, a cousin of the painter Jean-Honoré Fragonard, was at first director of the Lyons school, then later moved to Alfort, near Paris, to become director of the second school, where he displayed his preserved specimens of humans and animals still on exhibit there. Henri Bertin had been appointed comptroller general of France, and he obtained the authorization to open the veterinary school from Louis XV, a monarch greatly interested in medical matters. After Fragonard was drawn elsewhere Bertin had his friend Claude Bourgelat, a master horseman, appointed director.

Increasing prosperity was in part an increase in herd animals for food and transport, including urban and military transport, and with that increase came epidemic disease which threatened to eliminate large investments. Louis XV's interest was in accord with the rise of a cadre of professional animal specialists, from traditional farriers to equestrians and scientific veterinarians, who were developing a common language and common techniques of treatment. The formation of veterinary schools was the institutional outcome.

Between 1762 and the end of the century, twenty towns and cities around Europe saw the opening of veterinary schools. When the London Veterinary College accepted its first class in 1791, its first professor was a graduate of the Lyons school.

The training in these schools at first concentrated on the diseases of horses. The most striking exhibit in Fragonard's veterinary museum is an anatomized man riding an anatomized horse. Those choosing to specialize in the not very prestigious practice of animal medicine could best profit by planning a career tending to the mounts of aristocrats and wealthy bourgeois, and learning to maintain the equine engines of war and of trade. But the schools could not ignore the many, frequent epizootic infections that spread among a range of animals in rural areas. With an eye toward showing their usefulness to government sponsors, the veterinary schools encouraged students and graduates to study and address sudden disease outbreaks in the regions where they practiced.

Only months after the Lyons school began its first class, Bourgelat sent a group of students on a mission to control an epizootic (nature unclear) intensifying in the Dauphine region. That they succeeded in saving animals, mostly through dedicated nursing, was a benefit to them and the school.

The establishment of the veterinary schools in turn encouraged the formulation of advice on animal diseases. The Société Royale d'Agriculture in 1765 offered a prize to the author of the best essay on control of rinderpest and other spreading maladies.

Denis Barberet in his prize-winning essay singled out *charbon* as a disease equally able to attack animals and humans. Rinderpest and the poxes may have taken a greater toll of animals, but *charbon* could be spread from the intact carcasses and hides of diseased animals. Barberet's suggestion that regulations requiring the destruction of the carcasses of animals dead of *charbon* was taken up by other writers and eventually adopted nationally.

Barberet did not write that *charbon* could be transmitted directly from animals to humans. That was the inference of Nicolas Fournier, who in his 1769 *Observations et experiences* was concerned about the poor all unknowingly receiving a dose of *charbon* with the cheap meat sold to them by butchers.

Fournier was not as effective in distinguishing from each other the lesions of various diseases in animals, and he attributed sheep pox and anthrax equally to *charbon malin*. He conducted the unique investigation of following the fleece of infected sheep through the washing, carding and drying of the wool, carrying with it the atoms of anthrax ferment (*atomes de ferment charbonneux*) each step of the way, without losing the capacity to cause infections. Contagious corpuscles or molecules were the medium for the observed spread of the disease from animal body to product to humans.

A suspicion that there were minute particles bearing the essence of infectious disease had crystallized with the invention of the microscope.

In 1658 the Jesuit polymath Athanasius Kircher had written (*Scrutinium physico-medicum...*) of seeing under his compound lens the *contagium animatum* of plague. Kircher argued for infectious corpuscles and he asserted that they were alive: tiny worms brought about by putrid vapors rising from beneath the ground.

Fournier called *charbon* a ferment, but he did not go so far as to say it was alive. He was associating it with the bubbling eruptions that seemed to be shared by wounds, decomposing flesh, rotting plant matter and fermented beverages like wine and beer.

In 1774 Philibert Chabert, a farrier who had become an instructor at the veterinary school at Alfort, was asked to prepare instructions for the colonial authorities on dealing with the epidemic on Saint-Domingue. Chabert ran through the veterinary standards of cleansing with humorally moderating preparations of vinegar, honey, garlic, camphor, angelica root and juniper berries. Chabert said that clean water had to be used to clear the stagnant water bearing its load of *animalcules* and their eggs from the stables. Without actually examining the animals he could not tell what the disease was, but the account of worms infesting the dead animals caused him to call it a pestilential fever and advise that it be treated accordingly. He also recommended hiring a pupil trained at Alfort or one of the other veterinary schools to assist the officials charged with preserving the profitability of the island's economy.

Chabert did not discuss the many human deaths in Saint-Domingue from eating infected meat. Fournier's concern for the line of disease transmission into the laborers and the poor of Burgundy did not extend to any concern of Chabert's for the slaves on Saint-Domingue. But Kircher's worms were found in the animals.

Worms were the most convenient way to think of the transmissible principle of anthrax and other diseases. Aristotle, as always drawing theory from observation, had attributed the sores of animals in the same pasturage to small biting rodents and lizards, a category that also included worms. Vergil had referred to the *pestis* of snakes attacking domestic animals, though he did not use snakes to explain the disease of livestock during the dry period.

Linnaeus precipitated the causative worm of the communicable lesions and bleeding in the dramatic name *Furia infernalis*, and pictured it as a spiked thread carried from the grasses of pastures into the soft and vulnerable areas of animals. Worms could be minute, could readily multiply or even be generated spontaneously under the right conditions, and were often found in the wounds and bodies of animals and humans. They had been imagined as the causative factor of pain and disease since remote antiquity. Early microscopes enabled physicians to see ferocious-looking animalcules, and to see the piercing, tearing, gripping equipment of mites, ticks and worms just a little too small for the naked eye to capture. They might be the source of the bites and wounds on pastured and stabled animals, and they might enter the animals' flesh and blood to cause disease.

The *pestis*, the living agent, and the *morbus*, the disease symptoms, existed in a free association waiting to be explored. There were many diseases because there were many pests, though there might be a fundamental pest that causes all disease. Physicians, veterinarians and bacteriologists freely developed their own theories, often holding opposed beliefs simultaneously, accepting that diseases were environmental and microbial at the same time.

The study of animal diseases was becoming the study of comparative medicine. Disease agents were found that affected both humans and animals, in similar and in different ways, and animals could serve as test cases for experiments that could not be attempted with humans. At the same time that experiments and observations advanced comparative medicine, ethical and anti-vivisectionist movements attempted to limit the use of humans and of animals in medical experimentation.

The establishment of veterinary schools and the emergence of a veterinary profession challenged both traditional specialists and medical practitioners for primary expertise in the treatment of animals. Trained veterinary practitioners were more likely than local specialists to be able to compare a local disease event with other instances elsewhere and arrive at a proper diagnosis. Communication networks maintained among graduates fostered a common language of veterinary science.

Anthrax, usually known by distinct local names, was an important term in this common language. One trend was toward associating the names of animal and human afflictions with common lines of transmission and similar symptoms. Diseases that clearly could move between humans and animals had to be caused by effects that simultaneously encompassed both humans and animals. This could be the environment, climate and weather, the presence of water and the type of soil; it could also be a poison that passed among those afflicted. The rising comparative medicine emphasized the corpuscular theory.

Pox, anthrax, rabies, and glanders, the diseases most observed to affect both humans and animals, were the subject of observation and experiment. Edward Jenner had already shown that a disease peculiar to animals, cowpox or "grease" of horses, could provide protection against human disease when transferred to humans. Anthrax was not as much a threat as smallpox, but it had the potential to affect livelihoods and economies. The cost of anthrax to domestic production concerned governments, and ultimately its potential for deliberate transmissibility interested them as well. Those who focused on what was emerging as a uniformly caused infection focused on these two interests.

In 1774 Henri Bertin left his comptroller position to go to Guadeloupe and study the outbreak there first-hand, and he was replaced by the *philosophe* Turgot, who promoted the career of Felix Vicq d'Azyr, a young physician and excellent organizer who created a national disease surveillance network of interested specialists and saw to the publication by the royal press of papers on diseases of economic consequence. A 1776 collection combined Bertin's Guadaloupe study with papers on the Saint-Domingue epizootic. In that same year the new king, Louis XVI, approved the formation of the *Societe royale de medicine* .Vicq d'Azyr, who became its permanent secretary, had the use of armed forces to implement public health policy, destroy herds of diseased animals reported by his network and overcome local resistance.

The effort to examine local conditions leading to disease and seek solutions was manifest in the composition of booklets spreading the doctrine of disease contagion and suggesting preventive measures. A veterinary advice manual for the region of Moulins, France, in 1787 clearly outlined the ways in which the living and the dead bodies of animals sick with what the writer called *fièvre charbonneuse* could infect other animals and humans. Animals might die suddenly from the fever or they might linger a while and then die. Washing the animal, coming into contact with its waste, eating its meat, drinking its milk or being bitten by flies or fleas that had been nourished by the animal's blood—any of these could cause the lesions and the fever in humans.

This national, local and overseas development of veterinary surveillance and education was symptomatic of the latter years of the *ancient regime* in France. During the years of the revolution Chabert, Bertin, and Vicq d'Azyr lost their positions and ability to act in any concerted fashion to control epizootics. The interest in identifying the causes and means of preventing *maladies charbonneuses* was if anything enhanced during the French revolution, with at least one manual published by the national printing house offering farmers ways to "combat" the menace of the infection, as they had to combat reactionary forces and threats to their newly gained land. The struggle to claim the land from anthrax also was fought by Soviet farmers.

Among German speakers there was *Milzbrand*, "spleen fever," the basis of Swedish *mjoltband,* and among French speakers, *sang de rate,* also "spleen fever." *Milzbrand* became the German designating name for the animal and human anthrax conditions. The name came from the observation that fevered animals exhibited a listlessness thought to be an effect of spleen disturbance and the spleen of these cattle, when they were butchered, was enlarged, darkened, soft and sticky with small bodies, having a "blackberry jam" appearance.

Like the Oromo of Ethiopia, the farmers knew the disease from the inside of the animal. The spleen had long been used in divination, revealing by its appearance the influences that came to bear upon the animal and the world around. Ancient Tamil texts from India describe *pinnapada*, enlarged spleen disease with persistent cough and other anthrax-like symptoms. In the word *Milzbrand* and similar names, experienced farmers codified the relationship between the outward health of the animal and the state of an internal organ. Being able to tell what the spleen looked like from external signs made it unnecessary to look at the spleen and risk contagion.

With a growing knowledge of the infectious nature of diseased animal parts and products, veterinarians experimentally transmitted the disease from one animal to another. Organs or blood of dead animals fed to healthy animals caused them to come down with the same disease.

In 1823 Jean Barthélemy, a teacher at the veterinary academy in Alfort, France, injected the blood of a horse dead with *fièvre charbonneuse* into another horse and a sheep and caused them to develop the same symptoms. The following year another experimenter transferred *charbon* intravenously between animals. A number of others in various parts of Europe reproduced the results, one of them giving the fever to a sheep by having it bitten by dogs that had eaten the scrap parts of a sheep dead of *charbon*.

Veterinarians trained at the schools practicing in the towns wrote brief pieces on manifestations of disease which occurred in their areas, relating a local animal disease to other local infections and to a diagnostic type. In 1837 Jean-Charles Herpin, a graduate of the Alfort school, wrote of an *apoplexie charbonneuse de la rate*, an anthrax spleen apoplexy that suddenly killed a number of animals in his district. It clearly spread not from one animal to another but to most of the animals in a group that grazed in the same field. Several died while still standing. It was *apoplexie charbonneuse* because the characteristic black blood was present, and it was *de la rate* because Herpin found on opening up the animals that their spleens were enlarged.

While veterinarians experimentally transferred diseases from one animal to another, the evidence of transmissibility of glanders and anthrax to humans derived from a growing body of cases of accidentally infected stable workers and students. They gave evidence that the body fluids of animals showing signs of these diseases were somehow able to transport the diseases into humans through any breach in the skin. It was not the veterinarians but the physicians who began to examine under the microscope blood and tissue samples of animals dead of these diseases.

Who first saw distinct anthrax bodies is a subject of controversy. The German physician Aloys Pollender, looking for disease agents, saw *stab-*

*formige Korperchev* (staff-shaped little bodies) in the blood of five cows dead of *Milzbrand* in 1849 (he published his findings in 1855). Were these semi-transparent, straight, evenly thick bodies plants or animals? Were they the cause of the disease, vehicles for it, or did they have nothing to do with it? Pollender was not prepared to say.

The French physician Rayer and his assistant Davaine saw *petits corps filiformes* (small filiform bodies) in 1850 in *charbon*-infected sheep blood and reported the result that year. Rayer and Davaine had been asked by the General Council of the Department of Eure-et-Loire, where *charbon* was endemic, to investigate the contagion and suggest preventives. They combined experiment with observation, injecting sheep with the blood of sheep showing signs of *charbon* and after the injected sheep developed signs of the disease, comparing the appearance of their blood under the microscope with the blood of animals dead of naturally occurring *charbon.* They were able to equate symptomatically different diseases of sheep, horses and cows with the *pustule maligne* of humans through discovering the same bodies in the blood and tissues of all.

Davaine remarked in his report that the bodies he saw in the blood of both naturally and artificially infected animals showed no spontaneous movement. This incurious remark has cost Davaine credit in the history of bacteriology. It was only in 1863, after Pasteur's early publications on ferments, that Davaine was prepared to see these *bacteridies* (a word derived from Latin with the same meaning as Pollender's *stabform)* as the source of deadly decay in the blood. Because the bodies did not move under the microscope there was no reason at first to think they were alive, or peculiarly related to *charbon* symptoms.

Friedrich Brauell had the sad but unique advantage of being able to examine the blood of a technical assistant who had died of *Milzbrand* after autopsying animals. This was in 1857, and Brauell looked for and saw Pollender's *stabformige Korperchev* reported two years earlier. He also located identical bodies in the blood of sheep dead of *Milzbrand.* Brauell's observation was the first time that bodies associated with *Milzbrand* symptoms in both animals and humans were seen in the blood of both. Brauell found the same rods in the blood of one other human he could be sure died of anthrax (a crematory worker, mentioned earlier), but when he looked into the blood of embryos found in animals dead of *Milzbrand,* he could not see the characteristic bodies. He concluded that they were by-products of putrefaction since they were only found in the dead. He did not consider the possibility that the placenta filtered out the noxious elements, preserving the fetus from the death of the mother.

One experimenter may not have been aware of another's results. It took a war to make scientific relations more fluid. In the meantime, the evidence accumulated element by element for anyone situated to notice the pattern. The next piece was added by a Paris veterinarian, Henri Delafond, concerned with a local epizootic (1860). Delafond had earlier written a treatise on the humoral and climatic causes of *charbon*, but in his investigation of the *charbon* sickening the horses of the *Compagnie des Petites-Voitures*, an urban livery service, Delafond found minute *batonnets* (staffs) in the horses' blood. He cultured the bodies in blood serum and, suspecting they were a kind of mold, tried to force them to produce spores, but like Pollender and Brauell he was not sure whether they were the cause or the result of the infection. Delafond had, however, located the commonly observed corpuscles as the causative agent of an epizootic, and surmised that they had a spore stage.

Delafond published his findings the following year (1861), and soon after that died of causes unrelated to his research. In that year Louis Pasteur, seeking ways to reduce spoilage for the French dairy industry, published a paper on the fermentation of butyric acid, produced when butter goes rancid. Casimir Davaine read the paper in the *Comptes rendus* of the Academy of Sciences.

Pasteur wrote of *animalcules infusoires* (infusory small animals) living without oxygen and determining fermentation. He gave an elegant description of tiny, rounded, rod-shaped animalcules that rigidly moved in dance-like glides and pirouettes. And he reported that the animalcules were not affected by carbonic acid gas (carbon dioxide) but vanished when a stream of oxygen was passed through the fluid containing them. This observation would be of importance for Pasteur's later work on vaccines.

Davaine drew an analogy between these animalcules and the *batonnets* he and Rayer found in *sang charbonneux*, blood of sheep dead of anthrax. That the *charbon* rods did not move mattered less than their similarity to Pasteur's animalcules in shape, size and action. Death by *charbon* was a process of fermentation in the blood like butter growing rancid.

In the course of further examination Davaine found the rods in blood throughout the body and not just in the spleen. He thus dispensed with the focus on the identifying pathology of the spleen, and conceived of living *bacteries* causing a lethal ferment as they multiplied in the blood generally. Pasteur had enlightened Davaine to a living source of fermentation which he could use to trace its effects within the body, and escape vague environmental beliefs of miasma and putridity as the source of spreading disease. Ferment was the result of tiny living animals, and distinct from decay. A wound was the appearance of living ferment in the skin, not its decomposition, which happened after death. Davaine's mentor Rayer had prepared an anatomical atlas of skin diseases, which included plates showing the progress of glanders and *charbon*.

This is where Davaine and Pasteur diverged from one stream of contemporary investigation of anthrax: they looked to the microscopic and chemical changes in the anthrax body rather than concentrating on organ signs and environmental conditions, as others did.

The English veterinarian James Beart Simonds studied "splenic apoplexy" in animals on farms in Somerset, where it began to kill livestock after 1855, and he presented his findings in a lecture to a council meeting of the Royal Agricultural Society of England in 1862. While the great enlargement of the spleen was characteristic of every case he saw, it was secondary to changes in the constitution of the blood. He could find no explanation in the quality of the pasturage, poisonous plants or contaminated water. He concluded his lecture with the hope that the cooperation of the chemist, the botanist and the animal pathologist would lead to the adoption of effectual preventive measures. Simonds carried the environmental and anatomical study of the disease as far as he could without having access to the bodies Davaine was finding in the blood.

Providing a thorough description of the disease agent in his second paper of 1863, Davaine used the name *bacteridies* to emphasize that they are rod-like in shape but are not neutral objects. He could not find them in dried *sang charbonneux* (anthrax blood), yet injecting a healthy animal with that same blood would cause the *bacteridies* to be generated there, and the symptoms of *charbon* to appear.

During the 1860s Davaine pursued a concerted research program to study the infectivity of the *bacteridies*. Having converted L.-A. Raimbert, a physician who previously believed that *charbon* was a form of environmental irritation, together they performed experiments connecting human *pustule maligne* with animal *charbon* by means of the *bacteridies*. Always conscious of a need to verify his results with colleagues, Davaine had Raimbert excise a *pustule maligne* from one of his patients (the usual way of treating the condition), examined it under the microscope to identify the *bacteridies*, then injected guinea pigs with the same material. He could show the presence of the *bacteridies* in the guinea pigs' blood after they died of *charbon*.

Davaine attempted to prove that the *bacteridies* were the sole cause of *charbon* by injecting infected blood into a pregnant guinea pig. The female died within two days, her blood and the placenta full of the rods, but the fetuses were alive and free of infection. Administering placental blood to healthy guinea pigs caused them to die of *charbon*; the blood of the fetuses didn't have such effects. The infectious bodies were blocked from entering the fetuses by the placental filter. Davaine reflected upon the ability of the blood to spread disease through the particles it carried. The dried blood carried in the dust of stables was the most likely vehicle. He extended a series of experiments Raimbert had begun, causing *charbon* in animals by injecting them with parts of bluebottles (stable flies) which lived in stables where animals ill with *charbon* had been kept.

The particles were visible in liquid blood and they caused *charbon*, but they were not visible in dried blood or on fly parts, yet they also caused *charbon*. There were no pure cultures of the animalcules that always caused the disease in animals. This gave opponents of the theory that the disease had a distinct particulate agent their best argument.

Returning to the Hippocratic miasma, several skeptical commentators thought flooding waters and the resulting sickly, humid atmosphere were a more likely cause of this disease than animalcules in the blood. It was like other diseases of putrefaction and decay, which also left particles in the blood. Basing it on miasmas preserved the environmental nature of anthrax against the attempt to specify its contagion in observable microscopic bodies.

In the mid–1860s several veterinarians injected sheep with the blood of sheep dead of *charbon* and the sheep did die of *charbon*, but their blood did not contain the animalcules.

In the introduction to his 1876 paper on the etiology of *Milzbrand*, Robert Koch sidestepped the debate on whether or not the rods cause anthrax and asked how they are related to conditions under which anthrax is known to occur: damp areas, wet years, August and September when ground temperatures achieve their maximum, anthrax districts formed each time herds are driven into certain pastures and watering areas. Koch was well situated to isolate the factor in the blood that tokened the occurrence of anthrax.

After service in the Prussian army during the Franco-Prussian War (1872), Koch, retaining a rank in government service, was appointed to the potentially lucrative but arduous post as district physician in Wollstein, in a part of Prussia predominantly Polish. This area periodically was afflicted with *Milzbrand*, spleen fever. Koch did find the filiform shapes in the blood of dying animals, and he used the all too readily available infected tissue to conduct his own experiments. A police officer who confiscated the body of a cow dead of *Milzbrand* allowed Koch to take what samples he needed.

In his effort to win academic interest in his researches, Koch addressed Ferdinand Julius Cohn, a professor of plant physiology at the University of Breslau (Wroclaw). Cohn had been working with *Bacillus subtilis* (the "hay bacillus") and shortly before Koch asked him to view his results, Cohn had found that the bacillus forms spores. In his book *Uber Bacterien* (1872), Cohn referred to Davaine's assertion that particles found in *charbon* victims' blood were alive and were the cause of the disease. Cohn emphasized the view that the rod-shapes were alive and actively reproducing by giving them a Linnaean name, *Bacillus anthracis*, from the Latin word *bacillus*, "a small staff," deliberately distinguished from "bacterium," a large stave. Though skeptical that a rural doctor like Koch could achieve the results he claimed, Cohn found Koch's demonstration convincing, and offered to publish his paper in a journal he edited.

In his first paper on "The Etiology of Anthrax," Koch recalled Cohn's surmise that some types of bacilli became dormant in the form of spores before being revived by a change in conditions. His investigation centered on determining the natural history of the bacteria to learn if they did produce spores. The paper was illustrated with a color lithograph of drawings independently made by both Koch and Cohn, showing spore formation in *Bacillus anthracis* and *Bacillus subtilis*, which was the subject of Cohn's paper published in the same issue. The two men, one a respected professor of botany and the other a doctor with a rural practice, had separately seen the same process in bacteria. This provided support for their assertion that bacteria were alive and had a natural history.

Koch described his investigative procedures, which laid the basis for medical bacteriology. He was not only imaging bacteria. He was developing an experimental method to discern and verify the effects of disease-causing bacteria. He chose mice as test animals because they were abundant and easy to keep. Finding that they wiped off bits of bacilli infested spleen he placed on their tails and coats in an attempt to infect them, he used an old bullet extractor to pull their tails through a hole in the lid of a jar that held them, nicked their tails and placed the infested matter on the wound.

Koch used the traditional method of examining the spleen of a dead mouse to establish it had died of *Milzbrand*, confirmed with the microscope that the bacilli were present, and used the spleen tissue and blood to infect another mouse on to twenty repetitions. Each time, the bacilli proved as infectious as the last. In doing this Koch was replicating experiments of passing infectious material from one animal to another which others had performed with sheep and horses, but with mice, an animal not previously known to be susceptible to *Milzbrand*. The serial passage was designed to test the proposition that the bacilli were the reproducing agent of disease and were not diluted from one animal to the next, as a poison would be. Serial infection also demonstrated that it was the particles in the blood that caused *Milzbrand* and not some other substance in the mouse.

Koch used the bacteria-bearing mouse tissue to test the susceptibility of other animals to developing anthrax symptoms upon injection. Sheep and cows he knew were vulnerable; frogs and chickens he found were not. Koch found that the bacilli proliferated in the blood of guinea pigs, but not in the blood, instead almost exclusively in the spleen, of mice or rabbits.

To demonstrate that the bacilli were not just inert particles of poison, Koch used an electric incubator to warm blood serum or aqueous humor from a bull's eye seeded with bacilli to study how the bacilli changed under different temperature conditions. He did not see the particles moving or dividing, but he did see them elongate and form within themselves smaller, harder bodies, the spores Julius Cohn had predicted.

Koch injected the spores into the transparent and nutritious aqueous humor of a bull's eye and suspended a droplet surrounded by a ring of oil from a glass slip over a slide placed on a warmed microscope stage. The spores visibly opened and yielded bacteria which in turn formed spores when Koch raised the temperature.

Koch made a conscious decision to focus on the bacilli themselves rather than on the pathology of the disease in body tissues. Through a regime of experiments Koch discovered that to form spores the bacilli required moisture, access to air and temperatures above 15 degrees Centigrade. Spore formation had an optimum temperature between 15 and 25 degrees, and proceeded more slowly below and above that.

The bacilli themselves were fairly fragile: they disappeared when dried, cooled or deprived of air. They vanished entirely from an enclosed corpse of an animal they had killed, leaving only spores which were difficult to single out. This may have been why earlier observers couldn't find spores in animals that had died of *Milzbrand*.

In the form of spores the bacilli were durable and able to spread and enter new hosts, primarily through being consumed with fodder, pasture grass and contaminated water. Though he learned that the spores could be revived after drying, Koch did not recognize inhalation as source of spores entering the animal.

From his first etiology paper onward, Koch returned to the old knowledge of when and where *Milzbrand* occurs and he made practical suggestions for animal husbandry. Animal deaths could be reduced by treating the spores as the primary medium for the spread of the disease and restricting the spread of the spores. Koch, giving a scientific basis to measures taken since Vergil's time, suggested deep burials and destruction of all parts of animals known to have the disease. He mentioned that one health official had practically eliminated *Milzbrand* by lowering the water table of the land where cattle were kept and buried, so that ground water would not be a medium to carry the spores to the surface. The usual practice of suspending and bleeding an infected animal prior to butchering, he warned, just distributed the spores on the surface of the ground, so it didn't matter how deep the animal was buried.

Burial and incineration were already measures taken to halt anthrax plagues, but Koch's advice that the burials be deep and the burning thorough were not only to keep the spores out of natural systems. They were public health measures aimed at keeping the spores out of human commerce.

Koch recalled that the people hired to bury dead animals during the day often dug them up and butchered them for consumption later. As the animal was dismembered its blood might make contact with the blood of the butchers through cuts and abrasions on the skin, and cause superficial or even systemic infections.

Eating the meat, organs and marrow of the dead animal could convey into the human body spores that had developed after the animal carcass was opened. If the animals were out of reach, the workers were less likely to access them and contribute to the further spread of the disease. The temptation of meat, hide and other products even of a diseased animal was as great for European peasants as for African nomads.

Knowledge of anthrax's natural history helped explain how the disease spread and how it could be controlled, and it also dispelled mistaken notions. Bacilli from the blood and organs of an animal were given the opportunity to take on a form in which they could move into other animals through grazing in places stained with the blood and wastes, but buried cadavers alone could not generate bacilli or spores. The cadavers were enclosed and airless, and the temperature at any depth of burial was not sufficient to permit spore formation.

In his later papers Koch scorned the reasoning and methods of Louis Pasteur. Pasteur was renowned both for his technical discoveries in his profession of chemistry and for having applied his science to lessen the ravages of disease and spoilage in the French brewing and silk industries. He was called upon to address the *charbon* decimating livestock on farms outside Paris.

Despite common support for the germ theory of disease, and occasions when one praised the other for a significant achievement, Koch's animosity to Pasteur had a nationalist coloring. The Franco-Prussian War, of which Koch was a veteran, had ended in a victory for the Prussians, the coronation of the Kaiser Wilhelm I of Germany at Versailles in 1871 and the imposition of heavy reparations on the French, much of which had to be borne by the agricultural sector. France lost the Alsace-Lorraine region to the newly consolidated German Empire. Apart from its industries Alsace-Lorraine was a major producer of hops for brewing. The reparations were part of German policy to contain France and reduce its ability to field armies like those Napoleon had led across Europe earlier in the century. Pasteur's discoveries are credited with enhancing agricultural production to the degree that the French were able to pay the reparations.

Pasteur proved that the yeast found in the fermentation tanks was the active agent of fermentation, and not a by-product, as was long assumed. And he showed that microbes could affect the yeast and reduce the quality of the product. He advised greater control over the introduction of outside elements into the brewing process, which resulted in more consistently successful wine. And, of course, his findings led to the protection of milk from spoilage through heating—pasteurization.

Introducing the report of his field research on *charbon*, Pasteur wrote that for a long time it was believed that *charbon* arose spontaneously: "The nature of the land, the water, pasturage, methods of cultivation and maturing cattle, all were invoked to explain its sudden appearance." But the work of Davaine and Delafond in France and of Pollender and Brauell in Germany had called attention to the presence of a microscopic parasite in the blood of animals dead of this disease. Gradually it came to be understood that animals afflicted with *charbon* picked up the disease germs (*germes du mal*) in the outside world and never developed illness spontaneously. Pasteur therefore connected his own research disproving spontaneous generation specifically to anthrax.

This belief became better defined when in 1876 Dr. Koch of Breslau demonstrated that the *bacteridie* in its vibrion or bacillus form can form genuine corpuscle-germs or spores. Pasteur thus used all the words available to name the particulate agent. Both Pasteur and Koch were opposed by critics who believed that attributing changes in substances to living things was a reversion to old vitalist theories.

In the case of anthrax, both Koch and Pasteur were trying to explain "spontaneous" instances of anthrax in animals that were not associated with other infected animals. Critics of the germ theory of disease asked how sudden illness was more readily explained by germs than by circulating poisons. How could the germ theory provide suggestions on how to prevent the illness?

Pasteur submitted to the minister of agriculture and the president of the General Council of Eure-et-Loire, a region particularly beset by *charbon*, a proposal for a research project. The mayor of the village of Saint-Germain placed at Pasteur's disposal one of the fields of his farm, where Pasteur pastured a small flock of sheep raised according to local custom and tended by a pair of students being trained at the Rambouillet school to apply science to sheep herding.

The sheep were fed hay sprayed with artificial cultures of *bacteridies charbonneuses*, full of the parasite and its germs. In spite of the immense quantities of spores ingested by the sheep, a lot of them escaped death, often after having been visibly sick. A smaller number died suddenly with all the symptoms of *charbon*, after an incubation period that varied from eight to ten days. They perished with all the fulminant symptoms often noticed by observers who thought that the incubation period was much shorter.

The mortality of the test flock was increased by mixing in with the hay dried thistle with sharp stems and leaves. Autopsies of the experimental animals showed the same internal pathology as autopsies of animals pastured in the fields or kept in stables and that died of natural *charbon*. Different conditions, same disease. These results permitted the conclusion that the disease starts in the mouth or the back of the throat and spreads.

Pasteur, drawing upon Koch's identifying the bacillus, demonstrated that the potency of *charbon* could not be attributed to poisons carried in the medium of bacteria culture. He cultured the bacilli, took a sample of that solution, infected a mouse, and repeated the process on through two hundred mice, with the anthrax retaining its potency in each new subject.

The juice of grapes does not ferment if the yeast-containing dust of the vineyards doesn't coat them before they are pressed. Now Pasteur theorized that earthworms consumed anthrax spores from the decaying bodies of buried animals and carried them to the surface, where they released them in castings. This explained why a particular field was always generating new *charbon* deaths long after diseased animals ceased to be pastured there. Furthermore, the seasonally dried dust from the worm castings could be carried by the wind into the animals' fodder.

Koch injected mice and guinea pigs with the castings of earthworms which had lived in anthrax-contaminated soil and also with the soil itself. He found the soil infectious and the castings not. He wrote that Pasteur was ignoring the obvious observation, that the blood and other fluids of infected animals poured onto the surface was the source of anthrax, and the earthworms were unnecessary. Koch seconded this with a microscopic examination of soil he knew to contain anthrax. It was impossible to distinguish anthrax spores from many other spores seen there. Only animal tests could establish that the soil was infectious.

And how could earthworms spread anthrax in Siberia, known for serious anthrax deaths, if the temperature of the ground is so low year round?

Koch dismissed Pasteur's surmise that anthrax infections resulted from spores entering ruptures in animals' mouth tissues when they masticated thistles and other rough plant matter containing spores that traveled from earthworm casts. The swollen lymph glands found in the mouth region of sheep are not surprising since the mouth is the only place anthrax can enter sheep, whose thick coats prevent spores from entering the skin. In animals the oral glands will swell no matter where the spores enter, and the usual site of bacilli proliferation is the intestines and occasionally the respiratory tract.

Spontaneous anthrax might originate in the soil itself, Koch speculated. Whether there were corpses buried there or not, anthrax seemed
to come about in flooded areas. And decaying vegetable matter was an
excellent medium for the multiplication of bacilli. Bacilli growing and
sporifying in the soil under the observed conditions of temperature and
humidity could account for the otherwise inexplicable cases better than
buried corpses, earthworms and prickly fodder.

"However, according to my observations," Koch wrote in "The
Anthrax Inoculation" (1882), "anthrax bacilli can multiply and form
spores on decaying vegetable matter independently of animal cadavers.
Apparently, they live this way in swampy areas. Experience shows that
animals in such areas often become infected even where anthrax cadavers have never been buried." Where Pasteur made striking demonstrations of the validity of the germ theory of disease, Koch found reason
to downgrade his efforts.

Henri Bertin, a descendant of the founder of the Lyons veterinary
school, publicly doubted that Pasteur's germs were able to cause *charbon* in any animal, say, a chicken. Pasteur challenged Bertin to try. After
Bertin failed to infect a chicken with anthrax, Pasteur delivered to his
office a hen testably dead of anthrax. Pasteur had injected a hen with
anthrax-infected blood, attached the hen's feet to a board and immersed
the bird in cold water. The normally high temperature of birds inhibited
the proliferation of the bacilli and the cooling bath brought the temperature down to a level congenial to bacterial proliferation. Koch dryly
wrote that other experimenters had induced anthrax in birds without
traumatizing them severely, implying that Pasteur's methods would leave
room for questions about the lethal role of germs.

Koch's sharpest criticism was reserved for Pasteur's anthrax vaccine.
(A separate chapter on vaccine history will follow this development in
more detail.) The vaccine originated from Pasteur's research on another
affliction of economically important domestic animals: chicken cholera.
Pasteur's staff left cholera cultures unattended over a long holiday week-
end. When they returned they found that the potency of the cultures to
infect animals was greatly diminished.

Pasteur had made the observation that sheep pastured in fields
where animals dead of anthrax had been buried withstood injections of
anthrax cultures. Recalling Edward Jenner's discovery that those who
were deliberately infected with a mild version of smallpox had reduced
likelihood of developing the serious disease, Pasteur tested the attenuated cholera cultures on chickens and found that they resisted coming
down with lethal cholera when inoculated.

There also was a precedent for preventive infection coming from
the long-term European struggle with a devastating viral disease of

cattle, rinderpest, which the Italian physician Bernardino Ramazzini had tried to prevent by running threads (setons) containing infectious material through the hide of cattle. Not making any reference to veterinary precedents, Pasteur applied the preventive infection principle to anthrax, deliberately weakening cultures with, he said, oxygen infusions.

Koch's final paper on anthrax came after Pasteur's most dramatic display. On the challenge of Dr. Rossignol, a veterinary surgeon and landowner skeptical of the germ theory of disease, Pasteur inoculated test sheep at the Pouilly-le-Fort farm with the attenuated culture of anthrax bacilli, then injected both the test sheep and controls with a virulent culture. In a moment that was dramatized in the contemporary press and eventually in a Hollywood film, Pasteur and scientific observers arrived at the test pens to find all the sheep on the ground, but as they approached, the inoculated sheep rose up while the controls remained down. Only one of the vaccinated sheep, a pregnant ewe, died; none of the unvaccinated sheep survived.

Pasteur was widely acclaimed, and he made plans to produce an anthrax vaccine commercially. He had given another boost to existing livestock industry and laid the basis for a new industry, vaccine production. He promoted the vaccine in France and overseas by supplying it for tests conducted by his assistants. Koch resentfully alluded to the proclamation at the scientific meeting where Pasteur read his paper on the Pouilly-le-Fort trials that Pasteur was "the new Jenner." Of course, Jenner, in testing the efficacy of cowpox inoculations against smallpox, was attempting to save human lives, while Koch and Pasteur were trying to reduce the numbers of deaths of commercially valuable animals.

Koch's objections to Pasteur's immunization procedure turned around the difference between induced infection and natural infection. The dispute between Koch and Pasteur over how anthrax spread was about the peculiarities of anthrax, but their dispute over the anthrax vaccine and immunization has implications far beyond the prevention of this particular disease.

Koch's own tests of Pasteur's methods and those of his colleagues made it clear that if the inoculation was strong, it was just as likely as a natural infection to kill the animals, and if it was weak, it was useless. According to Koch, Pasteur's attempts to induce a "natural infection" with a strong anthrax culture may not have represented the severity of a real natural infection, which Pasteur, author of the earthworm theory of contamination, could not appreciate.

It was impossible to tell if Pasteurian inoculations actually did protect animals from anthrax. The tests that were made gave inconclusive results, there were too few of them, and Pasteur himself had a tendency to report only those results that favored his inoculation. In his 1882 paper

"The Anthrax Inoculation," Koch declared, "Pasteur's inoculation does not have a significant practical value."

Besides not being effective, the inoculation, in Koch's view, might actually prove dangerous. Mass campaigns of inoculating sheep, the livestock animal most vulnerable to anthrax, increased the possibility of infecting uninoculated sheep. By concentrating anthrax poison in sheep not evidently suffering from the disease, concerted inoculations risked exposing humans who had contact with the wool or ate the meat of recently inoculated animals.

The discovery that attenuated anthrax cultures could provide immunity was of great value, Koch concluded, and some day Pasteur's flawed approach might be improved. It certainly was premature to suppose as Pasteur had that all diseases caused by microorganisms are susceptible to prevention by inoculation. With anthrax there was evidence that people had caught the disease, recovered, then caught it again.

Koch favored public health measures over individual treatment, believing that they were most likely to prevent disease bacteria from spreading in the first place. Pasteur favored inoculation which could be administered when needed and that could reduce the likelihood of virulent individual infections.

Anthrax was primarily a disease of cattle which only peripherally affected human beings. The special cases of woolsorters and ragpickers disease showed how far the spores could spread from animals. Anthrax interested humans in terms of its effects upon animals, and because they could provide the means for its study.

The cattle and other animal-raising industries were growing throughout Europe and America, and they were generating peripheral industries based on animal products. Ever larger armies were becoming more a part of how urbanizing European nations related to each other. Cities and armies had to be fed and their populations used animals for transport.

Pasteur and Koch's careers rivaled each other as their nations did. They were compatible with each other as they attempted to find ways to reduce the effects of disease on animals and humans in an urbanizing and militarizing milieu.

Pasteur inquired of a St. Petersburg professor if there was any resemblance between *la peste Siberienne* and *sang de rate*, and in late 1881 he wrote to a Russian official in charge of horse breeding, the Director of the Studs, to propose vaccination experiments. The Director replied some months later that such a program did not accord with the views of the administration, but four Russian scientists would be sent to France and to Germany to study the vaccination methods.

Soon after Koch's paper on Pasteur's anthrax inoculation appeared, Pasteur responded to a Berlin veterinary professor's request for a vaccine sample with an offer to arrange a public test of its efficacy. Pasteur's assistant, Louis Thuillier had in late 1881 successfully demonstrated the vaccine in Budapest, Hungary. Conducted by Thuillier in early 1882, the first Prussian trial on 50 sheep "bought in a village where anthrax is unknown to the memory of man" did not succeed, which Pasteur blamed on the breed of sheep chosen. In a second trial the inoculated test sheep survived a challenge with a virulent strain of anthrax while unprotected sheep did not. A market was established for Pasteur's vaccine in Germany, and Koch faced the embarrassing criticism that his authoritative research had no useful outcome.

The following year a French expedition assembled by Pasteur was sent to Egypt at the request of Ottoman authorities then in control of the country. Their task was to discover the cause of an epidemic that had begun in the port city of Damiette and was spreading down the Nile. There were also European national interests in this expedition: cholera had spread to European cities in the past and governments were eager to forestall this reverse invasion. John Snow's discovery that cholera was spread in drinking water did not inspire preventive programs. The bacteria researchers might be able to locate the germ of the disease and find how to eliminate it before it returned to Europe.

In 1880 Koch was appointed a member of the Imperial Health Bureau in Berlin, the capital city of the Empire, and there he continued his research into sterilization and disinfection in his own laboratory. Refining the research methods he developed for anthrax, Koch identified the bacterial agent of tuberculosis, a disease of domestic animals and humans, and received the further honor and emoluments of appointment as an imperial privy councilor. Koch was beginning his practice in Hamburg when the 1864–75 cholera pandemic reached the city, and he was familiar with the disease. When the Secretary of the Interior decided in August 1883 to answer the Egyptian call for European expertise to meet the new cholera outbreak, he selected Koch to head the expedition.

The German Cholera Commission arrived in Alexandria, Egypt, to find the French team, the "Mission Pasteur," already at work dissecting cadavers and conducting animal inoculation studies. The mission included Louis Thuillier and Emile Roux, Pasteur's assistants. They claimed in letters to have discerned the microbe of cholera in tissue samples, though they were unsuccessful in causing experimental animals to come down with the disease. Koch later dismissed the germ the French had discovered as misidentified blood platelets.

The Egyptian epidemic waned and, lacking further material, the French turned their attention to rinderpest. During this research Thuillier came down with cholera and despite being administered iced champagne and ether injections under the skin by the French and Italian doctors present, died in a state of asphyxia. Koch and other members of the German expedition fixed laurel wreaths on Thuillier's coffin, spoke eloquently of his contributions and served as pallbearers. Koch eventually went on to India, where cholera was endemic, and there identified the cholera vibrio. Koch's relations with Thuillier from anthrax to cholera trace lines between science, nation and individual careers that cannot be reduced to borders.

After his success with cholera, and a further vindication of his sanitation advocacy when it broke out again in Germany, Koch felt pressure to produce a dramatic cure. His vaccine for tuberculosis (tuberculin), made from attenuated cultures, turned out to be an excellent test of exposure to the bacteria but not a treatment. Koch also distinguished from each other the bacteria that cause bovine and human tuberculosis. His laboratory in Berlin became the training ground for a generation of German, Russian, English and Japanese medical bacteriologists.

Pasteur, who had been granted a research institute of his own by the French government, was successful in creating a vaccine for rabies, another zoonotic disease with stark, dramatic effects on animals and humans, and a disease which had long been associated with anthrax.

In 1896 Koch, who had been promoted to a brigadier general in the German state service, traveled to German colonies in South Africa to attack the problems of rinderpest. The disease had long been controlled in Europe through drastic herd destruction measures. Koch did not determine the active agent of rinderpest, a viral disease, but he did develop a vaccine using the blood of animals that had survived an attack.

In the following years he studied in Europe and in Africa a number of diseases that affected both humans and animals, such as malaria and trypanosomiases, and diseases predominantly of animals, such as babesosis.

Koch traveled extensively, and Pasteur remained in France, where he died in 1895, too soon for the award of the first Nobel Prize in 1901. Koch's former assistant, von Behring, who devised a vaccine for diphtheria, won the first Nobel Prize in Medicine and Physiology in 1901. Koch did not receive his Nobel Prize until 1905.

Koch developed a repertory of methods of culturing bacteria in flat, open-faced covered glass dishes named after Richard Petri, to display the development of bacteria within a clear medium of gelatin or agar. Repeating the discovery of the bacterial cause of anthrax as a sad farce, one of the first anthrax hoaxes to be recorded in the United States in the 1980s arrived in the form of gelatin in a Petri dish.

Koch's work on tuberculosis led him to formulate a series of postulates for scientifically establishing that a particular bacterium caused a specific disease. The bacteria had to be culturable from the blood or tissues of animals showing symptoms of the disease, and the pure culture had to cause symptoms in an experimental animal. He then applied these postulates in retrospect to his anthrax research.

Anthrax entered the world as the first object of this pure culture method, a support for the germ theory of disease, possibly preventable by batch-produced vaccine, in a conflict between a rising European power and a declining one, on the fading boundary between country and city, the sharpening boundary between animals and humans. As anthrax became divorced from its past of plagues, biting agents and black pustules, it came to embody Koch's pure culture cut loose in the world, uncertainly contested by Pasteur's vaccine.

# 9

# Seeing Anthrax

The word anthrax named a sight, a jewel clinging to the surface of human skin, but that was just a sight without a cause. There were other sights sharing the same fluid. As the external malignant pustule of humans and animals became associated with other external pathologies and internal effects such as an enlarged spleen, a problem of causation arose.

What became bacterial anthrax was several different visions of disease in humans and animals. Besides carbuncles and pustules there was splenic apoplexy, *apoplexie charbonneuse,* described by farmers and veterinarians as a mysterious sequence of illness in a formerly healthy animal. James Beart Simonds, based on his observations of cattle in Somerset, in 1862 recorded the signs of an afflicted animal.

> The animal stands with its back arched, it has a difficulty of progression, a staggering gait and a twitching of the muscles. Paralysis succeeds. The countenance is dull and dispirited, and the head pendulous; a frothy saliva comes from the mouth, the breathing is labored and difficult, and the pulse augmented, becoming tremulous and indistinct as the disease advances. Colicky pains come on, and when the infusion into the intestinal canal takes place these pains are associated with diarrhoea and blood-coloured evacuations. The urine is frequently discoloured with blood. The animal falls and generally dies in convulsions.

Animals dying of splenic apoplexy did not show external signs that distinguished their disease from many others, or from the effects of climate, weather or feeding habits. It was necessary to delve inside, to the organs and the blood, to find the underlying cause that linked farm stock to woolsorters and tanners and separated one kind of carbuncle from another.

108

This stage of resolution remained characteristic of anthrax even as it was identified and broken down into ever finer living if motionless pieces. The particles themselves had to be identified as more than a shape different from other shapes in the flesh and blood, and capable of inducing ferments or causing disease wherever they were placed.

The development of microscopy converged with the visual representation of bacteria. Microbiology was practiced long before there were microscopes, in the cultivation of bacteria and yeasts to make wine, beer, cheese, yogurt, tofu and many other foods, in tanning, and in linen production. The science of microbiology was looking into the substance of these visible products to discern minute elements.

Historically and in individual careers, microscopists slowly learned to separate and classify types of microbes and investigate their internal structure. Improving microscope quality accompanied by more efficient lighting of the specimens helped a variety of interested investigators describe an ever greater variety of minute things previously invisible. They did not agree on the shapes of what they saw, whether they were alive or not, and how they affected visible processes.

Athanasius Kircher, a copious illustrator, did not illustrate his microscopic observations of plague samples, and the earliest pictures of microbes seen through a magnifying lens are in the published works of Leeuwenhoek and Hooke. The general shape of the filaments and their motions were the identifying features. From the start, however, the microscopists tried to associate minute observations with properties in the visible world, the buoyancy of cork with its hollow cells or the generative properties of sperm with its vigor.

Once the larger, motile protozoa were classified separately, coloring agents added to the specimen field helped outline the smaller bacteria and fungi. Vegetable dyes, indigo and carmine, and preparations such as India ink, were used to define anthrax bacilli, probably the first pathogens visually identified (1849–50), though they were not at first identified as pathogens.

The existing association between the microscopically visible bacilli and the macroscopically visible disease of animals and people brought Koch to his own studies and experiments. Koch's techniques were developed as he attempted to isolate and grow the agent of tuberculosis, which is smaller, slower to multiply and more difficult to culture than the anthrax bacillus.

Adapting an existing technique of making blood films on glass slides, Koch used an artificial dye product of the German chemical industry, aniline, to make the bacteria stand out in tissue samples. Koch also was a patron of microscope construction and microscope illumination technology. His use of improved lenses and light condensers in conjunction with stains allowed him to manifest two visions of bacteria, a structural outline produced in oblique light and colored interiors in direct light.

Dissatisfied with his drawings of the bacteria, Koch made photomicrographs of the bacilli colonies. His mentor Ferdinand Cohn, more concerned with the classification of the bacilli, made drawings and then photographs of segments of the colonies (magnification and resolution were not high enough to picture individual bacilli) which he compared with other bacteria and fungi.

Early microscopists used drawings to communicate their finds through publication, to give other microscopists the opportunity to compare observations. As magnification and resolution of the image increased, line shapes in drawings acquired internal structure. Koch and Cohn combined their drawings in a single colored lithograph that illustrated their first joint publication. They were showing to their colleagues that they had independently seen very similar structures, which could be verified through other microscopes. The chance that forms seen under the microscope (or through the telescope, for that matter) are artifacts of the instrument and circumstances always has to be considered.

The idea of bacteria as a cause of disease which Koch and others were promoting required better ways of repeating the act of isolating bacterial forms and separating one type from another and from artifacts. Improvements in the quality of the instrument can only go so far in guaranteeing focus on the same form. The development of certain techniques of manipulating samples to show the same image was essential to the experimental verification of the germ theory.

The blood film sample remains the technique of choice for visualizing anthrax bacilli because the medium sustains the bacillus and does not cause it to dissipate.

The vegetative cells of *B. anthracis* are large, measuring 3 to 5 microns in length and approximately 1 micron in width, and their internal structure, including the formation of spores, is not difficult to make out if carefully stained. A spore when fully formed is 2 to 6 microns across. A human hair is about 70 microns wide.

The external shape of the bacilli had given them their Latin name (*bacilli* meaning "little ceremonial staffs"), and eventually the long-stranded colonies were compared to railroad boxcars lined up in a row. They could float independently of each other, be encapsulated or not, form the spores internally, or as vegetative cells develop into colonies, and the colonies could have a coarse, rough appearance or be smooth.

When a smear of anthrax-infected material is applied to a layer of agar imbued with sheep's blood and left overnight exposed to air, the characteristic colony that results is relatively large, white to gray-white in color, growing in a pattern of tight curls turning toward the center

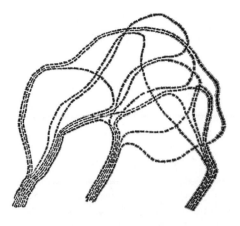

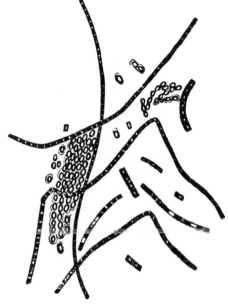

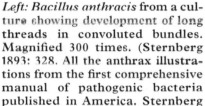

*Left: Bacillus anthracis* from a culture showing development of long threads in convoluted bundles. Magnified 300 times. (Sternberg 1893: 328. All the anthrax illustrations from the first comprehensive manual of pathogenic bacteria published in America. Sternberg was surgeon general of the United States Army from 1893 to 1902, an important advocate of scientific medicine and an accomplished photomicrographer. His manual is illustrated with his own photographs and with engravings taken from European bacteriology atlases.) *Right: Bacillus anthracis* from a culture showing a formation of spores. Magnified 1,000 times. (Sternberg 1893: 329.)

that caused Koch to compare it to the mythological Medusa, whose head was covered with writhing serpents. The formation of this colony is diagnostic of anthrax, though unlike Medusa's serpent hair strands, the coils do not move.

The shapes and sequences that the nineteenth century microscopists and bacteriologists identified as anthrax are the distinguishing vision of the bacteria. The presence of the bacterial capsule, the morphology of the colonies, the degree of motility (for anthrax, none) and the presence of forming spores all remain approved tests for the detection of *Bacillus anthracis.* Culturing bacteria on an artificial medium, using a variety of culture methods, creates appearances on the surface of the medium (the degree of spread and concentration) which then can be inspected further under the microscope.

The Danish bacteriologist Christian Gram in 1884 published instructions for using the aniline dye crystal violent with iodine and an alcohol wash to give lasting color to certain microscopic bodies. The technique resembled a cloth dyeing process which required a mordant to draw the molecules of coloring into a fabric matrix and a wash to fix them there. As the Gram stain was adopted by more researchers, it was discovered that not only did it make bacteria colorfully (purple-brown) visible, it dyed some types of bacteria more resistively than others, just as some types of fabric were more accepting of dyes than others and more likely to hold color with repeated washings.

The bacterial cell wall retains the dye, and the chemical characteristics of the cell wall decide whether it will retain the dye or not. Besides being a visualization technique, the Gram stain is also a chemical test. Bacteria can be divided into Gram-positive and Gram-negative groups, with some falling in between, depending on the length of time they resist discoloration with solvent washing. *Bacillus anthracis* is a strongly Gram-positive bacillus in its vegetative state. It holds the color for a long time when treated with solvents.

Gram-positive bacteria have thick cell walls with a high peptidoglycan and low lipid content. The difference between Gram-positive and Gram-negative bacteria has to do with the effect of the decolorizing solvent on the structure of the cell walls and the lipids lining them. The solvent washes the lipids away from the thin Gram-negative walls, and the dye leaches out, leaving the bacteria colorless. Thick Gram-positive cell walls dehydrate and shrink when exposed to a solvent, and the bacterial pores, the transport mechanism between cell wall and outside fluid, close down, trapping the dye inside despite the loss of the lipid lining. Subtle differences in the cell wall structure from one bacterium to another create discernible variations in the degree of staining. Some bacteria, for instance *Bacillus anthracis*, receive Gram stain so consistently that they serve as an index type of Gram-positive bacteria.

The division of bacteria into Gram-positive and Gram-negative is a major biochemical distinction. But the Gram stain will not dye the encapsulated bacteria. The capsule is extruded in some strains of bacilli when they multiply in living tissues. It can be induced by incubating vegetative cells in defibrinated horse blood for at least 5 hours, or by culturing the isolate on nutrient agar containing 0.7 percent sodium bicarbonate with incubation at 37 degrees Centigrade in the presence of carbon dioxide. In nature the capsules form when the conditions in an animal's body following death achieve these characteristics.

John McFadyean, a graduate of the Edinburgh veterinary school in 1876, the year of Koch's first paper, took additional medical training to specialize in comparative physiology and eventually became dean of the Royal Veterinary College in London. McFadyean was an advocate of scientifically grounded veterinary practice, and made a number of contributions to the scientific and educational foundations of his profession.

In 1901 at an international conference on tuberculosis, McFadyean publicly disagreed with Robert Koch's stand on the non-transmissibility of bovine tuberculosis to humans, having discovered that a large number of Britain's milking cows suffered from the disease, and that there was evidence of it being transferred to children through the milk.

McFadyean also improved on Koch's visualization of anthrax bacilli. He found that the artificial dye methylene blue prepared to form polychrome methylene blue and applied to a sample can stain encapsulated bacilli. A standard procedure to reveal encapsulated bacilli is to spread on the slide a drop of blood from an animal thought to be infected, let it dry and cure it in alcohol, then apply the McFadyean stain. If *Bacillus anthracis* is present, the resulting characterisitic texture will include the bacillus cells among pieces of the capsules.

Neither Gram nor McFadyean stain shows the presence of anthrax bacilli exclusively. They expose a number of chemically similar bacilli perhaps well enough for an experienced observer to identify them.

*Bacillus anthracis* may not move, but it does change under certain conditions and it does multiply. Casimir Davaine in his early studies determined that an individual *bacteridien* divided every two hours. This meant that if not checked a population of the bacteria would double every two hours. After twenty-four hours a single bacterium would have become two to the twelfth power, or 11,096, and after forty-eight hours, 16,777,216. Davaine estimated that a person dead of anthrax would have billions of bacteria in his blood. The great quantities of bacilli observed in the blood of animals dead of *charbon* lent support to this conclusion.

Davaine's vision of *charbon's* pathology was mechanical. The bacilli increased to the point that they crowded out bodily processes such as the circulation of the blood. Any curative measures had to address the increasing mass of bacilli. Davaine therefore recommended caustic agents such as carbonic acid, which was observed to kill quantities of the bacteria and inhibit their potential for exponential growth. This could not be an effective approach to preventing or curing anthrax in animals because caustic substances damaged tissue as well as eliminated the bacilli.

Besides making the bacilli visible for the first time, Koch also addressed the invisible destructive masses that Davaine calculated. He found that even a one part in a thousand mercuric chloride solution would kill the living bacteria, but the spores were much more difficult to neutralize. It would take exposure to two percent aqueous solution of chlorine or bromine liquid or a one percent mercuric chloride solution twenty-four hours before it was certain all the spores in a sample were no longer viable. All these exposures were more than enough to kill a human being or a large animal, which gave an idea of the tenacity of the spores.

Koch's experiments with anthrax, many performed for the first time with any microscopic life form, set a standard for experimental technique, and in turn made the anthrax bacillus a standard for pathogenic bacteria.

There are echoes of Koch's experimental technique and an advance of the anthrax standard in the work of Kurt Schimmelbusch, who had his apprenticeship in Koch's Berlin laboratory. In 1893 Schimmelbusch published the results of experiments attempting to gauge the lethality of multiplying bacilli in mice, at the same time contributing to contemporary studies of sepsis and wound infection.

Schimmelbusch nicked the tail of a mouse with anthrax culture and then waited varying periods of time before amputating the tail a distance from the site of the wound. He concluded that unless the tail was amputated two centimeters from the injection within an hour, the mouse would be dead within twenty-four hours. This result gives a measure for the infectivity of a pathogen in an animal of any size by comparing the animal's body mass to that of the mouse.

Experiments like this used standardized equipment, procedures and life forms, the anthrax bacilli and the mouse, to measure biological processes. Anthrax was participating in a growing professional vision of infection, prevention and sanitation. It became the model organism for teaching bacteriology to the generations of scientists and doctors following Koch. At the University of Michigan Medical School in the early 1890s, Alice Hamilton and her fellow students "followed Pasteur's law in [F.H.] Novy's laboratory, isolating the anthrax bacillus, cultivating it, injecting it into an animal and recovering it again." The number of students who continued to do this over the coming years is reflected in the number of papers and dissertations on anthrax. The future physician Harvey Cushing wrote to his father from medical school on April 3, 1893, that he had decided to make anthrax the subject of a paper he had to write, though it was "not very practical question from the standpoint of practice" because he was unlikely to encounter any cases of anthrax infection.

The various visual images of anthrax were compiled in the atlases and manuals of bacteria published around the turn of the century. In the *Manual of Bacteriology* (1893) of United States Surgeon General of the Army George Sternberg, anthrax is a black and white graphic of cell colonies, a culture form in a test tube and invasive particles colored blue in black cell specimens. Sternberg did not reproduce photomicrographs of anthrax colonies by the heliotype method as he did for several other species of bacillus. An expert photomicographer, Sternberg preferred to illustrate photographically bacteria species that had not been shown before.

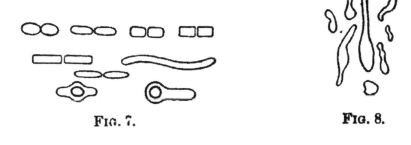

FIG. 7.                    FIG. 8.

FIG. 9.

The shape of *Bacillus anthracis* (above) and their division (below). (Sternberg 1893: 23.)

Eduardo Garcia del Real's *Atlas de Bacteriologia* (1908), a Spanish language version of the Lehman and Neuman *Atlas*, has colorful chromolithographs of *Bacillus anthracis* dish and test tube cultures. The dish cultures on fluid media were formed by brushing a sample on the surface and then counting the time until characteristic textures began to appear. The type of bacteria would then be known by comparing the culture appearance with illustrations in the manual. The cultures initiated by sticking a straw or wire covered with infectious material into the center of a solid, transparent medium in a test tube also had a geometry and coloring that would allow identification of the bacteria by comparison with lithographs. These ways of seeing the bacteria would be transmitted from medical text to medical text until improved photographic techniques created a new range of pictures. Other ways of visualizing bacteria drew upon their interaction with the entire body of the host.

Eli Metchnikoff, a Russian biologist, imagining a thorn piercing a starfish, studied cellular response to invading bodies. Metchnikoff did not find a good reception in Germany, where Koch's followers, while defending the germ theory of disease, were developing their own humoral theory of host response. The experiments of von Behring, Kitasato and Ehrlich demonstrated that the immunity animals acquired upon exposure to bacteria was a property of blood and tissues and could be transferred from one body to another.

The German microbiologists were hostile to Metchnikoff's work as Koch was to Pasteur's, as much for national as for intellectual reasons. When Metchnikoff visited Pasteur he was offered a laboratory. Yet Metchnikoff, who wrote his scientific papers in German, was more Koch's heir than Koch's own students were.

Koch's postulates, strict as they were in linking disease symptoms to bacteria, required numbers of experimental animals to be infected to verify that a cultured bacteria caused a specific disease. It became apparent that some individuals died and others did not. Bacteria may always cause disease, but the same bacteria didn't always cause the same disease to the same degree of severity in every creature infected. Some hosts of bacteria were more immune to their effects than others were.

Metchnikoff theorized that a special class of cells, the phagocytes, devoured and destroyed invading bacteria. Despite being accused of reverting to the old vitalism, as Koch was for saying that living cells cause disease, Metchnikoff persisted in his experiments.

In a study of the response of the water flea *Daphnia* to infection by a parasitic fungus (1884), Metchnikoff cited Koch's 1877 paper describing the response of frogs and other vertebrates to anthrax bacilli. Invertebrates responded to invaders by attempting to digest them, while vertebrates, Metchnikoff noticed in Koch's work, had a class of white blood cells that specialized in engulfing foreign bodies. All these defensive cells ate and digested outsiders, hence he called them by the Greek name "phagocytes," "eating cells." Koch had noticed that the anthrax bacilli were ingested by what he called amoeboid white blood cells. But Koch's observations of cells in a neutral culture medium, rather than in the cells of a living animal, created artifacts that prevented him from seeing how the phagocytes function.

Metchnikoff repeated some of Koch's own experiments injecting frogs and other vertebrates with anthrax bacilli, but he observed the effects directly in the cells of the animals. The frogs kept at room temperature did not come down with anthrax symptoms and Metchnikoff was able to watch the anthrax bacilli being engulfed and digested by the phagocytes. Animals kept at 37–38 degrees Centigrade, even the frogs, did die of anthrax, their white blood cells engulfing far fewer bacilli.

Metchnikoff examined phagocyte reactions in animals that had been immunized with Pasteur's attenuated anthrax vaccine. Only one subject, a rabbit, survived injection with virulent anthrax, and in its blood Metchnikoff saw an increase in white blood cells containing bacteria. The result neatly supported the effectiveness of Pasteur's preparation, while sustaining Koch's view that it worked only in a few cases, at the same time elucidating its action in terms of Metchnikoff's own phagocyte theory.

Metchnikoff's work, like Koch's and Pasteur's, far exceeded the study of any one bacterium. Anthrax had become a model bacterium because it could be gathered in the wild and cultured in the lab, its natural history was known and experiments using it could be measured against an existing literature. Phagocytosis advanced the understanding of disease process that was wanting in cell culture science, and it made the static bacteria dynamic antagonists of bodily defenses.

Eventually phagocytosis would have a specific application to the pathology of anthrax infections in the human body. The phagocytes engulfing the encapsulated bacteria do not destroy all of them, but transport some of them to the lymph nodes where they multiply uncontrollably.

Nineteenth century bacteria, even the motile ones, were of a fixed shape and size. The staining procedures affirmed this. Even if they were motile they were isolated in their motion. Twentieth century bacteria were involved in mass movements and characteristic conflicts. Metchnikoff watched Koch's bacilli being engulfed and he saw them influencing cells in the host's body. Where Koch had made still photographs, Metchnikoff described a movie.

At the same time the bacteria were getting larger, they were becoming individual isolated cells and patterns of cells in colonies. The combination of stains, microscopy techniques and lighting yielded an anthrax graphic that showed the outlines of the bacterial cell as a repeated pattern. Koch's two microscopic visions of the bacteria, a structural one with slanting light and a colored one with direct light, both became textbook identifiers as soon as it became possible to print them. The structural vision became a black and white graphic. Eventually the anthrax pattern it showed could even be used as the design for a necktie.

By the end of the 19th century the various standardized images of anthrax were being collected with images of other bacteria in atlases, manuals and textbooks of bacteriology. In his *Manual of Bacteriology*

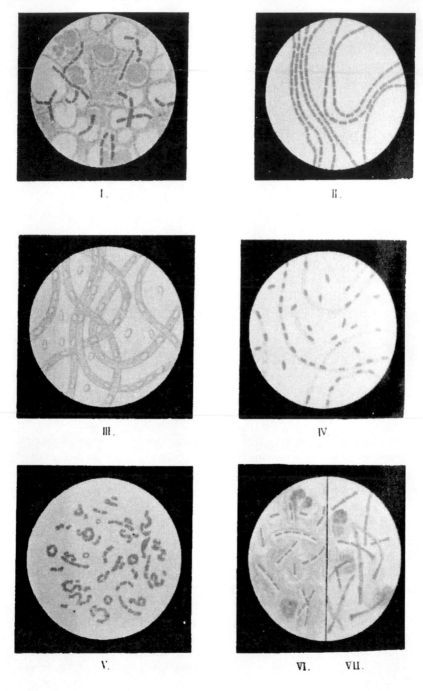

I.

II.

III.

IV.

V.

VI.     VII.

Sternberg displayed black and white engravings showing the shape of individual anthrax cells, of anthrax colonies and test tubes with characteristic cultures, chromolithographs (colored prints) of anthrax incursions into animal tissue and heliographs (printed photomicrographs) of comparable bacilli cultures. The visually identifying characteristics of cultures in a medium held by a test tube were often illustrated in these publications by showing the test tube in color if possible, beside the bacteria colony. Eppinger's *Hadernkrankheit* study of 1895 contains only one chromolithograph, of bacilli in a finely drawn tissue section and a test tube with an active culture. By the early twentieth century photographs of the cells and tissues replaced the engravings, which were retained only in graphics of colonies in strands with spores developing. The Beaux Arts anthrax design of the late nineteenth century manual was succeeded by a functionalist cellular design in, for instance, Soviet bacteriology manuals (see page 122).

In the developing vision, anthrax and all other bacteria were cells visibly reacting to chemical reagents. The chemical properties of bacteria cells extended from systems like the Gram stain to new visions specific to types of bacteria.

In 1911 the Italian serologist Alberto Ascoli described the use of the antigenic properties of the bacterial capsule to make a test for the presence of anthrax bacteria in blood or tissue samples. Ascoli produced a reactive serum by injecting anthrax cultures into rabbits and, after the infection had become established, removing samples of the blood abounding in antibodies and filtering it clear. When an anthrax-infected specimen was carefully added to a test tube containing the rabbit serum, and the test tube was heated, any antigenic capsules in the sample would interact with the antibodies in the serum and precipitate a visible band between the two fluids.

The Ascoli thermoprecipitin test was the standardized visualization of anthrax immunology. A chemical manipulation caused the results of an antigen-antibody reaction to appear, revealing the presence of anthrax. The test integrated the cellular and humoral theories: for the test to work

*Opposite:* **Preparations of *Bacillus anthracis* each magnified 1,000 times. I. Preparation of infected rat tissue; II. Agar culture, one day at 22 degrees; III. Unstained preparation of a 36-hour culture at 37 degrees. Spores are beginning to appear; IV. Agar 36-hour culture at 37 degrees, stained and showing spores; V. Involuted shapes in a stick culture at two weeks; VI./VII. Guinea pig lung tissue (left) and rabbit liver tissue (right), both showing sporifying colonies. (Garcia del Real 1908: plate 43. A Spanish-language edition of the bacteriology atlas published by Lehmann and Neumann 1896, including reproductions of its color plates. Garcia del Real, formerly a military physician, was a lecturer at the University of Santiago.)**

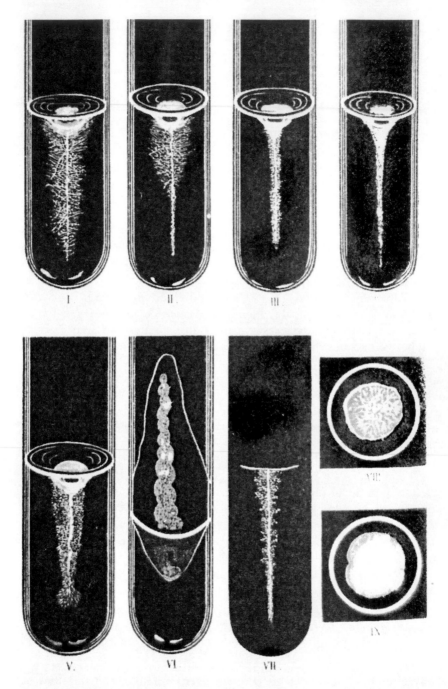

Stick (solid medium) test tube cultures of *Bacillus anthracis* at three days, 22 degrees Centigrade. I and II typical; the rest atypical. VII atypical seen from above, five days a 22 degrees. IX typical seen from above, five days at 22 degrees. (Garcia del Real 1908; plate 41.)

the white blood cells (phagocytes) have to have multiplied in the presence of anthrax bacilli as the result of chemical signals preserved in the serum of blood previously exposed to the bacilli.

The Ascoli test does not distinguish anthrax from related bacteria, which may produce antigens that also cause the precipitin reaction. It is still used to detect the presence of bacterial capsules in food and other animal products. The test is the first of a series of unrelated procedures that yield appearances diagnostic of anthrax biochemistry and do rely on direct observation of the bacilli. Adding penicillin to an anthrax culture produces a typical visible pattern confirming the presence of susceptible bacilli. Introducing a specific bacteriophage, a virus that enters and destroys bacteria, into an anthrax culture causes another characteristic pattern to appear. Both of these culture plate appearances correspond to sub-microscopic activity visualized on the surface of the culture.

The discovery in the 1950s that the copper-based blood of the horseshoe crab turns blue and coagulates in the presence of Gram-negative bacteria and their toxins provided the basis for a rapid test for these common bacteria. The most that the limulus amoebocyte lysate test can accomplish toward making Gram-positive bacteria like anthrax visible is by the absence of a reaction. Its incorporation into rapid detection antibioterrorism devices has created an industry somewhat to the detriment of horseshoe crabs.

Anthrax biochemistry became anthrax genetics with the molecular analysis of anthrax, starting with the discovery of anthrax toxins and their corresponding genes. Standard chemical primers can show the presence of certain anthrax genes in samples expressed with the polymerase chain reaction. Anthrax is now a collection of proteins, amino acids and the base pairs of nucleic acids that code for their generation.

The molecular vision of anthrax is only the most recent envisionment of the bacilli in terms of ever finer components, which it shares with many other life forms. Like all the other visions of anthrax, the molecular vision contrasts anthrax bacilli genes with others in a system, this time the digital configuration of contrasting base pair sequences.

The visual appearance that gives anthrax its name, the black eruption on the skin or the outpouring of black blood from the orifices of an affected animal, is really a manifestation of bacteria, toxins and genes. This in turn allows the old anthrax to be separated from the odd assortment of carbuncles, bubos, ulcers and rashes that it participated in before the underlying cause was identified. The black surface of anthrax also has been subject to a specifying vision.

One of the earliest pictures of an anthrax lesion, a plate from an anatomical atlas Conrad Heinrich Fuchs published in 1843, distinguishes *anthrax carbunculus* from *anthrax malignus*, and the spreading black

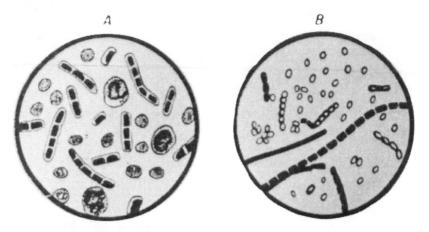

Siberian microbes magnified (a) in the blood of an infected animal (b) spores and strands of the Siberian microbe. (Terentev 1946.)

malignant pustule certainly looks more menacing than the contained car-buncle. A tradition of dermatological drawings and photographs give ever more detail to the distinction to the stages of the eruption caused by the bacillus. The widely disseminated *Portfolio of Dermochromes* pub-lished by Eduard Jacobi of Breslau in 1893 contains color photographs of wax models of skin diseases. Malignant pustule is illustrated by an appearance on an arm (see page 85).

The black eruptions are the result of the bacterial toxins entering the red blood cells and causing them to break down and release the iron atoms bound in the hemoglobin. The iron then forms oxides with the free oxygen, and the resultant mass absorbs rather than reflects light. How the toxins accomplish this on the molecular level is still not known.

The black eschar, to give it the correct dermatological name, is only the final stage of a series of appearances on the surface of human skin into which anthrax spores have entered: a vesicle, then a pustule, an ulcer and finally the eschar. Each of these outwardly visible stages of anthrax infection is connected to a cellular stage in the vegetative development of the bacteria, their confrontation by defensive cells, and an immuno-logical-molecular stage in the release of toxins and antibodies.

Within the invaded body, human or animal, a further sequence of cellular and molecular events either halts the progress of the disease or moves it along. These events form a pathology with its own appearances, some of them so visible to farmers, butchers and anatomists that they give anthrax a distinct name: *charbon* (French, carbon), *Milzbrand* (Ger-man, spleen fever) or *geilsiekte* (Afrikaans, gall-sickness) from the enlargement and distortion of those organs. Those internal effects are in turn related to external changes in the environment. A hot, dry spell following heavy rain affects the gall bladder or spleen and sickens the animal.

In some animals the course of the internal infection and its outward manifestations are different from the appearances and timing in other animals. Cows, sheep and goats are prone to peracute infections that cause them to develop a fever then suddenly die, even while still standing. Horses suffer acute infections that center on neck glands. Dogs, cats and pigs experience chronic, systemic infections from which they might even recover.

In humans the enlargement of the mediastinum, the tissue between the lungs, is an early sign of anthrax, and the cardinal's cap is a postmortem appearance unique to internal anthrax in which the proliferating bacteria have caused the blood vessels in the brain to rupture, spreading veil of blood over the cerebrum. Prior to the isolation of anthrax toxins, it was believed that the internal pathology of anthrax was due to the build-up of bacteria in the blood vessels, causing ruptures and anoxia in tissues.

Anthrax was visible on or in the body, or between bodies, and that visibility was extended from the identification of its causative agent to the molecules of its biology. In the twentieth century it developed forms otherwise discernible.

# 10

# The Anthrax Bombs

Responding to tests of Pasteur's vaccine, Koch warned that administration of anthrax to healthy animals could as easily be destructive as it was protective. A twentieth century survey of anthrax in America found that the vaccine administered to animals was a significant factor in causing the disease where it had not occurred before.

It was not much of a step to see the defensive vaccine as a potential weapon, which then is defensively prohibited. Hitler could ban chemical and biological weapons because he was gassed in the trenches during World War I, then extend his wartime experience in a more lethal form to millions of Jews. Nixon could abandon biowarfare except for defense when development of defense was the same as development of the weapon. The shield was a weapon which in turn could serve as a shield.

The dialectical environment of national conflict in which anthrax was isolated and characterized in the first place continued to define anthrax throughout the twentieth century. It is remarkable how consistent this has been: in the general conditions of the Franco-Prussian War, staged again and again in its invasions and economic warfare, and with them the scientific rivalry between Koch and Pasteur and their schools. The scientists of one side think they know what the scientists of the other side are doing because they know what they themselves are doing with the same materials.

The protection-assault dialectic is fundamental to imagining germ warfare. It yields the idea of "defensive" germ warfare, in which vaccines are deployed against biological agents that are being developed by the vaccine users. The defenders might even be attacking those they defend, or themselves.

Germ warfare centers most tightly around inoculations which are both protective and aggressive, but then advances into clouds that neither protect nor attack. And germ weapons can simply, stubbornly be treated as any other weapon.

When it parts from the fundamental attack-resistance of inoculations given to animals, anthrax germ warfare becomes a fantasy modeled on woolsorters disease and other nebulous states of delivery. The black skin eruptions and the contaminated animal products are forgotten in the cloud of spores.

As long as anthrax is in the hands of specialists, it remains in the controlled space of the laboratory even when applications are proposed. One of the applications is a military phase in which it is made into bullets and bombs. Once it escapes into the public imagination it is assimilated to plagues, poisons, air pollution and bad food, which return it to miasmas, flung cinders, and other magical entities.

The scientists and technicians who specialize in the uses of germs also can be defenders or assailants or both, as their publicists, backers and opponents portray them. They can work for us or work for the enemy, or both. The history of germ warfare is a history of managing the ambiguity of both germs and the specialists in germs. Like the rare firefighter who sets fires to have work, the germ warfare specialist can induce an attack to publicize and fund his readiness to deter attacks.

Germ warfare differs from "conventional" warfare in that it can be clandestine, implanted secretly and used as an accusation that the other side was so low and unethical that they would resort to such a means. Yet it can use the bombs and bullets of conventional warfare to achieve its ends. There was no exchange of fire in germ warfare, only an exchange of propaganda while sustaining the environment of creeping fear that makes germ warfare seem possible.

Chemical warfare, which preceded germ warfare, and nuclear warfare, which followed it, are both attempts to control forces otherwise at play. But germ warfare, unlike the others, is a human attempt to assume control of forces that previously were at the whim of gods and nature. Germ warfare is the waging of nature by other means.

The major anthrax weapons production programs in the twentieth century, the British-American and the Soviet, were undertaken because the producers feared the other side was producing anthrax and could imagine how and why they were doing it. As with conventional weapons, one gun barrel faced another and didn't discharge lest the other might. There was leakage both of imagined anthrax and of anthrax spores. Other conflicts received anthrax from the major confrontations.

The first documented attempts to use anthrax offensively during wartime were by Axis agents against Allied supply routes during the First World War. The wartime germ attacks were secretive, were uncovered slowly if at all, and were not very effective, unlike the front-line artillery barrages or chlorine and mustard gas attacks. If the attempts had been successful they might have been better documented. Germany's extensive covert program of bacteriological warfare was only revealed to the general public some time after the war, in the confessions of the saboteurs and the deliberations of an international war claims commission.

The purpose of the program was to infect horses and mules being gathered for transport to Europe, where they were needed as draft animals to carry personnel and equipment. The United States supplied Britain and France, the Allies, with materiel, and finally entered the war on their side. The Axis powers, primarily Germany and Austria-Hungary, needed to cut supply lines to and within Europe through active warfare (submarine attacks on shipping, for instance) and sabotage.

Anton Dilger, a German-American physician who had specialized in wound surgery at Johns Hopkins University, joined the German Imperial army in 1914. The following year, leaving active duty due to a nervous breakdown brought on by medical attendance in a bombarded building, Dilger dedicated himself to sabotage and returned to the United States with anthrax and pseudomonas (glanders) cultures, intending to infect draft horses and mules.

He and his brother Carl set up a laboratory to grow the cultures in Chevy Chase, Maryland. Using cultures supplied by Dilger, Captain Frederick Hinsch organized teams of men to inoculate horses gathered for shipment to Europe in the port of Baltimore, Maryland. Dilger tried to set up a second lab in Saint Louis, Missouri, a rail center for shipment of draft animals and cattle, but the cold winter weather killed the cultures. His involvement in an incendiary attack caused him to flee to Mexico, where he remained for the rest of the war.

Whether these attacks had any serious effect on the animals was unclear, because the disruptions of war were already inducing diseases in livestock, and limiting protective vaccination. There was enough of a spike in reported cases of human anthrax (cutaneous) in 1916 for the U.S. Surgeon General to include a special section in his Annual Report (1917), but the report did not link the increase to enemy action.

Both during and after the war the Germans were accused of spreading or attempting to spread biological agents to sicken both humans and animals. Apart from an induced glanders epidemic that reduced the supply of mules to Europe from Mesopotamia, the German germ warfare program does not seem to have had much success. That chemical agents actually were used was nauseatingly apparent to soldiers of both sides fighting the trench war in Europe, but disease outbreaks were more readily explained by war conditions than by human spreading of agents.

As part of their Pamphlets on the War series the London publisher Hodder and Stoughton issued (for a penny) "Microbe-Culture at

Bukarest." Boxes of high explosives were found at the German Legation in Bucharest, Rumania, according to official documents. Dr. Babesh of the Rumanian Institute of Pathology and Bacteriology responded to the Prefect of Police's request that he analyze the yellow liquid in some vials also found in the legation. Thin-oblong bacteria with undulated filaments showed under the microscope, two guinea pigs died after being injected and colonies growing in gelatin and potatoes were recognized under the microscope as "carbon bacilli." Dr. Babesh responded, "I can declare positively that this first phial contained a very virulent culture of the anthrax (carbon) bacillus." The second vial contained glanders bacteria.

In a diplomatic note, the pamphlet continued, the Rumanian Minister of Foreign Affairs declared that the staff of the Imperial legation had violated all the rules of neutrality [Rumania was a neutral power during the war] by introducing secretly into the Rumanian capital ... bacillus-cultures which were intended for the infection of domestic animals, and were in consequence likely to produce terrible murrains, as well as maladies transmissible to human beings."

The rumor of clandestine germ attacks by the Germans persisted long after the war. An attempted use of anthrax in the First World War, the only one for which there is physical evidence, was uncovered in the police museum in Trondheim, Norway It consisted of a set of sugar cubes with tiny glass vials in them that had been stored in the museum since they were taken from the personal luggage of Baron Karl Otto von Rosen, who was arrested in January 1917 in the northern town of Karasjov. The baron's luggage also contained packages of dynamite labeled "Swedish meat" and vials of curare. He claimed to be an agitator for Finnish independence (from Russia), but the Norwegian police suspected German sympathies. Analysis of the contents of the vials seventy years later showed that they contained anthrax spores.

From the location of the baron's capture, near a major northerly supply route, it was inferred that he intended to insert the cubes into hay fed to horses and reindeer. The vials would be broken by the action of chewing, the glass shards would create mouth lesions for the spores to enter, and the animals would sicken and die from ingestive anthrax, throwing into disarray the shipment of goods that was bypassing the German U-boat blockade of the British Isles, and precipitating an outbreak among humans. This was an attempt to create a weapon using Pasteur's findings on how anthrax entered animals.

The discovery of the vials, apart from underlining the continuing rumor of German biological warfare during the First World War, foregrounded a change in the use of the bacilli. The other known attacks were by injection, in effect an inoculation program intended to destroy the animals rather than immunize them. The plot uncovered in Norway took advantage of the ability of the anthrax spores to withstand drying and to become infective if swallowed.

Wet injections might be used to transmit any number of diseases to animals and in fact glanders was more frequently attempted in that medium, because unlike anthrax it then might spread directly from animal to animal. The glass vials utilized a property unique to anthrax—its spores—to spread it to a number of animals at the same time. If enough animals were debilitated and died, then perhaps plague conditions would ensue with the disease spreading from the animals' undisposed bodies before they could be burned or buried deep enough. But the Germans were also accused of attempting to spread plague itself through the time-honored methods of depositing infected corpses in public places and poisoning wells. And of dropping "plague" bombs on British troops during the war.

The imagination of how cultured germs might be used in warfare was based on earlier epidemics blamed on enemy activity. Imagining what an enemy might do with germs then served to help plan germ campaigns against the enemy, or at least to sell defensive measures to the funding authorities.

The next step in the development of anthrax as a weapon left behind the live culture inoculation approach and concentrated on delivery through the spores. As animals ceased to be vital in wartime transport, the technology of anthrax was modified to have broader effects on agriculture, to replicate an anthrax epidemic which might also include humans.

Another important proposal for the dissemination of the bacteria, prefigured in the unverified accounts of plague bombs, was the controlled explosion.

An international convention in the Hague (1899) had agreed to ban the use of projectiles solely to spread asphyxiating gases, but the German general staff believed they were within the limits set by the treaty when they released chlorine gas on enemy positions during the battle of Ypres in April, 1915. Masks worn by miners had been issued to German troops, and the Allied troops, though forewarned, suffered from the attack.

This and subsequent releases of gas brought the Germans only mixed success on the battlefield, and they may have cost them more in the negative propaganda that helped persuade America to enter the war. The gas attacks created the image of the gas-masked soldier, and implanted the graphic image of warfare waged through poisonous clouds—which might be made of noxious chemicals, bacteria or radioactivity—as a threat as well as an act.

Poland, a country pieced back together by the peace agreements at the end of the war, advocated an international convention that would prohibit wartime use of biological and chemical weapons. In 1925 European powers signed the Protocol for the Prohibition of the Use in War of Asphyxiating, Poisonous or Other Gases, and of Bacteriological Methods of Warfare. The protocol entered into force in 1928, and European countries generally observed its provisions in warfare.

The Geneva Protocol was the first important multilateral agreement prohibiting chemical and biological weapons. It also was restricted by a lack of a verification mechanism, did not apply to civil conflicts, and was not signed and ratified immediately by all the parties to the League of Nations conference that wrote it. France signed in 1926, Poland in 1929, the United States in 1970 (Senate confirmation followed in 1974), Slovakia (after it became an independent state) in 1993 and Taiwan not at all. Most signatories reserved the right to use these weapons against an antagonist who used chemical or biological weapons first, and all, including France, had weapons development programs that included defensive and retaliatory instruments prohibited by the protocol.

"The explosion of anthrax bombs no louder than the popping of a paper bag" is how Bernardo Marx, the protagonist of Aldous Huxley's novel *Brave New World* (1932), describes the horrors of the Nine Years War that led to the establishment of the reformed society which he is trying to escape. Later, Marx expresses his acceptance of the world regime by exclaiming, "What use is truth or beauty or knowledge with anthrax bombs popping all around you?"

Huxley even knew how anthrax bombs would sound. They were like puffballs bursting with spores. Poor eyesight had kept him off the battlefield during the First World War and he had not actually heard any bombs explode. His abiding curiosity about science, and his family and social connections with prominent biologists, placed him in the social and intellectual milieu that was to test real anthrax bombs within a decade. There were discussions of the possibility well before that and Huxley apparently was party to them. His grandfather, Thomas Henry Huxley, Darwin's great defender, was certainly intimate with developing biological science, and his brother Julian Huxley was a prominent biologist. John Burdon Sanderson's relative J.B.S. Haldane, also an important biologist, was a convert to Hinduism and a pacifist, and did not mention anthrax bombs.

Projected use of anthrax bombs in a future war was a token of the skepticism with which the Geneva Protocol was received by many Europeans. There would have to be managed changes in the hereditary make-up of humanity before such weapons could be foresworn. For Huxley, the anthrax bombs ended the world which created them and initiated the new world order. The artificially bred hierarchy into which people were born with pre-assigned social rank and social destinies made the world safe from weaponized anthrax, but at the cost of personal liberties.

Anthrax took the place of poison gas as the horror weapon that would force a new, socialized peace, but only in Huxley's vision. Other imaginings of future war exaggerated existing weaponry and alignments. When H.G. Wells conceived antagonistic use of a bacillus (*The Deadly Bacillus*, 1895), the bacillus was not anthrax but cholera, employed by an anarchist who persuades a gullible scientist to give him a culture which he plans to release into the London water supply.

In his anthrax bombs Huxley epitomized the military vision of one section of his own class, a vision which would communicate itself to Japan, America and South Africa.

Around the same time Huxley published his novel, an American military doctor, Major Leon Fox, wrote a paper entitled "Bacterial Warfare: The Use of Biologic Agents in Warfare." Fox's paper was aimed at the very possibility that Huxley expressed, of bacterial weapons, but its force was mostly to deny their potential. Fox questioned the viability of bacterial agents when delivered by bombs and projectiles, but he relaxed his qualms when it came to anthrax. Recalling the use of chlorine at Ypres, Fox suggested that an aerosol cloud of spores might serve as a potent weapon if the spores could be dispersed alive.

Fox's paper crystallized and guided military thinking for a decade. It was translated into German, Russian and Japanese and eagerly read by staff officers, doctors and politicians. It was republished in 1942 in the same military medical journal, soon after the attack on Pearl Harbor.

The revelations of German biological warfare during the First World War, made public in France, Britain and the United States during the late 1930s, fueled preparations to respond to any German germ campaigns. In 1934 a story appeared in British and French newspapers that German agents had tested dispersion of bacteria (*Serratia marcescens*, as it is now called) in Paris Metro and London Underground subway systems, in an attempt to measure the likely effects of a bacterial bomb.

This was the first alleged use of a bacterial stimulant to gauge civilian targets. The evidence that the tests actually took place was flimsy. After Hitler came to power in 1936 German research on bacterial weapons was limited by his decree forbidding their development. The other powers did not know this, however, and recalled German activities during the First World War, and the reputed tests since then.

There is no record of tactical anthrax weapons actually being tested anywhere until 1942. Then, unbeknownst to each other, but almost concurrently, British and Japanese military research units detonated anthrax bombs under test conditions.

Prior to and during the Second World War, British weapons developers at a sequence of facilities ultimately known as Porton Down designed and tested "unconventional" weapons, which meant weapons in violation of the 1899 Geneva Convention. The experiment station was originally set up in 1916 to test chemical weapons and protections against them, but a germ warfare program rapidly was put into place after the German attack on France.

The purpose, germ warfare advocates claimed, was defensive and retaliatory. The enemy would be the first to use these weapons and we must be ready to respond in kind. As with conventional weapons, germ weapons were just as easily offensive as defensive.

Other agents had been studied in laboratory tests, but anthrax was the first choice of the British team because there was a chance that the spores would survive an explosive dispersal; they were known to survive fire that burned animal corpses. The enemy combatants would then breathe the airborne spores in sufficient numbers to suffer a battlefield equivalent of woolsorters disease. The British anthrax bomb was by design an aerosol bomb.

A privately funded Canadian germ warfare program had actually preceded the British one, and in 1940 was studying non-explosive dispersal of psittacosis (a bacterial fever) through sawdust and other particulates, which would avoid Fox's problem of the destruction of the agent upon explosive dispersal. And the Japanese had studied and were already practicing non-explosive dispersal of plague using the typical vector, fleas, but dropped from airplanes rather than hopping from rats. The British, and following them, the Americans, concentrated on using explosions and therefore anthrax spores

After improvising fermenters to produce anthrax spores in quantity, Paul Fildes and David Henderson of the Porton Down Biological Department on July 15, 1942, detonated a bomb containing spore slurry upwind of fifteen sheep immobilized in wooden crates arranged in an arc, their heads pointed toward the bomb. The only sheep that did not die of anthrax were located at the far ends of the line.

The spore cloud produced by another bomb detonated nine days later was carried by a change of the wind and only half of the sheep were exposed. Those exposed died on schedule.

Spore-filled bullets were fired into a steel casing containing live sheep, several of which also died from anthrax. The personnel inside armored interior of tanks might be killed by anthrax and the tanks rendered useless. In these tests there was an urgent attempt to make anthrax spores into a lethal enhancement of projectiles, as depleted uranium would later be used.

The test results supported Leon Fox's surmise that if anything would survive explosive dispersal in sufficient numbers to be an effective agent, it was anthrax spores. And for the Porton Down team the tests provided evidence to overcome the barrier of Fox's judgment against germ warfare, especially the resistance of the Americans, to whom they turned to mass-produce anthrax and the bombs to deliver it.

The outdoor explosions had been conducted on Gruinard Island, a private estate off the coast of Scotland. The sheep that died in the experiments were autopsied, and the remains were buried by being covered with rubble off a seaside cliff. One of the corpses was carried by the tide to the mainland and was scavenged by a shepherd's dog, which then died and spread spores to the pastured sheep, which also died. The time-honored mode of anthrax spread reasserted itself on the periphery of the careful tests.

Gruinard Island itself became so saturated with spores that the government set it off limits for fifty years. During the mid–1980s the island was bombarded with formaldehyde and seawater to destroy the spores, but it remained uninhabitable until the 1990s.

After Gruinard no longer was usable, the British team turned to Canada, where a program was established on Grosse Isle in the St. Lawrence River to mass-produce anthrax in tray cultures and prepare it for bomb delivery. Not enough anthrax was being produced fast enough for the British biowarriors, who turned to America with its mass production capacities.

Fildes and Henderson brought the evidence that bacterial warfare really was possible to George Merck, head of the United States War Research Service, which was formed to investigate biological warfare, and to officers of the Chemical Warfare Service. They offered British technological advice if the Americans would agree to make anthrax spores in quantity. They placed an immediate order for three kilograms of botulinus toxin and later anthrax bombs.

The Americans established development, testing and production facilities, and they tested anthrax bombs. The war was ended in the Pacific by the earlier launched, more rapidly progressing work of the Manhattan Project before the anthrax factory near Vigo, Indiana, got beyond producing simulant.

Realizing that their bombs would not be ready for some time, the British resorted to a lower cost means of deployment requiring less anthrax. In 1942, during the Battle of Britain, Operation Vegetarian, referring ironically to Hitler's well-known avoidance of meat, had factory workers forming millions of linseed oil feed cakes which were then imbued by pumps with anthrax spores. The cakes were to be dropped en masse on German farmland where the cattle would eat them and die in droves, causing Germans to become vegetarians. There were test drops on Gruinard Island. But the 1944 Normady invasion was staged before the cakes were ready in sufficient numbers and the plan was never executed. The cakes were destroyed after the war except for a few kept as museum specimens. Project Vegetarian had reverted to the older German method of using anthrax to sabotage animals, combined with a non-aerosol bombardment.

In 1998 veterans of the Porton Down program disclosed to a reporter of the *London Daily Telegraph* that the Porton Down team planned in 1944 to saturate Hitler's clothing with spores, so he would die in agony. They changed their plans, however, when it was argued that this would only make Hitler a martyr and consolidate German resistance to the projected invasion. Hitler lost his chance to attain the apotheosis of Herakles.

As the bombs were imagined spraying the enemy with spores, defensive vaccines were sought to protect troops from any spores that might come in their direction. Tests and manufacture of anthrax were performed by men in gas masks and protective clothing, and there were few instances even of cutaneous anthrax. But such gear was not practical on the battlefront.

Drawing upon a line of vaccine development that had preceded Pasteur, Cromartie and Watson at Fort Detrick in 1944 produced an anthrax vaccine for humans. Animals and humans treated with a lesion extract from which bacteria and spores had been filtered showed resistance to more virulent anthrax. A Porton Down team led by Harry Smith in the mid–1950s identified the specific toxins that made the bacteria lethal. This discovery in turn led to the realization that anthrax toxins cannot function as isolated poisons as botulinus toxin can, because the toxins must be in the presence of the encapsulated bacteria. Just as well to use the spores in bombs.

The Japanese, whose biowarfare program was not known to the general public until the mid–1980s, had not scrupled to devise vaccines and did not seem to be involved in the same attack-defense anthrax dialectic as the Western powers. Anthrax did exist in Japan and occasionally affected cattle, but technical knowledge to create bioweapons arrived with bacteriology. Japanese industry had not contracted the woolsorters model, and the military imagined their bombs differently.

Anthrax bombing was among the many forms of germ attack devised by the Japanese Unit 731. General Shiro Ishii, a well-traveled physician and the inventor of a porcelain water filter, headed the "water purification" unit located near Harbin in Manchuria. The American microbiologist Murray Sanders, sent to interview Japanese bacterial warfare scientists in September 1945, learned from Ryoichi Naito, an English-speaking physician who had worked on toxin development, that

Ishii returned to Japan from a tour of Europe in 1932 convinced that widespread acceptance of the 1925 Geneva Protocol prohibiting biological weapons signified how potent such weapons must be. Perhaps it is fortunate there was no protocol prohibiting fission weapons. Tomosada Masuda, close to Ishii in command of the unit, told Sanders that the capture in 1935 of five Russian spies carrying glass vials containing anthrax spores, cholera and dysentery bacteria precipitated experimentation on military use of bacteria.

Naito described the anthrax bombs conceived and tested under Ishii's command. There was first a steel jacketed "Ha" bomb that blew the spores it contained into test animals with flying shrapnel. This was followed by the "Uji" bomb which refined the same principle by employing porcelain rather than steel as the bomb casing. The charge was placed on the outside of the bomb shell, which could contain more spore fluid. The fine slivers of flying ceramic were more likely to inject subjects with a deathly load of spores.

The Uji bomb was designed to distribute the spores over wide area and to disappear, leaving no evidence that a bomb ever had been dropped. The very delicacy of the material, however, made the bombs difficult to manufacture in quantity. Naito also described a radio mechanism on the ground that would cause a series of bombs released from an airplane to detonate when they reached the optimum altitude to spread their payload.

The information that Sanders collected made it seem that these bombs were designed to kill animals and seed the land with spores, that they were aimed at disrupting the economy rather than primarily intended to kill troops or civilians. Animal kills and the accidental deaths of a few laborers were the only lethal outcomes of the project.

Ishii himself was not captured, and an elaborate funeral in his home village passed him off as dead, but he was soon made available on order of the American occupational authorities. The first interview he gave only described early bacteria bombs (perhaps the earliest anthrax test bomb detonated anywhere, in 1937), indoor aerosol experiments with animals and a modest tray method for growing bacteria, similar to one the Canadians independently developed.

As more rumors of human experimentation reached the Americans, and the Russians demanded interviews with Japanese bacterial warfare specialists, Ishii made a deal to reveal all findings in exchange for immunity from war crimes prosecution.

Ishii told Norbert Fell, an American military bacteriologist pressing him to make full disclosures, that he considered anthrax the best agent because "it could be produced in quantity, was resistant [to bomb blasts], retained its virulence and was eighty to ninety percent fatal."

In the aftermath of his visit, Fell received a number of reports from Japanese scientists working in Ishii's unit, one of which described British bacterial warfare trials. Humans tied to stakes were subjected to bomb detonations, or confined to a chamber where bacterial aerosols were sprayed with a flit gun.

In other words they were treated the same as animal test subjects. The shrapnel and infected wounds killed the bomb victims, and inhalational infections killed both bomb and spray victims, though not all of them. The Japanese attendants reportedly left the victims untreated if they survived the original blasts to determine how long they would live.

The Japanese experimenters attained woolsorters disease, inhalational anthrax, in animals and humans through bombs and sprays, but they did not try to create an anthrax cloud outdoors, which was the primary aim of British and American experimentation. The results of the tests on human subjects, including autopsy reports, were among the records the Japanese gave to the Americans in exchange for freedom from war crimes prosecution. The great attraction of Ishii's work was his actually having tested airborne, ingestive and cutaneous germ assaults on human subjects, and he performed autopsies which were recorded in verbal descriptions and slides of tissue samples. In all the years of observing anthrax, Europeans had not built up such a body of data.

Some of Unit 731's delivery methods, such as feather bombs and insects to spread plague and anthrax, would reputedly show up again during the Korean War, when the hard-pressed Americans were accused by the Chinese of dropping anthrax-bearing insects on villages. The use of hatpins and other piercing objects to inject victims with anthrax and other bacteria was planned as an assassination and terrorism technique during the struggle of the apartheid government in South Africa to maintain itself against the African National Congress. The hatpins were again proposed in addition to a number of other piercing objects to create wound entrances for the bacteria.

One Unit 731 technique of anthrax delivery which had a fairy-tale wickedness about it was chocolates prepared with spores and distributed to children. Dr. Wouter Basson, who headed the apartheid regime's Project Coast, also ordered and tested anthrax cigarettes, and had anthrax and botulinum chocolates prepared. The testimony of the veterinary surgeon Mike Odendaal at Basson's trial on May 24, 2000, described testing anthrax cigarettes for the viability of the spores and injecting soft chocolates with liquid anthrax medium. Odendaal did not know what was done with the preparations, which he gave to another Basson confederate, and Basson himself denied knowledge of them. Basson also allegedly planned to use umbrellas, hatpins and a collection of other devices for cutaneous attacks with toxic agents.

The anthrax chocolates may have been an independent invention; the cigarettes certainly were. In general, however, the heritage of Unit 731's technical innovations spread worldwide to both military and spy organizations after the war, and even before the report reached the general public. South Africa more effectively transmitted Ishii's innovations than the Americans did, and several of the Americans possibly involved in the 2001 anthrax letter attacks had South African connections.

Sei-ichi Morimura's sensational novel *Aka no hoshoku* (*The Devil's Gluttony*, 1981), never translated into the English language, was one of the first Japanese revelations of the activities of Unit 731. This book, journalistic exposés and lawsuits by Chinese survivors all followed the death of Ishii and others who had been directly involved in the Japanese biowarfare program.

Aum Shinri Kyo's 1995 anthrax attacks may have an adaptation of a tradition of biological weapons to the needs of urban terrorism. Instead of anthrax bombs, however, Aum employed aerosol techniques more consistent with Anglo-American germ warfare.

During the Second World War the Americans set up a plant near Vigo, Indiana, to manufacture the quantities of anthrax required for bombs to be sent to Britain. The plant never got beyond testing with a simulant, *Bacillus globigi*, a supposedly harmless organism that sporifies under the same conditions as *Bacillus anthracis*. This and a testing facility in Louisiana, where no outdoor tests ever were conducted, were closed down after Hiroshima, and adapted to other purposes.

The Cold War led to defensive study of the possibility of airborne germ attacks. With Gruinard Island too contaminated for further testing, the British turned to conducting seaborne tests of detonations that sent clouds of bacteria over animals towed behind a ship traveling remote stretches of the Caribbean. As with their earlier tests, the testers were attempting to gain precise battlefield-simulating knowledge of the motion of bacterial clouds under varying air conditions.

The Americans sprayed their wartime store of *Bacillus globigi*, and the simulant bacterium *Serratia marcescens*, over populated areas in the United States then attempted to gauge the likely success of attacks using real pathogens. The experiments were also a Cold War gesture designed to convince the Soviets that the Americans and their allies were prepared both to defend themselves against such attacks and deliver pathogens to civilian targets from the air.

Improving the technology of battlefield and wide-scale delivery through bombs called into question the value of anthrax as the medium of choice. Fox's and Ishii's arguments for its superiority (ease of production, long lasting form, lethality) still applied, but it was the very lethality of anthrax that caused weapons developers to rethink its usefulness in a period of localized conflict and mass media propaganda. Anthrax might kill too easily to realize the aim of the use of bioweapons to incapacitate opposing forces and civilians. Another bacterium primarily affecting animals but communicable to humans, *Brucellosis suis*, recommended itself.

Bombs designed to scorch the earth by disseminating spores in a liquid medium became a fixture of low-cost weapons planning long after the war. Among the germ warfare devices United Nations inspectors found in Saddam Hussein's arsenal after the Gulf War in the mid–1990s were liquid anthrax bombs, probably derived from Soviet models or purchased outright from the Soviets. By then these bombs were considered outmoded.

The anthrax bombs were an attempt to make a tactical weapon out of bacteria. This use of anthrax resembled the use of radioactive waste in non-fissionable "dirty" bombs designed to spread radioactivity over a wide area, injuring all living things within that area and making the land uninhabitable. Both anthrax and radioactivity were lethal materials that could be concentrated in a warhead and disseminated by explosion.

The threat of an anthrax-laced explosion was a stronger weapon than its actual use. In the minds of many military planners, anthrax-based and other biological weapons were second to the atomic and hydrogen bombs, which also were used only in tests after the Second World War, to display nuclear capabilities, and not in actual warfare. Iraq and other powers projected biological weapons like anthrax and chemical weapons because a credible showing of nuclear weapons would require more time and a much greater investment.

The anthrax bomb still depended upon the inoculation concept. Rather than individual cattle, an entire area was to be saturated with spores. The conceivable defense, however, remained individual injections with an attenuated culture of the bacteria. As the United States prepared to attack Iraqi forces occupying Kuwait, the commanders attempted to secure sufficient anthrax vaccine to protect frontline troops. The frontline troops, however, were not uniformly cooperative; some were convinced that the vaccine caused disease.

Many military planners believed that the best defense against chemical and germ weapons was bombing raids and the threat of nuclear retaliation. There was some concern that bombing the bunkers where Iraqi germ warfare agents were likely stored would release them into approaching American troops.

The Americans and their British allies in the Gulf War recognized that there was another method of germ attack, aerosols, that might be used with anthrax, because they also had been working on this method themselves for decades. Inoculations and bombs were clumsy and inefficient ways of delivering the agent, and they were conceived to affect animals and humans as anthrax itself did during its naturally occurring transmission. Aerosols could affect human populations directly, without needing to embed spores in the earth or in animals and go through a cycle of infection before reaching humans. With aerosols, the immediate and collective debilitating effects of an anthrax infection could best be realized. Armies, military installations, even entire cities could be subdued without a need for animal hosts.

Aerosols do not have any protective strength; they are strictly for attack. They are based on the woolsorters disease model of anthrax and not the disease-vaccine, offense-defense model. Vaccines might be called for to protect potential victims from an aerosol attack, but the aerosols themselves are not both offensive and defensive like vaccines.

Fire extinguishers, paint and insecticide sprays were among the first military applications of aerosols, but they were created to spread and deposit chemicals. Anthrax spores had to remain suspended in the air. The artificially spore-imbued atmosphere of textile mills that had produced woolsorters disease became the basis for the technology of anthrax aerosols and defense against them.

Plague and botulinum toxin aerosols were also planned, but the hardiness of anthrax spores recommended them for this use. It required drying the spores to make them airborne and likely to be inhaled in quantity by human victims. The dryer and lighter they could be made, the more easily they would permeate the breathing space of an area. It was also essential to reduce the spores' tendency to clump together, which could weigh them down and limit their travel.

Research on how to aerosolize anthrax spores needed only to look at the atmospheres generated in factories. Potters and miners came down with diseases from the dusty air they breathed. Milling wheat, sugar cane, and other natural products in industry created a powdery air that invaded the lungs, caused a variety of diseases and could even explode.

Textile mills had their peculiar particulate environment, and resultant lung condition in long-time workers, bissinosis. Anthrax spores when added to that air caused infections with a much more rapid onset than the slow diseases of dusty trade workers. Textile workers were exposed to machined fogs of sharp particles for decades, but it was only when anthrax entered the mix that workers came down with acute conditions.

Weapons developers had before them the natural experiment of an unprotected office employee walking into a mill building and developing inhalational anthrax. And of course they could experiment with exposing animals to the mill environment to study the onset of the disease under known conditions.

Though quantities of spores were collected from the respiratory passages of mill workers who did not come down with the disease, and animals had to breathe thick atmospheres for long periods of time before they became sick, weapons developers proceeded with their anthrax plans.

High speed milling and anti-electrostatic treatment to reduce clumping can make the dried anthrax spores fine enough to become and remain airborne while still viable. There is a specific size tolerance, around 3 micrometers, large enough to enter respiratory passages and stay there and small enough to remain suspended. Adding an anti-static powder such as a clay or glass particulate can allow the anthrax spores to enter the air like smoke. In the dramatic scene that ends the first part of Richard Preston's book *The Demon in the Freezer,* a scientist examining spores from one of the 2001 anthrax letters becomes apprehensive when he sees the spores fly up into the air from the tip of tool he is using to lift them out. A perfectly airborne anthrax had been engineered. But the scientist most fears that it is being used to carry smallpox.

By effective treatment the insinuative nature of the spores is enhanced, and this process can be sold as means to subject entire cities, or armies, to a woolsorters disease environment. Britain, Canada, the United States and the Soviet Union from the 1940s onward set up facilities to mass-produce anthrax bacteria for use in weapons.

Anthrax spores were such a promising package for the delivery of biological warfare agents that researchers tried to generate a spore-like form for bacteria that did not sporulate, and for viruses. They accomplished this by lypholizing the bacteria—forcing them into a dormant state which can survive drying, temperature changes, sunlight, and caustic chemicals. Plague packaged like anthrax was the goal.

Even as they solved the technical problems of producing a lingering spore aerosol that many people would breathe, the anthrax weapons developers needed to face the fact that not everyone exposed to anthrax gets sick and not all those who get sick die. A non-infective strain, no matter how successfully delivered, would have no weapons value at all, as the Aum Shinri Kyo cult members found when they sprayed anthrax spores from a fixed blower and from mobile units in Tokyo in 1995.

Geneticists determined later that Aum Shinri Kyo was using the anthrax strain used to vaccinate cattle, the Sterne strain, and it had little effect on the intended human victims. They had tried to use the unmodified shield as a weapon. The cult members found sarin gas released in the subway more to their purpose. Efforts also were made to reverse Sterne's procedure and make encapsulated bacteria viable for release directly into the air, enabling them to infect victims directly without going through the spore state.

A traditional weapons planning mentality prevailed in the design of germ warfare anthrax aerosols. What was delivered had to be lethal. While the mechanics of milling and treating the spores could be worked out and tested with neutral substances, achieving the needed level of virulence was a matter of finding a strain that could be counted on to cause the disease once the effort had been made to prepare and deliver it.

The most virulent strains were obtained by careful collection from the wild. A single cow that died of anthrax in Texas was the source of the Ames strain isolated by the veterinarian Dr. Michael L. Vickers, and later used in American weapons development. Prior to its destruction in October 2001, the anthrax specimen collection at the University of Iowa at Ames was perhaps the most extensive in the world, but the collection gave its name to the most lethal form of the bacteria.

Ken Alibek, who as Dr. Kanatjan Alibekov worked to increase the potency of Soviet germ weaponry before he defected to the United States in 1992, described in a confidential interview how the Soviets acquired a particularly strong strain of the bacilli. In 1953, Alibek claimed, a large quantity of spores was inadvertently spilled into the sewers of Kirov, the site of the first large-scale anthrax production facility. The Soviets were producing anthrax weapons in large volume as part of a program to create a response to the West's superiority in nuclear weapons.

Three years later the senior scientist at the facility, mindful of the evolutionary possibilities, thought that the rats in the sewers should by then be carrying a very strong strain of anthrax. Rats are highly resistant to anthrax, so any form found in them must be persistent indeed. A team was organized, and the hardy spores extracted from the rats they captured formed the basis of Strain 836.

This strain was prepared as spores in an aerosol and accidentally released into the air from another facility in Sverdlovsk, in 1979, killing (officially) sixty-four people. The Soviets at the time made great efforts to have the Sverdlovsk deaths attributed to ingestive anthrax from bad meat. A 1927 epidemic of lethal gastrointestinal disease in Yaroslavl, which killed twenty-seven people, mostly single males, was attributed to sausages made from the scrap parts of animals dead of anthrax. The pattern of this epidemic was imposed on the Sverdlovsk cases: ingestive anthrax (a caution against bad processing and black market meat) was substituted for inhalational anthrax, which was an industrial affliction.

The Soviets were attempting to avoid disclosing how deadly the airborne spores were by masking the outbreak with the more generalized problems of bad meat. Or they were attempting to convey to their enemies just how effective their spores were while keeping a lid on public objections to the location of the military facility.

The American inhalational anthrax deaths in late 2001 were briefly obscured by the aftermath of the terrorist attacks on the World Trade

Center and Pentagon, but they actually were a rogue release of a preparation of the Ames strain, by persons and for purposes unknown.

Successful transformation of anthrax bacilli into an airborne bioweapon realizes the imagined contagion of the disease but supposedly under human control. This designer plague is referred back to the primitive state of human anthrax infection, through the handling and consumption of animals dead of the infection and their products. Woolsorters disease defaults to butchers disease.

If there have been actual uses of anthrax bioweapons other than the Aum Shinri Kyo and U.S. postal attempts, they have not been reported. The one likely use of anthrax as a weapon in warfare reverted to ingestive anthrax.

During the war of independence in Rhodesia in the late 1970s, the white colonists and their South African allies allegedly implanted in pastures animal feed cakes impregnated with anthrax spores, a crude but effective means of attacking the enemy through his livelihood. The enemy was the native peoples who were treated as rebels against the European-dominated government.

The technology to produce easily transported anthrax feed did make the transition from Britain to South Africa during the postwar period. The feed cakes were distributed both in Rhodesia and in South Africa in an attempt to ruin the land itself. Those able to subsist outside the developing white-dominated economy were considered rebels and subversives. Anthrax was one of the weapons, drawn from conflicts elsewhere, that could be used to reduce people's capacity for independent livelihood.

The use of anthrax made the South African conflicts ecological wars. The result was contamination which eventually affected all parties. The model of anthrax was derived from the desperate measures of countries defending themselves against invaders by making the invasion very unprofitable. Only this was colonialists defending their control of the land against those who were living on it through cattle. By seeding the cattle and thus the ground itself with anthrax, the South African whites were attacking themselves in the long run. They initiated a history of anthrax infections where none had existed before, and they introduced a strain of anthrax that people who had long lived with cycles of infection had no resistance to.

Indeed, Dr. Meryl Nass, the epidemiologist who studied the spread of anthrax in Rhodesia during the late 1970s (and later emerged as a major critic of anthrax vaccines), found that cattle were coming down with black blood fever in areas where anthrax was not known before. She was able to trace the infection to human sources long before the post-apartheid Truth and Reconciliation Commission began its investigations.

The extensiveness of the distribution of anthrax feed, and the number of cattle affected, brought into play the risk model of anthrax and a large number of cases of ingestible anthrax. People who had invested their livelihood in cattle were eating the fallen cows and coming down with lethal infections in far greater numbers than was usual even during an outbreak. That anthrax might have been the Black Death was credible from the plague-like spread of disease.

An alternative explanation of the Zimbabwe outbreaks was the failure of what had been an excellent veterinary program which included regular vaccination of the cattle against anthrax. Certainly war conditions had caused an upsurge of anthrax elsewhere. But Nass believed that a breakdown of preventive measures did not explain the distribution of the disease, which affected as many as 10,000 people, killing 182, entirely in the areas set aside for native peoples, not on white-owned farms or in tourist areas.

The pattern that had been set in Rhodesia continued in Zimbabwe over the years since independence in 1980. As the government condoned the takeover of white-owned farms in 1999–2000, there were periodic outbreaks of anthrax, for instance one in November–December 2000 that killed 50 cattle in a communal farm in Mhondoro and then killed nine people and caused 630 to be hospitalized. Zimbabwe inherited Rhodesia's excellent veterinary services and programs of cattle vaccination. It appeared unlikely that the anthrax outbreaks were the result of normal anthrax cycles since they were unrelated to the weather conditions that usually produce anthrax in cattle.

The white farmers blamed the supporters of Robert Mugabe's government who were invading white-owned farms and herding their cattle across boundaries. But this is more a political explanation. The anthrax infections resembled those that occurred twenty years earlier during the war of independence, which, Mugabe claimed, was being continued as the use of the land was being distributed to his supporters.

In the continuing Zimbabwean anthrax visitations it is difficult to distinguish between actual scorched earth germ warfare aimed at animals and people dependent on them, the anthrax heritage of the earlier warfare, new strains distributed by the movement of people, and the use of anthrax to focus the wickedness and stupidity of the opponent. It has all the elements of a plague condition, in which even scientific understanding and preventive technology become part of the continuing spread of the disease.

The Zimbabwean anthrax complex remains on the level of cattle-human ingestible anthrax, which refers back to the earliest occurrences of the disease and needs only the basic technology of culturing the bacteria to proceed deliberately. The spread can be accomplished through the animals themselves. No laboratory is required.

In America and Europe (as well as urban Africa, India and South America), where the imagined anthrax partakes of anthrax aerosols and the woolsorters model of anthrax atmospheres and where anthrax has become divorced from the agrarian circumstances of its transmission, the imaginary anthrax has ample play. But it comes back to the old plague in the end, with its confusions, excuses, inescapability and search for the perfect victim.

# 11

# Vaccine History

British cattle farmers had to cope with a serious outbreak of cattle plague (rinderpest) in 1865. A Royal Commission, headed by Burdon Sanderson, investigated the spread of the disease, and in their three reports offered the results of applying current theories to a practical problem.

Charles Darwin, in the twenty-seventh chapter of his *Variation of Animals and Plants under Domestication* (1868), quoted a passage from the commission's Third Report:

> It has recently been ascertained that a minute portion of the mucous discharge from an animal affected with rinderpest, if placed in the blood of a healthy ox, increases so fast that in a short space of time 'the whole mass of blood, weighing many pounds, is infected, and every small particle of that blood contains enough poison to give, within less than forty-eight hours, the disease to another animal'.

Darwin's interest in the commission's report stemmed not only from his position as a landowner and cattle keeper. In their findings of a multiplying poison he saw evidence for his theory of a "peculiar formative matter" which had equal power to transmit every single character possessed by either parent to their offspring. This usually is seen as Darwin's closest approach to genetics. His "formative matter," however, was much more general. It included microbes, toxins, poisons: all the invisible corpuscles capable of multiplication within a living system and providing a template for that multiplication. It was not much of a step for Darwin and followers like Thomas Henry Huxley to see the unseen particles of formative matter in a state of competition through natural selection ultimately give rise to the flora and fauna of a region.

The agent of rinderpest (cattle plague) later found to be a virus (poison), could be included with microbes among the "contagia" capable of increasing in volume and influence whenever they entered a living system. In his *Introductory Report on the Intimate Pathology of Contagion* (1869), Sanderson characterized all contagia as colloidal substances, and he cited experimental evidence that rinderpest contagia when filtered through parchment paper ceased to be contagious. It would be possible to make direct studies of the composition ("intimate nature") of infectious matter.

Sanderson's work on rinderpest paralleled Jean-Baptiste Auguste Chauveau's studies of vaccinia and variola, the agents of pox infections in humans and animals. In order to compare smallpox with cowpox, Chauveau separated the vaccine lymph removed from active lesions into distinct segments: minute particles, leukocytes and clear liquid. He did this by adding a solvent which dissolved the soluble bodies and rose to the top of the fluid. He carefully removed the lighter fluid and experimentally injected the residue into animal subjects to determine if he had isolated the contagion. Sanderson traveled to Lyons to learn Chauveau's technique, which he brought back and refined in his own laboratory. In his report Sanderson projected using this technique to identify the physical properties of any isolated contagion, to determine if it was alive and to analyze its chemical composition.

Smallpox was the model for this research because the very word "vaccine" came from the successful use of animal contagia cowpox, to prevent a human scourge, smallpox. The smallpox model was never very far from early vaccine development. There was a supply of vaccinia, cowpox, matter from the lesions cultivated in some people to provide injection material. By making studies of this and smallpox matter retained from human victims, it might be possible to identify a common element in other infections of both humans and animals, and find new vaccines to prevent diseases other than smallpox.

Both Chauveau and Sanderson eventually applied the separation technique to the contagia of anthrax, in an effort to isolate an immunizing fluid like that already known for smallpox. There also was a supply of anthrax contagia, matter from malignant pustules and the blood of afflicted animals, to support the experiments.

In Prussia, Edwin Klebs, who had gained knowledge of wound infections from his medical service in the Franco-Prussian War, showed that finely filtered residues of these infections continued to be toxic but would not multiply in living systems. Klebs discovered the same was true of filtered anthrax blood, and he overgeneralized his findings to project the existence of a single microbe, *Microsporon septicum*, responsible for a range of skin infections, including anthrax. Yet Klebs had provided evidence that the toxic component of anthrax was separable from its contagion.

Klebs, who had attributed all disease to internal pathology, evolved to seeking separable disease agents, which he identified as bacteria. Robert Koch cited Klebs' findings as evidence for the germ theory. Injecting the bacilli-free filtrate into test animals did not cause bacilli to appear in their blood. Both Koch and Klebs neglected the ability of the bacilli-free fluid to act as a poison.

It took Koch's more concerted studies proceeding in the same aftermath of war to establish the presence of the visible bacillus as a necessary condition for contagion. This germ theory of anthrax remained controversial, in the face of the ability of blood without the microbe visibly present to cause disease symptoms in animals that received it.

The old corpuscular theory of contagion had become separated into living and non-living contagia. Advocates of one or the other often would not accept the apparent versatility of infectious matter. Indications that contagia were both living and unliving would inspire and frustrate efforts to control them.

During 1878, his last year as professor superintendent of the Brown Sanatory Institution, Sanderson conducted two research projects on the anthrax poison. One project provided evidence it could be transmitted to humans through the meat, renderings and other products of animals that had died of the disease even though there were no bacteria visible in the products. This trend of research paralleled and supported the discovery of an anthrax agent in the imported goat hair associated with the occupational illnesses of textile workers.

Scientifically guided regulation of the food supply had begun with the analysis of adulterations of bulk flour and sugar, and was now acquiring further sophistication of microbial inspection and culturing tests. Anthrax entering the food stream through infected cattle products could be a source of disease in urban consumers, especially in rapidly urbanizing northern countries. The first pure food law requiring inspection of bulk food was passed in England in 1860, and around the same time the United States government established a chemistry laboratory as part of the Agriculture Commission, to study food adulterations.

Learning the variety of routes by which anthrax poison entered the chain of consumer goods put greater emphasis on stopping it at the source. The meat of anthrax-infected cattle traded to an unwary public had caused epidemics of anthrax poisoning (as opposed to anthrax infection). Regulation of slaughterhouses and inspection of meat by veterinarians and by public health authorities could curtail the entrance of poisons into the commodity stream. These preventive measures have forestalled anthrax so successfully that an epidemic can only be the result of the breakdown of safeguards.

The best way to prevent anthrax poison in particular from entering everyday goods was to prevent the cattle from becoming infected in the first place. The great investment that cattle represented was best secured by fortifying them against this disease. Governments had long since institutionalized preventive destruction of anthrax infected animals. Now prevention began to focus on controlling the poison.

Sanderson's other area of experiment on anthrax during 1878 was the immunization of livestock by using the poison as a preventive inoculation.

Sanderson continued the practice begun by Jenner of trying to develop a milder form of the disease agent which would then strengthen the one inoculated against natural strains. By transferring the blood of anthrax cattle to small rodents and then back to cattle, Sanderson diluted the poison to a protective dose. "The rodents die, but the bovine animals inoculated with their blood or with the pulp of their diseased spleens recover."

Sanderson did not have the time to take the next step and isolate a vaccine. His method was to dilute the "poisonous" blood to the point that it could be administered to healthy animals without inducing a serious infection. In 1880 his successor as professor superintendent, W.S. Greenfield, induced acquired resistance to anthrax in cattle by placing the contagia in one animal, transferring them to another, smaller animal, and so on down the line until the recipient did not die. The blood of the surviving animal became a protective vaccine. This procedure resembled Joseph Lister's method of achieving pure bacteria cultures. Greenfield did not attempt to manufacture the vaccine; he only announced his technique in the reports published in major scientific journals. As he later complained, his findings were obscured by developments on the Continent.

Jean-Joseph Henry Toussaint, a veterinarian and biologist who had studied with Chauveau, conducted independent experiments on an anthrax vaccine and delivered his results within weeks of Greenfield's announcement. Toussaint injected 8 rabbits with the extract of a piece of spleen taken from a sheep clearly dead of anthrax, not all at once but at various times after the death of the sheep. When these rabbits died Toussaint injected other rabbits already exposed to virulent anthrax with blood extract from one or another of the test rabbits. Toussaint's object was to define the concentration of the *charbon* poison necessary to protect unexposed animals without causing them to die of the disease.

Anthrax vaccine history began with a competition between Louis Pasteur and Toussaint, to demonstrate publicly the ability of a preparation to protect animals challenged with injections of virulent anthrax. There is no telling how many experimenters had already tried to prevent anthrax by injecting the blood of infected animals into those threatened by the disease. Rinderpest had already been treated by preventive infection. Chauveau had forestalled the spread of the 1865 outbreak from Britain to the French ports in part by a campaign of preventive vaccination.

Toussaint had previously collaborated with and competed with Pasteur in finding a vaccine for chicken cholera. At least initially, Toussaint maintained a chemical theory of vaccine action different from Pasteur's biological theory. Drawing upon the discoveries of his mentor Chauveau, Toussaint believed that filtering and heating (to 55 degrees Centigrade) the blood of anthrax-infected animals would yield a fluid not contagious but toxic to invading bacilli. In effect the bacilli could be killed by their own residual wastes.

This vaccine-making drew upon techniques of brewing and wine-making, and contemporary discoveries about the nature of fermentation. The yeasts and bacteria that produce wine are destroyed by the alcohol they generate, limiting the alcohol content of the final product. Heating destructively speeds up fermentation by causing byproducts to accumulate. Vaccines could be prepared by heat-curing the blood of infected animals, determining concentration and dosage, and administering the blood to healthy animals, which would then be protected from the multiplication of bacteria by decay products already in their blood.

At the July 27, 1880 meeting of the Académie des Sciences, Henri Bouley, inspector of French veterinary schools and Toussaint's chief supporter, read a note from Toussaint describing field trials in which four dogs and five out of six sheep vaccinated with Toussaint's formula survived injection with virulent anthrax. Following Pasteur's precedent with chicken cholera, Toussaint did not immediately disclose his method of vaccine preparation but presented it to the Académie as a sealed note. The note was opened and its contents revealed only after Académie members accused Toussaint (and Pasteur) of trafficking in "secret remedies." The sealed notes were a way of preserving the potentially valuable license rights to untried treatments while the maker confirmed their worth through public trials.

Pasteur was alarmed by the results of Toussaint's tests, not only because his priority was threatened, but because the results undermined Pasteur's biological theory of disease. There was no room for both germs and toxins where Pasteur was trying to prove that germs had any role at all.

Pasteur had shown in a series of experiments that the presence of other germs inhibited the growth of anthrax bacilli in urine, and it was already known that the bacteria of putrescence caused anthrax bacilli to disappear from a wound. Pasteur called this phenomenon "antibiosis," and it formed the basis for his strategy of using weaker or diluted strains of the same bacteria to forestall lethal infections. The observations of Sanderson and others that certain fungi would halt the growth of bacteria in a culture would have to be repeated under changed circumstances in the next century to bring about the first antibiotic, penicillin.

Pasteur was continuing his efforts to show that fermentation was a process dependent on living microbes and was not strictly a chemical process. Disease was like fermentation and, Pasteur maintained, had to be treated as if caused by living germs rather than as the result of a chemical poison.

Pasteur theorized that bacteria invading living tissue consumed nutrients embedded in the tissue. A vaccine could be created by introducing weakened bacteria which would use up the nutrients without causing a full-blown infection. Any virulent bacteria entering the tissues would then starve before they could reproduce extensively.

The contrast between chemical and biological theories of vaccine action continues in the controversy between proponents of "killed" pathogen vaccines and the proponents of "live" pathogen vaccines, most notably in the competing polio vaccines of Salk and Sabin seventy-five years later. Being able to tell whether or not the pathogen actually has been killed or eliminated from the vaccine body is obviously important. Toussaint advocated a killed vaccine and Pasteur a live one.

Toussaint himself was attentive to the residual toxic properties of his heat-treated vaccine as revealed by small animal tests, and he adopted carbolic acid as a means of killing the bacilli. In this he was following the lead Joseph-Casimir Davaine, who years earlier suggested that antiseptics, substances capable of preventing infection in wounds, including carbolic acid, could be used to reduce the virulence of anthrax-infected blood. Davaine never tested whether blood so treated would yield a vaccine, but Toussaint now did, administering carbolic acid treated anthrax blood vaccine to twenty sheep, sixteen of which shakily survived exposure to fully virulent blood.

Henri Bouley discussed the irregular performance of Toussaint's vaccine cultures with Pasteur's assistant Emile Roux. From this meeting Bouley took away a biological interpretation of vaccine action: bacteria cultures continued to live, grow and generate poisons even after extreme heat treatment. And Roux brought to Pasteur news of Toussaint's use of carbolic acid.

Toussaint soon changed his interpretation of how the vaccine worked, but he was unable to produce a consistent treatment, and his test results continued to fall short. At the Pouilly-le-Fort trials, Pasteur, claiming to create his vaccine by attenuating live bacteria with oxygen, actually used anthrax cultures treated with an antiseptic, potassium permanganate.

Pasteur also adopted the method used by Koch of passing infectious matter through a sequence of animals, injecting one with blood or an organ extract from an infected animal, timing the appearance of symptoms and injecting another. While Koch was only demonstrating that it was in fact the bacteria that were consistently causing the physical symptoms, Pasteur was studying the effects of multiple passage upon virulence.

Pasteur found that anthrax bacilli passed through guinea pigs became more virulent both for guinea pigs and sheep. His experiments in serial passage were more extensive with rabies; with anthrax they only provided a technique for modulating bacterial virulence.

Against the virulence achieved by serial passage Pasteur balanced the mildness and protective qualities achieved through chemical and heat attenuation. Pasteur's assistant Charles Chamberland had produced the potassium permanganate vaccine that Pasteur used in the Pouilly-le-Fort trials. Pasteur never said other than that, the bacteria were oxygen attenuated, prepared according to the same method he had used to create the chicken cholera vaccine.

Pasteur knew by this time that the attenuation had become hereditary in his bacteria cultures. A major reason for his being able to repeat his success and provide vaccine to others is that the cultured bacteria always retained this mild, protective property. The attenuation formula could be used to manufacture vaccines of consistent quality.

Pasteur proposed setting up a factory which he hoped would be a source of revenue for him and his family, but public funds were not available and he had to be satisfied with having his laboratory produce the vaccine. By the mid–1880s he was reaping about 130,000 francs a year from international sales.

Pasteur used a chemically attenuated vaccine in the Pouilly-le-Fort trial, but soon he discovered that he could make vaccine sufficiently weakened just by heat treatment, reverting to Toussaint's practice but with the significant innovation of using a two-dose schedule.

Pasteur's vaccine was administered to animals in two inoculations two weeks apart. The first vaccine was produced by incubating *Bacillus anthracis* cells at 42–43 degrees Centigrade for 15 to 20 days. For the second vaccine the cells were incubated for only 10 to 12 days. Pasteur I vaccine was demonstrably weaker than Pasteur II vaccine: it only caused anthrax symptoms in small experimental animals, mice and young guinea pigs, while Pasteur II sickened rabbits and adult guinea pigs. The livestock treated with the two dose schedule gained immunity through progressive exposure. They would then be expected to resist any wild anthrax they encountered.

Pasteur even experimented in treating animals with anthrax to protect them from rabies, testing experimentally the long association between the two diseases. Pasteur did not administer his anthrax vaccine to humans. Humans only suffered from anthrax through contact with animals which, if immunized, would not spread the disease to their keepers and consumers.

When Pasteur took on the challenge of creating a vaccine for rabies he concentrated on a treatment for humans rather than the animals that carried it, and his tests were on people desperate to escape the terrifying death that usually resulted from the bite of a rabid animal. Pasteur's 1885 rabies vaccine for humans was based on a dosage principle similar to the anthrax vaccine: progressively less diluted solutions of spinal marrow from rabbits deliberately infected with rabies were administered to a victim over a period of days. Young Joseph Meister had nothing to lose in being the test case for the vaccine, and he lived to guard Pasteur's tomb in the Pantheon.

Diluted doses reduced the effects of taking doses of higher concentrations, this was a well-known principle of consumption. The same might be observed in the response to alcohol and opium. Poisons taken in moderation affected the taker less poisonously, and made him able to resist more corrosive onslaughts. Germs were still not needed to explain the effects of the vaccine. Pasteur's success in reproducing vaccines was the result of his acting as if germs were the best explanation.

In 1984 Russian microbiologists celebrated the centennial of L.S. Tsenkovsky's development of a method of producing an attenuated vaccine against anthrax, Pasteur's demonstrated and profitable success, and his use of his results to advance the germ theory of disease, have obscured other developments.

The important innovation in Pasteur's vaccine was that it was not just a substance which magically conferred immunity; it was a technique which could be used to manufacture quantities of vaccine from supplied strains of anthrax using established fermentation techniques and equipment. Anyone who understood the principle of manufacture could attempt to make Pasteur's vaccine from available anthrax samples.

Robert Koch had scorned Pasteur's vaccine, and supported Toussaint's priority. But there was pressure on Koch to turn his discoveries into genuine gains. He saw Pasteur's vaccine adopted to immunize Prussian herds while his own work had not yielded anything so beneficial. When he attempted to apply the attenuation-progressive immunization principle to another bacterium he isolated, *Mycobacterium tuberculosis*, the result was very disappointing to the consumptives who flocked to receive the treatment.

When Eli Metchnikoff treated a herd in Russia with vaccine prepared according to Pasteur's procedure, he had to flee the estate owner enraged by the deaths of the animals. It was a matter of subtle brewing and good publicity.

Pasteur's anthrax vaccine was a principle of production which could be attempted wherever anthrax samples were available. But like brewing, the outcome, even when all the correct ingredients were present, did not always succeed so spectacularly.

Animals did die of anthrax after the vaccine was administered, and it could not be taken by humans. The British industrial health authorities did not even consider using the vaccine as a protection for wool and goat hair workers, but instead relied upon abating the spores present in the imported raw materials through washing with formalin.

Over subsequent years there was much experimentation with the Pasteur vaccine, to make it less likely to cause the disease it was supposed to prevent while at the same time retaining its effectiveness when transported far from the place of production.

Following Pasteur and Toussaint, anthrax vaccine history progresses one preparation succeeding the previous one and is based upon what has been learned about what does and does not work in a vaccine. Vaccine effectiveness is tested in the field, by applying it to the animals being protected, but it is created in the laboratory out of the previous vaccine.

In 1877 Pasteur and Joubert observed that animals contaminated with saprophytic bacteria and then exposed to anthrax survived the disease. This was compatible with observations long made that anthrax bacilli disappeared from the blood and organs of decaying animals. "These facts may offer great hopes from a therapeutic point of view," they wrote, but then Pasteur pursued immunizing against anthrax with anthrax.

The action of other bacteria against anthrax opened the possibility of curing anthrax by their administration, and in the 1880s several experimenters attempted to establish which bacteria would best oppose an existing anthrax entrance into the skin. "The most powerful antagonist of the anthrax bacilli is the diplococcus pneumoniae fibrinosae of Friedlander: in the experiments with it, all of the eight treated rabbits recovered," wrote Dr. E.O. Shakespeare in an 1888 compilation of treatments and experiments. "The next powerful is the staphylococcus aureus: all four of the rabbits treated by subcutaneous injections were cured." Following the standard set by Toussaint, Shakespeare describes the curative efficacy of bacteria in terms of how many of the 8 rabbits injected with anthrax cultures survived after they received an injection of one type of bacteria or another.

Shakespeare observes that there is no systemic anthrax in these antagonistic injections, and the bacteria seem to be destroyed at the point of entrance. Discussing the reaction to anthrax of animals already immunized with erysipelas bacteria, he dismisses the surmises that the formation of pus or phagocytes are the reason anthrax bacilli are rendered harmless. "It is manifest that the substance which kills the bacteria is produced by the cells of the body of immune animals; and it is probably always present in the body of these animals." The animal itself and not the bacteria produces the "poison."

This leads to the work of Dr. L.C. Woodbridge, who reported to the Royal Society that he protected rabbits from anthrax by injecting them with the filtered extract of anthrax cultures grown in alkaline solution of a "peculiar proteid body" obtained from the testis and thymus gland. Instead of injecting the animal with attenuated anthrax or another bacteria, Woodbridge achieved immunity by using the products of anthrax grown on body materials. Shakespeare equates this with Pasteur's rabies injection using an extract of spinal cord of rabbit exposed to rabies.

Achille Sclavo, a native of Alexandria teaching at the University of Siena, experimented with serum therapy, using the filtered blood of infected animals to confer immunity on humans, and in 1895 announced that he had achieved a successful anthrax therapy.

Emil Behring (later von Behring), a Prussian military doctor who had worked in Koch's Institute of Hygiene laboratory, developed serum therapy for diphtheria, a devastating infection especially of children. Von Behring's method was to administer attenuated bacteria cultures to guinea pigs (as Pasteur did), but then take the further step of filtering out the guinea pigs' blood serum and using that to immunize subjects. Animals could then be used to produce quantities of immunizing serum for humans.

A number of researchers were trained in von Behring's laboratory, notably Shibashaburo Kitasato, and from there the technique of serum therapy spread throughout the world. Von Behring received the first Nobel Prize in Medicine and Physiology, awarded in 1901, for his discovery of the humoral immune system.

Anthrax was not as serious a threat to humans as diphtheria, but protection against it had both commercial and military implications.

A proprietary secrecy still surrounds Achille Sclavo's serum therapy: the old practice of crafting nostrums, "secret remedies," that haunted Pasteur and Toussaint. Sclavo was reproducing in Siena the commercialization of von Behring's diphtheria antitoxins by Hoechst in Germany. Sclavo soon turned to using blood serum to create therapies for other diseases, and began commercial production of treatments for diphtheria and malaria.

In 1925 Hans Meyer, reviewing a history of human anthrax cases, judged Sclavo's vaccine together with the similar serum preparations of Mendez and Sobernheim, as "unproven" preventives. Efforts to create a human anthrax vaccine using serum therapy continued.

Sclavo's anthrax vaccine, not especially effective, remained in production for many years. Sclavo authored texts on infectious disease and military medicine, especially in the tropics, where his serums might hold some promise of preserving colonial soldiers and transport animals against exotic diseases. For his contribution to the local economy Sclavo was elected a citizen of Siena in 1900, and in 1904 with his students founded the Instituto Sieroterapico e Vaccinogeno Sclavo, which ultimately was purchased by the American biotechnology firm Chiron. Sclavo's name is on civic buildings and a school in Siena.

Protecting humans from anthrax still meant protecting animals and disinfecting their products. The history of Pasteur's anthrax vaccine in the field at first remains close to its history in the laboratory. The laboratory is the vaccine factory, producing the hopefully immunizing fluid and providing the expert personnel to administer it.

Rather than injecting heat or antiseptic-treated cell cultures, experimenters injected spores suspended in a dense fluid medium, such as glycerin, which was then administered in a single dose. It was necessary to test the relative virulence of each batch of spore vaccine on progressively larger animals. If it killed rabbits it was too virulent; if it didn't kill guinea pigs it wasn't virulent enough. These vaccines were slightly more effective than the original Pasteur formulation but the tedious animal testing was required to control quality.

Attempting to publicize the efficacy of vaccine and serum therapy to veterinary colleagues, L.C. Maguire recommends Pasteur's vaccine, which statistics show "has been thoroughly satisfactory. He also cites serum from hyperimmunized animals, and a combination of serum with anthrax cultures to produce long and short term resistance in animals. "This method," he continues, "has the great advantage of only requiring a single treatment of the animals, and the results obtained from it are quite satisfactory. In Argentine and Uruguay, this method of vaccination was employed from the spring of 1904 to September, 1905 on 140,000 cattle. 50,000 sheep and 2,000 horses. According to Sobernheim, no fatalities resulted from the vaccination, and almost everywhere a complete eradication, or at least a marked restriction, of anthrax was noted."

Anthrax vaccination trials in Argentina and Uruguay are a measure of European interests there as well.

A further innovation in the Pasteur vaccine came with the introduction of saponin as a component of the liquid medium carrying the anthrax spores. Saponin is a lather-producing compound found in a number of plants, evidently developed to discourage browsing animals by giving them an upset stomach. Its contribution to the anthrax vaccine is two-fold. It serves as a medium that suspends the spores in a more or less even distribution to keep them from concentrating as they would in less viscous fluid.

Glycerin might do this as well, but saponin also causes a strong inflammatory reaction at the injection site. This was thought to be a sign of saponin's cleansing action eliminating the bacteria but not their immunizing products. The saponin-caused inflammation allows the anthrax spores to enter and germinate, but reduces any immediate septicemia their germination would cause. The bacteria were then free to produce their anthrax-suppressive components inside the animal's body without immediate damage.

Early vaccine developers used antiseptics to clean the blood of anthrax cells. The antiseptics actually caused inflammation, were abandoned because they caused too much inflammation, and were reintroduced again in saponin. Vaccine media are tried according to changing theories of their immediate value, but that use is modulated by the specifics of their effects in the field.

Another pragmatic element in vaccine development was the discovery of the differing virulence of strains. It is not clear whether Pasteur and his colleagues realized it, but the effectiveness of their vaccine depended upon the reduced virulence of the strain they either collected or induced by chemical treatment and heat curing.

Vaccine development was enhanced by seeking out and collecting bacteria samples proven to be of greater or lesser virulence by their effects on the animal from which they were collected and upon test animals. Bacteria were identified according to classification schemes that marked their origins and maintained in colonies according to their known nutrient requirements.

Universities and vaccine producers built collections of bacteria in which the microbes were maintained in colonies, or in low-maintenance spore samples. The American Type Collection, begun by a group of scientists in 1925, included samples of anthrax bacteria, as did many other collections initiated over the following decades, but there also were several collections that specialized in anthrax samples, notably that at the University of Iowa-Ames, which was begun in 1928.

As new characteristics were discovered and new tests developed, the bacteria in these collections could be distinguished from one another and from new strains in ever greater detail. Index numbers and letters positioned single strains in relation to others in terms of virulence and other testable, standardized characteristics.

Isolates, samples of bacilli from specific observed characteristics, were used in vaccines with varying concentrations of saponin, in some preparations as high as ten percent. The severe local reactions the saponin produced were balanced against the degree to which the medium regulated virulence.

In the 1930s the South African veterinarian Max Sterne reviewed many of the papers advocating saponin-based anthrax vaccines and tested the vaccines, concluding that the saponin enhanced immunity rather than reduced virulence of the anthrax, and that a much smaller concentration (0.5 percent) gave the same result without severe inflammation at the injection site.

By culturing the bacilli on horse serum agar in a 30 percent carbon dioxide atmosphere, Sterne generated spores that reliably became unencapsulated bacilli. These bacilli had the potential to generate protective immunity without causing an infection. Sterne's 34F2 strain could be reproduced from an available sample of anthrax bacteria by following Sterne's preparation instructions.

Sterne suspended between 600,000 and 1,200,000 of these spores in 0.5 percent saponin in 50 percent glycerin saline solution to form a vaccine with minimum inflammatory effects and maximum protective value. He had found an anthrax strain and a vaccine formulation that minimized the disadvantages of the saponin suspension while maximizing the advantages of having bacteria germinate inside the protected host.

With modification of the spore concentration, Sterne's 34F2 strain and vaccine formulation became the worldwide standard for animal anthrax vaccines. The very limited variability of anthrax bacteria because of their sustained spore stage made the strain portable: the spores would always generate the protective unencapsulated bacilli. The Sterne vaccine was administered from Argentina to the Soviet Union and Australia, reducing anthrax visitations among animals, and by extension, among humans. Despite Sclavo's innovation there still was no widely used anthrax vaccine for humans.

Sterne himself warned, however, that some domestic animals, goats and llamas, for instance, were unusually susceptible to getting anthrax from the injection itself. The history of use of the vaccine shows that the bacteria germinating from the spores remain virulent and animals can contract anthrax from its administration. Aum Shinri Kyo was not using a completely harmless strain when it released 34F2 spores into the Tokyo air.

Pasteur had conducted his field trials based upon only a little laboratory evidence of vaccine effectiveness. He was sharply criticized for testing the rabies treatment on humans without being sure it would work. With the development of successor live spore vaccines, laboratory testing of the strength of the vaccine became essential. Sterne gauged the immune properties of a vaccine by using test animals of varying sizes, and attempting to breed mice with a fixed level of susceptibility to the anthrax strain he used.

Eventually the epidemiological measure LD50 came into use. This designated the dose of a pathogen that would kill half the population of a specific test animal. By determining the dilution and media required to kill half a number of guinea pigs, all of whom received the same dose of vaccine, the experimenter could determine the dose that would immunize cattle without ill effects. The testing of vaccines became a laboratory science divorced from the uncertainties of field testing. Once the LD50 dose was determined for a strain of anthrax and preparation of vaccine, the vaccine could be manufactured in a central location and shipped to users.

The Pasteur vaccine spread as a set of instructions continually tested in the field and modified accordingly. The Sterne vaccine spread as a specific strain of anthrax shipped as raw spores for culture or as a manufactured vaccine with instructions for its use.

With the spread of the Sterne strain, vaccine history divides into a stream of laboratory and manufacturing innovations on the one hand and an even more complex and obscure history of its reception in the field, among veterinarians, livestock raisers, government agencies and eventually agrobusinesses. The vaccine injects a new element into the local management of anthrax, and its use requires training of the technicians who will administer it and of the farmers who stand to benefit.

In his history of anthrax vaccines John Turnbull, following Sterne, identifies a cycle of vaccine adoption and modification among farmers. The protective efficacy of the saponin-suspended vaccines in herds previously decimated by anthrax made farmers critical of the skin reactions and fevers produced by newer vaccines. When the potency of the vaccines was reduced in response to these criticisms there was an upsurge of natural outbreaks, leading to the introduction of newer, more potent vaccines such as Sterne's, adjusted to moderate immediate reaction. The animal vaccines change as the result of interplay between manufacturer's lab tests and public relations with vaccine users.

As the animal vaccines were adopted the number of anthrax outbreaks among animals, and therefore among humans, declined. The limited statistics on human cases of anthrax show a progressive decline over the course of the twentieth century. Under the Factories Acts and Public Health Act of the United Kingdom, for instance, anthrax was a notifiable disease: instances had to be reported to a central bureau. The number of notifications charted yearly between 1900 and 1990 shows an allover trend downward, with a strong spike only during the 1915–18 war, when vaccination was relaxed and conditions encouraged the spread of animal and human diseases.

At least within the confined universe of the British industrial statistics, the vaccine had reduced the number of animal and human anthrax cases even before there was a human vaccine. The only factor that worked against vaccine effectiveness was war, not because of the use of anthrax as a weapon, but because the disruption reduced vaccination coverage. This would be used as an argument, however, to cover the upsurge of anthrax infections in Rhodesia-Zimbabwe in 1979–80. Vaccine coverage had broken down, and anthrax was being used as a weapon.

The Sterne strain served as the basis for a human anthrax vaccine. There was a demand for a human anthrax vaccine to protect workers in textile and tanning industries and veterinarians from cutaneous anthrax, but it was war and fears of anthrax used as a weapon that drove human vaccine development.

In 1943 Soviet defense forces sought protection against the germ weapons they believed the invading Nazis would unleash (or had unleashed) upon them, and they drew upon earlier attempts to adapt the spore-based animal vaccine for humans. Scientists at the Tblisi Scientific Research Institute, in Soviet leader Joseph Stalin's native Georgia, tested direct application of a solution containing a high concentration of Sterne strain spores to the scarified shoulder skin of human subjects. The unencapsulated bacteria that germinated contributed immunity while being subject to destruction by the body's own cellular immune system. Phagocytes could devour the unencapsulated cells.

The vaccine developers tested their product by injecting the immunized human subjects with live virulent spores and exposing them to anthrax aerosols. The resultant immunity was achieved at the cost of serious side effects, and could not be administered at all to a wide range of susceptible individuals. Yet the live spore vaccine manufactured in Tbilisi was used in the Soviet Union to the degree that the loss of Georgia on the breakup of the Soviet Union in 1990 caused regrets among biowarfare scientists, because the factory that made the vaccines was no longer in Russian hands.

Also reacting to a possibility of Nazi anthrax use, Americans sought an immunizing vaccine. Human vaccine development, like biowarfare later, was spurred by beliefs about enemy intent and capabilities. Euro-American scientists did not try to adapt the veterinary live spore vaccine, considering it too dangerous, but instead drew upon observations that preceded the discovery of anthrax spores, that there were poisonous components in the body fluids of animals infected with anthrax which could provoke immunity but not cause anthrax. Toxoids could provide vaccine-mediated immunity without injecting the bacteria themselves.

Davaine's antiseptics and Toussaint's chemical vaccine had remained an undercurrent and there were attempts to create spore and cell-free vaccine. In 1900 it was found that an extract of tissue infected by anthrax, filtered free of spores and cells, could induce some degree of resistance to infection in experimental animals.

W.J. Cromartie and D.W. Watson in 1944 worked at the newly funded chemical and biological weapons facility at Fort Detrick, Maryland, to isolate the "aggressins" of anthrax generated in skin lesions, in effect bacterial cultures on flesh. They were continuing a line of research that Sanderson, Greenfield and Toussaint took from Chauveau, before Pasteur's culture method became predominant. Fluid from these lesions progressively injected into experimental animals conferred resistance to fresh anthrax infection. A preparation of aggressins filtered free of anthrax cells and spores compounded with a presumably neutral medium could be injected into humans who then did not develop systemic anthrax after cutaneous exposure.

The Merck Corporation, founded by George Merck, the pharmacologist who headed the wartime biological and chemical weapons program, was the sole manufacturer of anthrax vaccines during and immediately after the war. But Merck soon abandoned the human vaccine as unprofitable, not wanting to invest in the tests required for licensure.

This aggressin vaccine was not tested in humans against airborne exposure until the 1950s, when in military tests a variant was used to protect volunteers who breathed spores released in a test chamber.

By then Harry Smith's team at the British bioweapons facility had identified the separate proteins generated by the bacteria: protective antigen, edema and lethal factors. Protective antigen (PA) was so named because it was found to be the operative component of the aggressin based human vaccine used in America and Europe to protect lab workers, textile workers and veterinarians in regular contact with anthrax bacteria. The presence of protective antigen caused the humoral immune system to generate resistance to multiplication of the bacteria, a mechanism which then became the object of research.

In 1950–55, 1,249 workers at four animal hide processing mills in the northeastern United States took part in tests of what was then known to be a protective antigen vaccine. Prior to these tests the yearly average was 1.2 (usually cutaneous) anthrax cases per 100 workers. The total number of cases during the test period, among vaccinated and unvaccinated (control) workers was 5 inhalational cases (4 fatal) and 21 cutaneous cases (none fatal).

None of the four workers who died of inhalational anthrax during the Arel Mills tests had received the vaccine. The tests didn't cause their deaths, but those administering the program were always faced with the fact that the vaccine might have protected these workers from infection. Perhaps this is why this was the only field trial of the vaccine for humans.

The protective antigen vaccine licensed by the British Department of Health depends upon growing Sterne strain bacilli to maximize the production of protective antigen while minimizing lethal and edema factors. It was never clear if either factor has a role in inducing immunity to anthrax infection, but it was clear that more than trace concentrations made the fluid infectious.

It is the role of protective antigen to enable the other factors to enter the cell, where they interfere with its workings. In their absence the protective antigen causes the blood of the inoculated animal to generate antibodies that protect against further infection.

In the United States during the early 1950s, the University of Michigan vaccine development center, which had inherited the rights to the protective antigen vaccine from Merck, developed a cell-free vaccine filtered from cultures of a non-encapsulating isolate derived from a cow that had died of anthrax in Florida. This was similar in design to other protective antigen vaccines, but with the addition of a neutral adjuvant, aluminum hydroxide (alum).

The vaccine was described as aluminum hydroxide adsorbed: the alum has the property of attracting molecules of protective antigen to its surface and thus is able to distribute it more evenly in solution. Its acronym is AVA, anthrax vaccine adsorbed. Like glycerin or saponin in spore-based vaccine, alum was a way of making sure that the inflammatory anthrax components were not concentrated in any one place but were spread sufficiently to emphasize production of protective antibodies.

The Michigan vaccine rights and production facilities was purchased by a private firm, BioPort, which became the sole producer of vaccine, now called Biothrax, required by veterinarians, researchers and textile workers. The vaccine was licensed by the United State Food and Drug Administration in 1970 and was for years the only licensed for humans anthrax vaccine available in the United States. Its production over the years has been troubled by problems with conforming facilities and standards to licensing requirements.

The extensive vaccination programs of the Gulf War period and after went ahead based on human trials of AVA at the U.S. Army Research Institute on Infectious Diseases (USAMRIID), where 1,590 employees received between 1973 and 1999 a total of 10,451 doses of the vaccine. Only 4 percent of the test subjects reported a local skin reaction and 0.5 percent had short-term systemic reactions.

The vaccines designed since Sterne employed unencapsulated bacteria because it was observed that the absence of a capsule made the bacteria vulnerable to phagocytosis and reduced the inflammatory reaction. In spore-based vaccines like those used in the Soviet Union, the spores germinated into unencapsulated bacteria that did their immunizing work and then vanished without causing an anthrax infection. In protective antigen vaccines like the licensed British and American varieties, there was only a fluid filtered free of spores and bacteria components and containing mostly protective antigen.

Instead of the saccharide capsule that other bacilli produce, anthrax bacilli were found to produce a poly-D-glutamate capsule with its own antigenic properties. Both the capsule and the three toxic proteins had to be present for the bacilli to be infectious.

Strains that did not grow the capsule still produced the proteins, and could be manipulated to produce more protective antigen in proportion to edema and lethal factors and thus serve as vaccines. Producing only the capsule, neither the capsule nor the toxic factors rendered the bacilli mildly infectious but also non-protective, not a good basis for vaccines. Being able to isolate and purify the toxic factors biochemically made it possible to identify their role in the working of vaccines, and led to an independent study of their chemistry.

The natural and induced variation in these aspects of the bacilli, and the ability to stabilize unencapsulated bacilli in cultures, indicated that these conditions were genetically mediated. Bacteria contain their genes on rings of DNA called plasmids. The presence or absence of specific genes, regions of plasmids, decided whether bacilli encapsulated or generated toxins or both. The two properties were independent of each other. The gene coding for the presence of toxins was designated pX01 and coding for the capsule was pX02. If both genes were present in a strain of anthrax it was lethal, if neither was there it was harmless.

Discovering the ability of the anthrax bacilli to vary genetically in ways that regularly corresponded to bacilli phenotype (capsule, toxins present or absent) organized vaccine history in retrospect. It was clear that the Sterne strain of anthrax used in animal then in human spore-based vaccines was lacking in the pX02 gene. Applying genetic analysis to old stocks of Pasteur's duplex vaccine revealed that he had either found or created through heat curing at 42–43 degrees Centigrade a strain of bacilli lacking the pX02 gene, encapsulating but without toxins. This strain alone would be mildly infectious but without a protective value because no protective antigen was present. The effectiveness of the vaccine must have come from residual traces of bacteria with both capsule and toxins, enough to spur antigen production but not enough to cause severe inflammation.

Vaccine history was a give and take between virulence and protective strength magnified by adjuvants and media. The ideal vaccine aspired to induced maximum protection with minimum infection, but that ideal was never achieved in human vaccines. One possibility opened by recombinant genetics was to experiment with including anthrax pX01 genes in the plasmids of the considerably less virulent, but still sporifying, *Bacillus cereus*. Live spore vaccines could then generate immunity without infection. This was a proposal for retaining vaccine history through genetics.

Uncovering the relationship of anthrax genetics to vaccine history created a potential to escape that history of attempted balance between toxicity and protectiveness. The old strategy of building antigens through mild infection with unencapsulated bacilli gives way to improved production of protective antigen. This in turn leads to blocking the infection process in its molecular biology by addressing subunits.

Protective antigen works as a toxic agent by creating a biochemical portal on the surface of a victim's cells which admits edema and lethal factors to the interior. Instead of using protective antigen to generate chemical defenses in victims' bodies, biochemists can attempt to construct substances that prevent the antigen from attaching to a victim's cells in the first place. Or they can set up reactions that interfere with the work of the toxic proteins.

Instead of being used to induce a chemistry that will inhibit the next, more serious infection, the bacilli are prevented entirely from taking hold, or that, at least, is the plan for future vaccines.

In November 2001 Rakesh Bhatnagar, the chairman of the Center for Biotechnology at Jawaharlal Nehru University, and Yogendra Singh, a scientist at the Center for Biochemical Technology in New Delhi, India, announced that their genetically engineered anthrax vaccine for humans was ready to undergo testing. The Indian science minister added, at a press conference, that the Indian government was moving quickly to approve the vaccine and he expected to have it available to the masses in six to nine months.

The vaccine was developed by creating "harmless mutant forms" of the three anthrax toxins, then introducing the genes for these mutated toxins into host organisms, where they would be replicated. The host organisms, which were not named, then could serve as factories for the harmless toxins, which would serve as a vaccine by generating antigens when injected into a susceptible human. Bhatnagar claimed that he could produce vaccine in a fermenter on an industrial scale, in a way answering the inability of BioPort to produce sufficient vaccine to satisfy the needs of the American military and the military's monopolization of existing vaccine stocks.

The results of this testing were not made public. In early September 2003 an online report of the *Proceedings of the (US) National Academy of Sciences* gave the results of initial testing in mice of "bivalent" anthrax vaccine developed by Julia Wang and colleagues at Harvard Medical School and Brigham and Women's Hospital in Boston.

Instead of trying to create antigens for all three toxins, Wang and colleagues included only the protective antigen. Produced by using *Bacillus licheniformis*, a harmless relative of *A. anthracis*, to purify the main chemical component of the bacterial capsule, the bivalent vaccine would deliver the protective antigen disguised as anthrax.

Once inside the body the vaccine would generate antigens to both toxin and capsule and provide a broader spectrum of protection. Further tests of the vaccine were a possibility.

The possible terrorist and germ warfare use of anthrax provided the economic impetus for the development of these vaccines. Germ warfare design of anthrax was an extension of the vaccines first aimed at humans through animals and then at humans directly, in which the balance between virulence and protection was abandoned in favor of exaggerated virulence.

As the history of vaccines involved a search for strains mild enough to induce protection, germ warfare research took advantage of finding fast-killing virulent strains. And as vaccine research sought adjuvants that improved protective factor production or at least reduced inflammation, germ warfare turned to delivery methods which could affect the maximum number of people through the lethal respiratory route, without the conspicuous inconvenience of injection.

The germ warfare version of anthrax (and of other pathogens) played against strategic vaccines and tactical antibiotics. Early treatments for anthrax were based on disinfection with carbolic acid or perchloride of mercury and early germ warfare use of anthrax was an attempt to spread cultures in advance of disinfection. Antibiotics and aerosolized germ warfare evolved in tandem.

Usually a preventive strategy was taken toward anthrax because antibiotics might not be able to control the proliferation of bacteria once that had begun. Paul Ehrlich's salvarsan, the first antibiotic, which was discovered by observing how stains attached to infected and uninfected cells, was somewhat effective against syphilis, but was found not so effective against anthrax. Each successive new antibiotic was tested against anthrax in the laboratory, but there were no opportunities to test them against actual infections in humans.

Physicians were pleased to find that fluoraquinalone antibiotics such as Cipro kept six of the victims of inhalation anthrax alive after the mailborne attacks of October 2001. The only victims to die were not diagnosed in time to receive doses of the antibiotics at an early stage of the infection. Prior to this, advanced inhalational anthrax had seemed incurable even with penicillin.

The recombinant genetics that might promise new vaccines could also be used to compose new strains of anthrax that defy vaccines and antibiotics on the biochemical level of their operation. The escape from vaccine history promised by molecular biology leads to an exaggerated new vaccine history in which ever more lethal invented strains are ranged against hopefully corresponding protections. The former operations of anthrax in nature are restaged in culture. So far, however, only in the imagination.

# 12

# The White Powder

At the Latifiyah Industrial Complex, United States troops approaching Baghdad in April 2003 found thousands of boxes of "suspicious white powder." The powder was contained in glass vials three to a box. A senior U.S. official in Washington said that the material is probably "just explosives," but it was found with atropine and "Arabic documents on how to engage in chemical warfare." The complex was enormous, and troops of the Third Infantry Division were still going through the site searching for weapons of mass destruction. Nothing more was reported on the matter.

It was white powder, gray powder, black powder, blue powder, colored powder, blue envelopes, vials holding dust, a petri dish with gelatin, telephone calls or the word "anthrax" (often misspelled) written on a letter or package. Or, at times, it was a displaced package of flour or sugar, a spill of plaster or road paint. It was situated or sent or threatened for different purposes and effects. When it actually was anthrax spores it was delivered in the same way to the same addressees as the hoaxes.

This anthrax was not the same as other earlier anthraxes because it had nothing to do with animals, the soil, or manufacturing processes, but it was not independent of the anthrax models for germ warfare that inspired the hoaxes. It was an image and a threat and only rarely an infection. It was the crystallized social precipitate of the corpuscles and contagia that had formed the interior of epidemic disease before its substance could be analyzed. The white powder is always fearsome prior to analysis.

Few people have seen large quantities of real anthrax spores to know their color and the texture. According to the scientists interviewed by Richard Preston, they are beige and dust-like in a mass. What was conveyed into the mainstream of images was that anthrax is a powder, probably white, which equated it to other powders, and that it is deadly, but not, it seems, to the person who uses it as a weapon. It is only deadly, or at least shocking, to the intended victims.

Anthrax flitted through American popular culture. A survey of the *Readers Guide to Periodical Literature,* an annual index of general interest magazines, shows that before 1972 there were occasionally articles on industrial or rural outbreaks of anthrax and the use of penicillin to treat the skin disease. In the volumes covering March 1972 to February 1980 there are no articles on anthrax listed at all. Then the Sverdlovsk deaths produce a burst of writings on "the Siberian ulcer" in science and political journals, which trail off over the following years. In 1991 there were three articles listed on the thrash metal rock band Anthrax, and only one on the disease anthrax, concerning the military vaccination program. The two certainly are related. From then on there is only a scattering of articles on anthrax or Anthrax until the year 2001.

Anthrax was one bacterium in a large repertory of available threats and dangers. The rumors of anthrax attacks during the world wars, the part-disclosed Japanese military experiments, the American and Soviet biowarfare programs during the Cold War supposedly ended by the 1972 treaty, and then events like the Sverdlovsk release of lethal spores in 1979 maintained a background of anthrax which news media and fiction-makers could draw upon.

The widely publicized Sverdlovsk events seems to have been the driving force behind a revival of anthrax awareness that occurred in the early 1980s. Soviet biowarfare had to be countered by American defensive and offensive capabilities.

Anthrax appeared occasionally in American television fiction as a disease of cattle, for instance in the Western serials *Big Valley* (1965) and *The Virginian* (1968). Both episodes have to do with the arrival of the anthrax vaccine in the Old West, the *Big Valley* episode even culminating in the Pasteurian rise of the apparently dead animal which has been protected by the vaccine.

Where anthrax is a threat to humans on television, it comes from the government. One episode of the drama *I Spy* (1966) had a character racing against time to find his partner who had been infected with the "anthrax virus." A 1980 (post Sverdlovsk) episode of the American television series *Quincy, M.E.,* featuring the adventures of an urban medical examiner who became involved in police work, combined the awakening fear of airplane hijackings with the reawakening fear of anthrax. The ransom money given to the hijacker was deliberately contaminated with anthrax spores, which then led to mysterious deaths and a potential epidemic which Quincy had to contain. Anthrax was in its plague mode, but it wasn't in the hands of terrorists, only the government.

Whether anthrax is a disease of cattle that threatens human livelihood or a virus poisoning humans, the television drama builds around the vaccine or antibiotics and their administration.

Also contributing to popular awareness of anthrax was the long history of military medicine ordering soldiers to receive preventive treatment in advance of anticipated debilitating disease. The development of human anthrax vaccines in Europe and the Soviet Union was geared to counter the threat of enemy use of the spores as an offensive weapon. It only later became a part of biowarfare defense and civilian occupational medicine.

Penicillin ("penacilin" as it was spelled in the letters that accompanied genuine anthrax spores in October 2001), discovered earlier but only produced in mass quantities in the early 1940s, had a significant role in keeping soldiers fighting during the Normandy invasion that closed the Second World War in Europe. German bacteriologists found that infusions of a bacillus (*Bacillus subtilis,* related to *Bacillus anthracis*), fed to troops in Northern Africa reduced the severity of the debilitating dysentery they suffered. Anti-malarial medications had been important in Vietnam. Experienced commanders looked to medication when they faced an enemy in Iraq known to be producing germ and chemical weapons. And germs were often equated with the enemy. Popular culture reflected this.

The germ-armed enemy was part of the image of the Cold War arsenals of America and the Soviet Union. During the protracted war between Iran and Iraq (1980–88) that followed the deposing of the Shah of Iran, the Iraqis had used chemical and bacterial weapons against the Iranians, against Shiites within Iraq, and against the Kurds, who were seeking to create an independent state. American policy condoned these actions, and American and European weapons makers supplied the Iraqis with cultures and equipment. A list of the specific cultures supplied to Iraq by the American Type Collection has been posted on the Internet.

Anthrax threats and hoaxes were unknown prior to the Gulf War of 1991. The Cold War and other, older scare patterns served as a platform. What seems to have introduced anthrax into the everyday stream of threats and hoaxes is knowledge of Iraqi weapons and the American military's preventive vaccination program. The Soviet Union had collapsed in 1990, but the Soviet threat, or at least Stalinism and bioweapons, passed on to Iraq. Revelations in the press about germ warfare planning by various countries after the announcement of Nixon's 1969 executive order and subsequent treaty negotiations did not immediately inspire anthrax threats. It took the background of the Iraqi threat and American response to do that.

On November 12, 1995, U.S. Secretary of Defense William Cohen announced an executive order requiring all enlisted personnel to be vaccinated against anthrax. The order was the result of long debate within the American defense establishment, and was not a spur of the moment decision in response to an immediate threat.

The arguments in favor of the vaccination program were also the arguments opposed to the program. It could be claimed that no one had suffered from anthrax during the Gulf War because of the extensive vaccination program and some had suffered because of the vaccination program.

The Gulf War immunizations were also an argument against a more extensive anthrax vaccination program. By then the vaccine had been implicated in Gulf War Syndrome, a constellation of health conditions affecting veterans of the war and their families. Gulf War Syndrome was attributed to agents used by the Iraqis against soldiers in the field, yet it also afflicted those who had not been in combat or anywhere near it, but had been vaccinated against anthrax and other diseases.

The anthrax vaccination program using the American protective antigen vaccine (AVA) produced by BioPort was progressive in the Pasteurian tradition. Injections were administered at zero, two, and four week intervals, followed by further injections at six, twelve and eighteen months and yearly boosters after that. Certain classes of people, pregnant women and those taking immune-suppressant drugs, were exempted. Service personnel were reminded and then reminded again of anthrax as they received the shots, which themselves produced site reactions and fever conditions in the recipients.

A brochure produced by the U.S. Department of Defense for distribution to troops required to receive the doses answered questions about anthrax, about the components of the vaccine (including formalin), about the safety of the vaccine and about the role of the vaccine in Gulf War syndrome. It affirms the threat of anthrax while trying to be reassuring about the vaccine.

There was very little record of human testing of the vaccine to support those who wanted to defend the program. The New Hampshire mill tests had been published and were not the most confidence-inspiring. Most tests of anthrax on humans were intended to determine how lethal the spores could be as a weapon, not how well potential victims could be protected.

The fear of an army debilitated by a cheap spray of spores motivated politicians and commanders more strongly than complaints of vaccine-caused illness. The decree was issued, quantities of vaccine ordered and service personnel were ordered to comply.

The Adverse Vaccine Event Reporting System (AVERS), a joint project of the Centers for Disease Control and the Food and Drug

Administration, did not receive many reports of strong and unusual reactions to the vaccine. BioPort and the Department of Defense maintained that the vaccine was a success.

Some soldiers, sailors and pilots receiving the vaccines after the 1995 order considered their reactions to the vaccine a serious illness in itself. Some refused to be vaccinated and either quit the service or were court-martialed for disobeying orders. Some expressed concern that their advancement depended upon receiving the shots. The effects of the vaccinations underlined the belief that Gulf War Syndrome was as much the effect of the vaccinations as of any biological or chemical weapons deployed by the enemy.

There were Congressional hearings on the vaccine program in 1998 and 1999, legislation halting the program was introduced and debated, and new vaccinations were halted several times then recommenced. By October 2002 Secretary of Defense Donald Rumsfeld, heeding a report issued by the General Accounting Office, was calling for a reevaluation of the anthrax vaccination program. At that time the number of highly trained pilots and other specialists leaving the service because they refused to be vaccinated had reached a crisis level. The vaccination program and the response to its implementation kept anthrax before the public.

Anthrax further entered into the general mix of fears when United Nations weapons inspectors in 1997–98 found anthrax bombs and aerosol equipment among other pathogens and chemical weapons in the Iraqi arsenal.

The remote background of occupational anthrax infections and the continuing outbreaks among livestock were seconded and finally superseded by lingering knowledge of weaponized anthrax. This knowledge took the form of a vague but terrifying threat: plague induced by enemy attack. A range of confused fears was associated with the word "anthrax," skin eruptions and airborne miasmas deliberately induced.

The medical profession had little direct experience even of cutaneous anthrax, and the pulmonary variety was a textbook matter. The physician who examined the first person to be infected with inhalational anthrax in Florida admitted later that he did not immediately recognize the clinical signs of anthrax. He ordered massive doses of antibiotics to reduce the infection while diagnostic blood samples were cultured. Fulminant inhalational anthrax was extremely rare and initially would be difficult to distinguish from pneumonia or the flu.

Knowledge of anthrax from the first was knowledge of a threat to life and livelihood. The vaccine controversy simply emphasized the aggressive potential of anthrax without revealing much about it. The strong response to a mysterious agent spread from the military to the general public. Together these rumors gradually established a milieu for the public to produce and react to anthrax scares.

A package received at the offices of B'nai B'rith in Washington, D.C., on April 4, 1997, contained a petri dish labeled "anthrachs." The layer of red gelatin resembling a bacterial growth medium was tested and found to be just red gelatin. Nothing about the package explained who sent it or why. Whoever sent the package wanted to be considered sophisticated enough to culture anthrax while being crude enough not to spell its name correctly. They didn't deliver it in a form that actually might conceivably infect someone if it really were anthrax.

On April 24 B'nai B'rith then received an 8 by 10 manila envelope oozing a red gelatin, and in one of the first biological threat motivated public health actions, 100 employees were quarantined in the building for eight hours and the two who came into contact with the envelope were made to strip to their underwear and were decontaminated with bleach spray. A typed two-page note mentioned anthrax and declared "the only good Jew is an orthodox Jew." The gelatin turned out to contain *Bacillus cereus*, which was being used at that time as an "anthrax stimulant" by the United States Armed Forces.

Jewish organizations and individual Jewish leaders were among the most consistent objects of anthrax threats, as they were of other kinds of threats. But they were not the only ones. Anthrax became another substance in the repertoire of menace regularly leveled against birth-control clinics, media offices, politicians and landlords.

On December 12, 1997, newspapers carried photographs of Secretary of Defense William Cohen at a news conference raising in his right hand a five-pound bag of sugar familiar to Americans from supermarket shopping. Announcing the inception of the military anthrax vaccination program, Cohen declared that a volume of anthrax equivalent to the sugar package could devastate Washington, D.C.

The white sugar materialized anthrax for people who did not have an image of anthrax before this. White sugar (and white flour, another white powder of resort) became established as a consumer commodity in the late nineteenth century as the result of a campaign by corporate refiners and millers to raise fears of contamination in cheaper dark sugars and whole wheat flour. Fear was again attached to sugar but now because of its whiteness, which did not resemble the actual appearance or texture of anthrax spores at all. Following Cohen's display there were demonstrations in the media of common, even culinary powders like cocoa being blown around to illustrate anthrax spread. This was as accurate a picture of aerosolization as white sugar itself resembled the spores, but it added an element to the precipitating picture of anthrax as a readily available substance that could easily be aerosolized.

A tension between secrecy and self-disclosure enhanced the public anthrax milieu. The powder itself was from an anonymous source and unlabeled, yet associated with something horrifyingly lethal, a good secret weapon. Some hoaxers just threw white powder down in a public place to cause panic. But often the hoaxer had a specific objective and let his identity slip out. The presumed ability of anthrax to affect large numbers of people caused some threateners to identify themselves or leave transparent clues.

On February 18, 1998, Larry Wayne Harris and William Job Leavitt were arrested by FBI agents at a medical complex in Henderson, Nevada (close to Dugway, a major military proving ground where biological weapons had been tested). The two had been reported to the FBI by a third man, Ronald Rockwell, who claimed they told him they had "military grade anthrax." Rockwell wore a recording device in a meeting with the men, but picked up little useful evidence.

Leavitt, an elder of the Church of Latter Day Saints, was soon released and went on a juice and water fast to protest the slur on the church implied by his arrest. Leavitt said Harris had told him he could provide him with preventive vaccine against anthrax attacks. That was the only true information Harris gave anyone. When FBI agents searched his home they found containers, some of which had samples of veterinary anthrax vaccine, and a device Harris used at survivalist gatherings to demonstrate how deadly germs can be spread, or might be spread.

The Montana Militia survivalists expelled and denounced Harris for his talk of mass destruction. The key to masked threat is anonymity and Harris was anything but anonymous when he said in a television interview that 500,000 people would die after a five-gallon container of anthrax is (hypothetically) sprayed over Manhattan. This is similar to other imagined anthrax, or for that matter smallpox or nuclear attack scenarios of the time.

A federal magistrate decided that there was enough evidence to schedule a full hearing on whether by continuing to claim he worked for the Central Intelligence Agency Harris had violated his parole from a previous conviction. The previous conviction was for being in possession of plague bacteria and threatening to spread them.

Harris had written and self-published a book entitled *Bacteriological Warfare: A Major Threat to North America,* and for a time posted it online. The "threat" of the title, like Harris' career, is a parody of the protection-attack theme. While urging preparedness against enemies, the book provides instructions for culturing anthrax and other bacteria in a crude form in fact unlikely to cause disease or immunity.

Harris was found in possession of veterinary vaccines and type collection bacteria, not of finely granulated spores. Keeping contact with the soil source of anthrax, Harris had claimed, in an earlier interview, to know where the bodies of animals dead with anthrax were buried and to have obtained his lethal bacilli by sinking a probe twenty feet into the ground at one of these sites.

Where Pasteur ascertained the source of anthrax infection in "accursed fields" and the Soviet weapons developers catalogued anthrax infected cattle burial sites, Harris was using that knowledge as imagery to create a drama of public menace as in some techno-thriller novel.

In April 1998 British customs officers told BBC news they had been warned of a possible plot by Iraqi agents to plant anthrax in duty-free bottles passing through King's Cross Station in London. Two weeks later a Health and Safety Executive spokesman announced that the Executive had known since 1992 that there was anthrax in the walls and ceiling of the building. The spores had been implanted there in imported horse-hair used to bind the plaster when the building was built in the nineteenth century. The rumor of authentic old anthrax, even a woolsorters imported hair anthrax, had been translated into a contemporary white powder threat.

Between October 30 and December 23, 1998, the United States Centers for Disease Control and Prevention (CDC) noted, birth control clinics in Indiana, Kentucky, Tennessee and California reported that they had received anonymous phone calls saying that anthrax had been put into their ventilation systems, or they received letters claiming to contain anthrax, with or without powder.

The CDC also felt called upon to deny that there was any relationship between the report and an anthrax letter received by the NBC news office in nearby Atlanta the same day they delivered the report. A letter containing black powder and an anthrax threat surfaced in the Columbus, Georgia, post office near Atlanta at the same time. "It is an unfortunate coincidence as far as I know," the Journal-Constitution quoted Dr. Bradley Perkins of the CDC.

The phoned threats and powder letters multiplied during 1999, to the point that Neil Gallagher, the assistant director of the FBI's national security division, said in early March that not a day went by without the bureau hearing about an anthrax threat somewhere in the United States. The letters sent to media organizations and politicians in late 2001 were typical of these mailings, except that some of them contained active anthrax spores.

In 1999 William Patrick, a retired U.S. government specialist in weaponized anthrax, accepted a contract from Science Applications International Corporation to study the anthrax hoax letters to learn how a real anthrax letter would affect the public. The contract was offered by Steven Hatfill, who had left USAMRIID at Fort Detrick to work for the private defense contractor. The analysis Patrick produced made him the object of an FBI investigation after the 2001 attacks.

"What we are witnessing is an increase in awareness and thus more frequent reporting against a background of previous widespread under-reporting," stated M.E. Hugh-Jones, commenting on reports of anthrax in his "Global Report 2000" that began the 4th International Conference on Anthrax held June 10–13, 2001. "This should be a lesson to us all that full reporting is not as frightening as not knowing," Hugh-Jones continued before surveying the "more active" previous year's outbreaks.

On August 7, 2001, Reuters carried a story that the Scottish National Liberation Army were claiming to have sent an anthrax bomb to St. Andrews University. The device, accompanied by a typed note stating "this is anthrax," turned out not to be a bomb and to contain no anthrax. The army members were annoyed that Prince William, the heir to the British throne, was studying at the Scottish national university, and chose as their imagistic means of delivery a device which the British army had destructively tested on Scottish ground, Gruinard Island.

After the October 2001 anthrax casualties in America, law enforcement authorities, who had reduced the intensity of their response to anthrax threats as a way of reducing the number of threats, were obliged to pay closer attention to seemingly out of place scattered powders or to anything labeled "anthrax." The fear of the unidentified package discovered in a crowded location such as an airport or the lobby of a government building became the fear of anthrax as much as the fear of explosives.

The anthrax deaths temporarily revived anthrax threat practice and internationalized it, expanding the context to anyone in contact with news media. As the news of people falling ill and dying of what proved to be anthrax spread throughout the world in late 2001, a number of incidents were reported that mimicked the superficial features but not the content of the mail attacks. The publicity given to the actual deaths drove further dissemination of the established threat practice.

During October 2001 the Ohio Bureau of Workers Compensation received around 40 claims of "non-accidental exposure to anthrax." All of these had by December turned out to be the result of workers coming into contact with an unknown powdery substance in the workplace or public safety workers responding to a call. In all cases the substance was found not to be anthrax. At the end of October the Bureau of Workers Compensation announced that all claims of non-accidental exposure to a biological agent would be referred to the bureau's medical advisor for review. Where the claimant tested negative for anthrax, the claim would be disallowed. Of those who filed claims, none were compensable. The white powder was not workers compensation anthrax in Ohio.

A number of individuals were arrested for writing "anthrax" on letters or packages, either as a joke or a means of intimidation in some personal dispute. A man sent a letter to the FBI at the wrong address so it would be returned to his landlord's return address and the landlord would open it and discover white powder and a threat. The FBI traced the letter and arrested the man.

Anthrax threats also became integrated with set of stories spread over the Internet over the previous year, of envelopes imprinted with the words, "A gift to you from the Kinderman Foundation" or "Just for you" and containing a sponge or a powder that reputedly sickened the person who opened it. The anthrax threats yielded a technological response, a counterthreat in the form of devices designed to detect and abate the disease. Numerous local and national organizations created brochures, recordings, and posted on their websites advice on how to deal with "suspicious" mail, or just with mail.

The sales of the antibiotic Ciprofloxin soared despite warnings from public health officials that over-consumption would compromise its effectiveness. Kits alleged to enable the user to find powder in the mail without opening envelopes (Spy Spray) were sold over the Internet. Air sampling contraptions which collected suspicious particles in a vessel, or were claimed to raise the alarm if any spores passed through a filter, were still being marketed a year after the 2001 attacks.

The news of the mail-borne anthrax attacks became known, and the environment of fear around the word "anthrax" became focused on spores, a living powder carried through the mail and spreading through buildings. On October 16, 2001, Ken Alibek, attempting to assert his expertise acquired in the Soviet biowarfare program, told members of Congress that anyone worried their mail might contain anthrax spores should iron the mail to "kill the spores entirely," or, as he later backtracked during a CNN interview, "the probability of the spores surviving is much lower."

The anthrax threat, perceived, made and responded to, spread with the news to other parts of the world, where it took the place of other threats or just crystallized anxieties on streets, in buildings, about the mail. From the viewpoint of news media it was as if a cloud of spores were spreading from America to the world. News media in Belgium, France, Italy, Russia, Ukraine, Austria, Israel, Morocco, Peru, Chile, Kenya, India, China and Malaysia all reported incidents with "anthrax."

The Swedish car manufacturer Volvo suspended its "Volvo for Life" advertising campaign after its October 10 mailing of envelopes containing packets with a few grams of white vitamin powder to encourage Volvo owners to have their cars serviced (energized) caused at least one recipient to panic.

In each instance the simple image of a potent white powder entered a peculiar set of local circumstances and generated events fed back into the news stream. The white powder as an image became the current globalized commodity. Moving out of the United States in early October, it reached other countries and was reported back via the Internet over the ensuing months. If there were white powder scares or local white powder traditions in these countries before October 2001, they were obscured by local adaptations of Amerithrax (as the FBI called the substance of the American attacks to distinguish it from these others).

The *Jerusalem Post* on October 22, 2001, reflected the complaint of the national postal service that "dozens of envelopes filled with sugar, flour and other harmless white powders have each cost the Postal Service and the security authorities tens of thousands of shekels and slowed mail delivery...." Conviction for committing such a hoax carries a three-year prison sentence, and at least one man was arrested for sending a white powder letter. Though not one single spore of anthrax was found, a postal authority spokesman said each piece of suspicious mail is treated with "utmost care."

Kenyan Health Minister Sam Ongeri on October 18, 2001, confirmed that packages labeled "anthrax" and containing a white powder were received by the United Nations Environment Programme in Gigiri. The next day the *Daily Nation* reported that letters addressed to private individuals and organizations such as the travel company Abercrombie and Fitch were being tested for the bacteria. Only a parcel received by Dr. Samuel Mwinzi, sent to him by his daughter from Atlanta, Georgia, but clearly opened and interfered with on the way contained a packet of powder testing positive for anthrax. Dr. Mwinzi and others present when the parcel was opened were given antibiotics, and none of them became sick with anthrax.

This was the first instance of a genuine anthrax mailing received outside the United States, the article proclaimed. Another piece printed on the same day reminded readers that anthrax is nothing new to Kenya, and described the recent deaths of two cows and the illness suffered by those who butchered the bodies or handled the meat, requiring treatment with antibiotics. The white powder imported anthrax into the cities and postal system while the disease already existed in the countryside. The national union of Post and Telecommunications workers recognized this by petitioning the government on October 20 to vaccinate them against anthrax. On Sunday, October 21, the paper carried the news that President Daniel arap Moi had announced his retirement, and there was no further mention of anthrax letters or white powders. The imported anthrax threat had passed, disappearing among the other poisonings that sometimes were asserted in Kenyan newspapers.

An envelope containing white powder received by the United States embassy in Rabat, Morocco, on October 20, 2001, tested negative for anthrax. The Moroccan Interior Ministry issued a press release calling "immature and irresponsible" the authors of a dozen or so letters containing white powder put into the mails in late October, and they warned of heavy penalties awaiting the authors of these misdeeds "that are alien to our traditions." A Casablanca entrepreneur soon confessed to having sent a threat letter to an industrialist against whom he had grudge.

Locales which otherwise did not usually receive international coverage became venues for anthrax threats, thus increasing the sense of a world-wide presence of anthrax.

Maharashtra Deputy Chief Minister Chhagan Bhujbal on October 24 received a white powdery substance in the mail, and the six office employees who came into contact with it were reported to be all right after the powder was tested at the Haffkine Institute in Bombay. In Tulasipur village in Orissa on October 20 a twelve-year-old girl and her brother fell unconscious, she immediately and he "after a while," fell unconscious after they opened a letter from a relative undergoing military training and "smelt a white powder." Both were taken to a district hospital, where they recovered. The powder was sent to a laboratory for analysis.

In Vizhikkathode village in Kottayam district of Kerala, South India, the giddiness postal employees felt when they opened a cover containing a music card and a letter was attributed to anthrax by the crowd that formed. There was no white powder, no anthrax inscription, only an unusual smell, and the fact that the enclosed music card was from Cyprus. Mail arrives in sealed covers in Kerala, and postal employees often investigate unusual pieces. Kerala, like Cyprus, is an international crossroads even in its small villages.

Perhaps someone in Vizhikkathode village knew that five days earlier, on October 13, 2001, in Larnaca, Cyprus, a man had been seen driving around town throwing white powder from a nylon bag. Officers wearing protective gear collected samples and determined that it was flour. "There is absolutely no cause for concern," Police Chief Nicos Stelikos assured reporters at a news conference. *The Cyprus Mail*, in reporting the events, added that the Ministry of Agriculture had provided United States investigators with facts on human anthrax cases in the 1950s and 1960s, and samples of naturally occurring anthrax spores, to help "crack down on terrorism."

Cyprus was an example of the successful eradication of anthrax from an area where it had been endemic. There had been no cases, animal or human, since the 1960s. That did not stop someone sprinkling flour from acquiring an anthrax aura in the news.

A spokesman for the British embassy in Beijing, Ben Fender, announced that "there was something that appeared to be white powder" inside a package that was found in the counsular section of the embassy in late October. The counsular and visa section of the embassy was shut down for several days.

*The Times of India* reported that on New Year's Eve 2001 two postal workers complained of giddiness, uneasiness and chest pain after they opened a sealed mail packet containing a pouch of white powder, a little of which spilled out, and a photo of Osama bin Laden. No note was found and the powder tested harmless. The newspaper, expressing the beliefs of those affected, labeled it an anthrax scare.

In America, as instances of actual anthrax infection trailed off in October, the white powder continued to appear on streets. The unofficial Halloween holiday, which has as its object a contained theatrical fright, produced a few white powder incidents and some arrests.

The discovery of spores entering United States House of Representatives and Senate offices through the mail caused infections and the closure of buildings, and precipitated a fallout of white powder in the vicinity.

Officer James J. Pickett, on November 7, 2001, poured two packets of a sugar substitute over a police post desk in the basement of an office building of United States House of Representatives in Washington, D.C. Pickett left a note reading, "Please inhale. Yes this could be? Call your doctor for flu symptoms. This is a Capitol police training exercize [sic]. I hope you pass."

Pickett didn't even need to use the word "anthrax" to be indicted by a grand jury for making false statements and obstructing police work. The federal prosecutor, countering criticism that the case didn't warrant an indictment, reasserted Attorney General John Ashcroft's determination to investigate and prosecute all anthrax cases where the facts support prosecution. Pickett defended himself saying it was all a joke, that the sugar substitute packets were visible on the desk and he had talked about it with a fellow officer before leaving. The white powder had become another illegal substance, like drugs, that brings criminal proceedings against any agent whatever the explanation.

When an employee of Wal-Mart in West Palm Beach, Florida, told her manager about "anti-religious" wording on some currency she was handling, another manager told her she had handled anthrax-contaminated money. The employee eventually sued the employer because of the mental distress she felt in possibly communicating the contagion to her infant son.

A Collier County (Florida) sheriff's deputy was treated with antibiotics in late October 2001 when the air vents in his patrol car delivered a blast of white powder, and he and another officer were sprayed with chlorine solution by firefighters before being taken to the hospital for tests. A spokeswoman for the agency said that any hoaxer found to be involved would be prosecuted.

The white powder was also spotted outside any envelope or container. On October 14, 2001, a customer of Kroger grocery store in Sugar Land, Texas, reported that he saw a white powdery substance on the exterior of a mailbox on the sidewalk in front of the store. A flight attendant discovered a white powdery substance on soda cans in the plane's galley shortly before the plane landed at Bush International Airport in Houston, Texas. The passengers and crew were delayed about 90 minutes while a hazardous materials team determined that the powder was a sugar substitute. An area near the Qantas check-in service in the international terminal of Sydney Airport was cordoned off on October 13 as investigators in protective clothing studied a white powdery substance found on pre-printed ticket documentation at the ticket sales office. The *Las Vegas Review-Journal* had declared that the number of anthrax scares in Southern Nevada was decreasing when Bureau of Land Management officials announced November 7 that a powdery substance found in the men's room of the Red Rock Canyon State Park visitor's center was not anthrax.

On February 14, 2002, the Friendship post office in Northwest Washington, D.C., was closed after a white powdery substance was discovered sprinkled over letters in the basement. A postal worker complained she experienced an "itching sensation," but it was not clear whether it resulted from contact with the substance, which turned out to be sugar. The suspected anthrax had a telegraphic dizzying effect whether manifest as a powder or not.

Skin discomfort was often associated with the perception of anthrax proximity. A scattered epidemic of itchy red rashes among school-age girls in a number of American schools after the anthrax deaths in the fall of 2001 paralleled and in some cases integrated the anthrax hoaxes. "Maybe the anthrax got into our school, and somebody touched it, and then if you touched that person you'd get it," *New York Times* reporter Margaret Talbot quoted a fourth grader at an Oregon school where the rash manifested itself.

The rumor of anthrax joined the variety of other stigmata used among schoolchildren to ostracize outsiders and band together. It became just one more contagion spreading through the schools. It also recalls the story Scott Ian told about why he chose the name "Anthrax" for the band formed when he was in high school in the late 1970s. His biology class had studied bacteria and his friends were asking each other, "what if you got anthrax?"

On November 13, 2001, Dr. Antonio Banafi, a pediatrician practicing in Santiago, Chile, received a letter with a Florida return address but with a Zurich, Switzerland, postmark. He placed the letter in a plastic bag without opening it and gave it to the Chilean Public Health Institute, who swabbed the letter and cultured anthrax from the swabbings. The Centers for Disease Control identified the strain as different from the Ames strain of the Florida infections. There was no white powder visible in the letter, nor were there any infections among Chilean mail handlers.

On December 5, 2001, police arrested Clayton Lee Waagener, a fugitive since his escape from an Illinois jail where he was awaiting trial on federal weapons charges. The FBI had information that Waagener claimed responsibility for sending anthrax to health clinics on the East Coast of America during early October in 2001 more than 280 letters with white powder identified in an accompanying note as anthrax. Waagener was captured because authorities discovered he was using computers at Kinko's copy centers to view anti-abortion sites, and they posted photos of him in Kinko's stores around the country. When he entered a store in Springdale, Ohio, a clerk recognized him and telephoned the U.S. Marshals Service.

Waagener's ability to use the Internet to gather the addresses of the clinics and to keep touch with his supporters was also the reason he was captured. The anthrax of information is different from the anthrax of the soil and cattle in that it has an identifiable author. The author of the weaponized anthrax is the state, which guards that authorship carefully and attributes it to other states. But as with other kinds of violence the state tries to monopolize, individuals and interest groups can use the image of anthrax for play and intimidation. Birth control clinics reported at the time of Waagener's capture that they had endured several previous waves of letters claiming to contain anthrax. Through the Internet, Waagener organized an established deployment of the white powder.

Seeing white powder out of place as the instrument of malign intent in turn makes any white powder out of place an instrument of malign intent and therefore anthrax. The identity of the powder is information in search of a focus. If the atmosphere is charged with the white powder equals anthrax equation then nothing more is necessary. Framework in the form of words and pictures are sometimes included to guarantee the force of the substance. The white powder in Friendship post office resolved into sugar as soon as anyone went near it. The white powder in Mumbai post office and countless similar incidents was endowed with purpose by a photo of Osama bin Laden. The letters were just among the occasional threat letters sent to clinics, schools, banks and government offices until powder fell out or the word "anthrax" was visible. The more elaborate precaution of testing and decontamination had to proceed before it reverted to an everyday substance.

In some cases the appearance of the white powder caused evacuations of buildings, which was no different from phoned bomb threats. For anthrax the phoned threat could be a claim that anthrax had been released into the ventilation system, which evoked knowledge of germ warfare preparations of the spores. The anthrax-motivated evacuations were accompanied in a few cases by compulsory showers and dosing with antibiotics, which the caller intended to make happen.

During a snowstorm on in Kansas City, Missouri, a white powder delivery caused the evacuation of a Planned Parenthood clinic. Police made the beleaguered occupants shower and endure a pat down outdoors in the freezing cold while still wearing their wet clothes. The threatener had achieved his aim.

A narrative developed, a kind of grimly comic folk story, that a powder spilled in some public place and causing a panic was actually sugar, salt, plaster, street painting medium or any of the many other white powders tossed about by construction, demolition and delivery activities always going on. This story appeared in local newspapers as a relief from the general tension of possible germ warfare. After it was repeated enough times, and there were no more anthrax deaths reported, the story died off.

Someone just frightened by powder they noticed spilled on the street differed from the victims of deliberate spills and letters sent to public buildings. For a time people could enjoy status as authors of spills or as their victims. Already existing conflicts entered a new phase of relevance and reportability when white powder was introduced.

Public officials complained that anthrax scares with their evacuations and investigations put a strain on resources. They responded by identifying, arresting and prosecuting those responsible for the threats. Though the number of threats continued to grow and proliferate in local jurisdictions, the response became more measured. Fewer people were required to put their clothes in bags for destruction and undergo decontamination procedures.

The political scientist Leonard Cole summed up the evolution of anthrax threats as a change in the reaction of local authorities, who between 1998 and 1999 became "more restrained and less newsy—stripping and washing victims with bleach solution was happening less often." Cole concluded that "raising awareness about the threat of bioterrorism should not require exaggerated rhetoric."

Anthrax had become assimilated into news currents, not as actual infections but as authored threats which received a standard reaction. The powder and aerosol imagery all were part of a recognizable repertory like repeated words in a language. In a parallel to the originally highly local nature of anthrax as a disease, the threats were within local settings for group and even individual purposes. Informational anthrax could be spread through the mails and by telephone, by people with a collective agenda, a personal grudge or a desire to entertain.

Authorities, as Cole indicates, adapted to informational anthrax by setting response protocols, as they had for bomb threats or hostage-taking. In an article on the elite police training program called, the Police Corps, Joe Klein describes a simulation that took place at Mineral Area College in Park Hills, Missouri, in November 2001. Two cadets respond to an "anthrax call," two people on the floor of an apartment near a plastic bag spilling out white powder. The cadets hesitate, waiting for a HAZ-MAT (hazardous materials) team, and are criticized by their trainer, who points out that anthrax is treatable and the white powder might have been cocaine. They should have entered the room.

By late 2001 the spilled white powder wasn't always anthrax. The milieu was dispersing like spores in the air, still breathed but not multiplying in the places and to the degree that caused visible disease. The terrorist attacks and the genuine deaths from anthrax in the U.S. prolonged the fad, which became attached to them.

On March 11, 2002, the six-month anniversary of the World Trade Center and Pentagon bombings, organizations and individuals in the San Francisco Bay area received letters containing a white powder and a racist message. All those addressed were Latinos or dedicated to Latino interests, from the Mexican consulate to La Raza Centro Legal and the Center for Latin American Studies at the University of California, Berkeley, to individual advocates and attorneys. Emergency teams were tied up collecting samples and decontaminating buildings.

The campaign appeared to be local in origin, and the work of an individual who expected connections to be made among the targets and with the terrorist attacks exactly six months earlier. The head of one organization that received a letter expressed the opinion to a *San Francisco Chronicle* reporter that the attacks were motivated by anti-immigrant sentiments.

The appeal to both anthrax and the environment of terror, as well as the use of web-based information structures, gave the episode a resemblance to Waagener's much broader birth control clinic mailing the previous year. This was the only anthrax threat reported during the period. The white powder seems to have become absorbed by the 9/11 terrorist environment, which suppresses the powder's free use and confines it to this fading association until it only retains a commemorative value.

There was even a sense of a cleaning up operation by mid–2002. Wearing gloves while opening the mail was less common; anthrax hoaxes again received little publicity unless they were concerted mass mailings. There were continuing reports of the FBI's investigation of the genuine anthrax which injured and killed people the previous fall. They were said to be close to identifying the perpetrator; a short list had been prepared and searches were undertaken.

On Friday, May 31, 2002, federal authorities charged Dean E. Wilber with a felony for mailing to United States Attorney General John Ashcroft a greeting card packed with white powder, and a letter suggesting it was anthrax. Wilber was apprehended because he had signed the letter with his own name. The delay—the letter had been sent the previous year— was because investigators needed to determine which Dean E. Wilber was responsible.

Wilber mailed his card at a strategic time: December 17, 2001, the busiest mail day of the year. After the card was received and opened, the post office the letter was mailed from in Cheyenne, Wyoming, was closed for several days, halting the movement of thousands of pieces of mail. Nine postal employees there were treated with antibiotics while the powder was tested. It turned out to be baby powder.

It is absurd that a little powder in an envelope can close down a major postal operation. That absurdity is what makes it possible. The fact that a concentration of anthrax spores is not a white powder is not reassuring information to a postal employee who has just handled a package containing both the powder and the word "anthrax." That it turns out to be baby powder is a relief. The drama is played out again and again, almost becomes routine, but it continues as long as the uncertainty remains.

A San Francisco anthrax scare shows the later condition of the white powder. On the morning of Saturday, June 22, 2002, four households in the Richmond District received hand-delivered legal size envelopes bearing the name of a fictitious Jewish charity and containing nothing but "some kind of white powder," as a police sergeant on the scene described it. The envelopes were delivered in the vicinity of a Jewish temple, but only one of the houses receiving the envelopes displayed a Jewish symbol. The most recent terrorist warning issued by the FBI concerned possible attacks on Jewish groups.

The "suspicious powder" that spilled from an envelope sent to the Nashville, Tennessee, office of former presidential candidate Al Gore on September 2, 2002, was routinely tested, but didn't cause anyone to be "transported." On September 7 the librarian at Marin General Hospital in Corte Madera, California, notified her supervisor that a manila envelope had been received with a misspelled and sloppily written message on the front, indicating anthrax was enclosed. Part of the hospital was closed until the results of tests determined there were no spores. September 11, 2002, passed with a few similar incidents worldwide.

American troops searched for weapons of mass destruction during the April 2003 invasion of Iraq. The white powder they found in the Latifiyah Industrial Area was safely in vials, box after box of them. Far from being deployed against them, it remained enclosed and unidentified in a warehouse, and the results of the tests were not widely publicized.

On Tuesday, April 22, 2003, a postal service center in Tacoma, Washington, was evacuated after a test indicated that a white powder found among some envelopes might be toxic. The center reopened that evening. Six postal workers were taken to a hospital in Fort Meyers, Florida, after they were exposed to a white powder when they opened an air freight container. Tests on the substance did not find it was toxic. Anthrax was not even mentioned; the white powder had reverted to being a poison first, then harmless. A South African scientist who offered to sell vials containing bioweapons to American agents offered anthrax only as one item in his stock. National Guard teams inspecting the ventilation systems of buildings were seeking signs of terror, but not specifically anthrax.

The notion of white powder as a fearsome object for a moment became clear when in late April 2003 it was reported that a corrosive white powder was appearing on the containment vessels of nuclear reactors. It was easily determined to be boric acid, which is dissolved in circulating water to make it better able to absorb radiation. Here was another white powder associated with dread, this time the difficulty in maintaining nuclear power facilities. Juxtaposed to this news was the announcement that scientists had mapped the genome of the Ames strain of anthrax.

The white powder is a powerful elementary substance in an age of genes and subatomic particles, the raw form of the corpuscles and contagia ancestral to these newer, better specified particles.

The white powder happens for the moment to have been associated with anthrax. Dry and so fine that it suffuses the air like weather, capable of coating and permeating any body whether animal, human, glass, paper or building, it makes the airborne germ warfare anthrax into the earthborn natural anthrax again. It arises from those hidden but carefully logged burials of cattle—its mysterious original source—and passes through an equally mysterious industrial process before becoming the white powder.

It is a luminous body that radiates from foreign envelopes and packages with indeterminate identities, from music cards and photographs of terrorists, child script and the name of God, from pornographic scenes or from the word "anthrax." It is a suspicion realized in dust and granules out of place, mapped on asphalt or in envelopes that should only contain paper.

The white powder is of the same species as radioactivity, a source of the unseen energy that affects masses of people and therefore affects individuals. Cesium chloride or boric acid radioactivity becomes a white powder as well. Cesium chloride has had its own career as source of workers' illness and unconventional warfare threat (dirty bombs). Sodium azide, an actually lethal white powder that inflates the airbags deployed to protect automobile passengers from injury during accidents, is all around us but largely unknown.

The white powder is one of the luminous bodies Daniel Tiffany writes about in his study of the modern lyric. It is an old image of matter becoming inexplicable shining energy just beyond scientific apprehension. As the Welsh writer Arthur Machen alludes to it in his story, "The Novel of the White Powder," it is the residue of an unthinkable supernatural act. Like astral phenomena, radioactivity, deadly beams of light and other projections of anxiety into energy, the white powder stirs fiction and movies. Like these luminous bodies the white powder is a material force with, perhaps, an author and an intended victim.

When the Third Infantry found the white powder boxed in vials at the Latafiyah Industrial Complex on the way to Baghdad, it is not surprising that it was (probably) an explosive.

It usually is not anthrax.

# 13

# Ground and Air

When the news of the anthrax envelopes spread to Kenya, together with a few of the envelopes, the reaction in the press was circumspect. This is a disease we know, commentators stated. In Kenya even urban civil servants like to see the animal that yields their *nyama choma* (grilled meat) alive then slaughtered and being prepared. For Muslims, the slaughter is a rite of welcome which will soon include roast meat.

Kenyans voiced the opinion that Americans and Europeans are afraid of anthrax because they have not experienced it as an everyday disease. In countries where hunters encounter a dead cow or gazelle in the wild, anthrax appears on the hands and in the blood. They may be willing to take the risk or they may not even be aware there is one when they butcher and eat the animal. Anthrax is a white powder only for wealthy professionals and officials influenced by international trends. For people in many parts of the world, it is still an affliction that arises from animals and need.

Pediatricians in Turkey and India, for instance, are familiar with anthrax because children spontaneously encounter it in their explorations of soil and animals, or because the children have no other food. The only anthrax epidemics—from the carbuncle described by Eusebius during the fourth century and the Saint-Domingue outbreak of 1770 to the Zimbabwean epidemic of 1979–80—have been the result of people obliged to eat contaminated meat. Clusters of anthrax affliction and death from Paraguay to Korea to Lebanon are due to communities sharing the remains of animals they could not afford to lose.

Of the approximately 2,000 cases of anthrax reported to the World Health Organization in the year 2001, most of them were cutaneous and ingestive anthrax suffered by people who handled and ate the meat. The nature of this report suggests that many cases go unreported. "As long

185

as there is poverty, we will have this disease," Dr. Huseyin Caksen was quoted in an article about how most of the world experiences anthrax.

The year 2003 saw more recalls of meat products in America than in previous years, but none of the recalls were due to anthrax contamination. The comparative prosperity of the country, and the existence of an industrialized system of meat production, processing and delivery, keeps desperate people from having access to infected carcasses. When national meat standard inspections were being developed in 1895, the microbiologist D.E. Salmon wrote that anthrax, while a serious contaminant of animal remains, is not a serious issue for meat inspection because anthrax-infected animals die before they reach the slaughterhouse. The more dangerous bacteria are Salmon's namesake (*Salmonella*), and other bacteria of decay with powerful toxins, which can multiply in parts of the animal without tell-tale effects on the whole animal and be incorporated into the product chain undetected.

As the open range vanished and cattle drives gave way to the feed-lot system of raising large numbers of cattle in confined areas, this observation continued and continues to be true. It separates the EuroAmerican experience of anthrax from the experience of much of the rest of the world over the divide of wealth. The Soviet authorities, calling upon memories of wartime starvation, blamed the 1980 Sverdlovsk anthrax deaths on contaminated black market meat eaten by bachelors. The reality was the military luxury of weaponized anthrax.

The division in anthrax is a class division masquerading as a national division. The disease is often attributed to foreigners with whom we have regular contact. It is "Persian fire" to the Arabs, "charbon" to the Americans, and "Siberian plague" to the Muscovites. It is carried by imported materials even though we have had it all along ourselves, and when it becomes installed in our factories we name it after the workers, "woolsorters disease" and "ragpickers disease." Anthrax is named differently from syphilis, which was "the French disease" to the English and "la maladie anglaise" to the French, among other rounds.

Having saved ourselves and our animals from the foreign threat of anthrax (and smallpox and ... ) we seem to need to restage it, but that doesn't place us any closer to the way it always has been. Humans have had such a role in perpetuating and disseminating anthrax that it is difficult to know how it always has been. Some hints can be gathered from the way it actually is.

Anthrax all the while lies underground ready for its opportunity to increase. That opportunity is a matter of soil conditions, temperature and humidity, which humans have only lately begun to affect on a large scale. The spores may seem to enclose intentions, whether malicious germ warfare or benignly defensive vaccines. The bacilli do exist underground, in buildings, packages and envelopes. Anthrax ground forms when soil, weather, agricultural and social conditions combine to favor the germination of the spores.

The spores are widespread and under specific conditions they germinate in the soil, go through a life cycle and return to spores without coming to human notice. Only when a concentration of spores develops and reaches a concentration of hosts does the mass intrude upon animal and human livelihood. Before humans domesticated ungulates there was an anthrax cycle including only animals. A browsing animal picked up enough spores to develop an infection and became a fertile ground for the spread of the bacillus to other animals of the same and other species. On dying the animal transferred its exaggerated burden of spores to the ground where they were equipped to remain until further contact with a nutritive living system, a cow's inguinal glands or breached human skin. Other spore-forming bacteria, the Clostridia for example, have similar cycles and some similar outward effects.

Animal hair, which regulates heat and serves as a social and sexual signifier, also picks up anthrax spores. The hair of certain animals, sheep and goats for instance, is structured so well to be a spore catchment that there may have been natural selection in anthrax to promote that. The animal's hide beneath the hair is made to resist the incursions of the spores, and it would require a cut of the hide through accident or combat to provide an entrance. Then anthrax would have to speed up its germination time and beat out Clostridia and other spore-borne bacteria, and the body's immune defenses.

Human skin is more susceptible to anthrax entrances than animal hide but human hair is less likely to pick up and carry spores, and does not cover the body to hold the waiting mass. Instead human culture makes opportunities for concentrated delivery through industrial processes and raw materials that come into contact with opened skin such as hides and wool. Human culture allowed the anthrax bacilli to break out of ground-ground or ground-animal cycles and enter places where no ground, or even no cycle, is needed. Humans have performed a similar service for microbes as varied as the vibrios of cholera, the plasmodia of malaria and the retroviruses of AIDS.

It is difficult to know how anthrax was before humans enhanced the existing cycles and created entirely new ones for the bacilli to participate in. Natural events have the strongest influence on the anthrax that actually occurs, and most human efforts have been aimed at preventing that occurrence from overwhelming human resources. If human concentration of domesticated animals created opportunities to magnify existing anthrax presence into a mutual disease, there also had to be climate and weather conditions that promoted the increase and dissemination of spores.

Anthrax was identified in Europe and America as a distinct epizootic and ultimately as a bacterium producing toxins in the aftermath of a protracted cold spell known as the Little Ice Age, which according to climatologists extended from around 1450 to 1850 C.E. The anthrax outbreaks recorded in antiquity and during the medieval period seem to have been localized. Vergil's description of an endemic seasonal visitation is typical, and the black death events of later periods seem to have included anthrax. There then is silence on the subject until *charbon* and *Milzbrand* begin to appear. The Saint-Domingue (Haiti) pestilence in the late 18th century has all the elements of the Vergilian *pestis*, including the human deaths, and it occurs in a warm climate toward the end of the Little Ice Age period, in an area where European colonialism has produced a concentration of cattle and of people dependent upon the cattle for food.

Of course the development of a world economy capable of shipping Near Eastern goat hair to European mills and the emergence of science with instruments and intellectual precision capable of tracing microbial causes were also factors in anthrax becoming defined. The world spore load increased as humans became aware of spores.

The spread of anthrax was the result of the increase in cattle in an area. The anthrax spores may have been there already. When the concentration of animals increased beyond a point, an anthrax cycle among the animals could begin. Anthrax could never be the kind of population control the pox viruses are. The poxes seem to have originated in insects, which have enormous population swings, and passed to a similar mode among reptiles and mammals. Anthrax needs more specialized conditions to emerge from the soil and into living systems. Humans knew these conditions long before they knew about bacilli and spores.

Before that scientific knowledge, the material nature of anthrax was a nebulous mass of corpuscles, a powder or a dust that caused many diseases. The specific conditions lay in the ground and a principle of quantity; of spores, cattle and people in the same place. The climatic conditions magnified an existing microbial base and a developing social system.

It was folk knowledge, then history, then systematic geographic epidemiology to know where the anthrax ground is located. "Accursed fields" which repeatedly caused disease in the animals that pastured there were sooner or later noticed to be the places where animals dead of black bane were buried.

That knowledge had a way of being forgotten or stored in obscure symbols, then resurfacing with a new outbreak. Unlike any other regular affliction of humans and animals, anthrax hid in the soil but could crop up spontaneously with the natural or human-induced travels of the spores.

Anthrax first appears in European scientific literature as a livestock affliction peculiar to a place. The French essayists and observers of *pustule maligne* during the 1770s were recording the rise of anthrax ground in specific regions of France and its overseas colonies and connecting the instances together with a common causal factor. The appearance of anthrax symptoms in a particular herd of animals tied the disease to the locale where they pastured. Customs governing the slaughter and disposal of dead animals were made to prevent the spread of diseases in a locale, and were adopted into general codes of law because of local experience. The early veterinary studies of *charbon* and *Milzbrand* were studies of particular areas of anthrax ground.

Blancou writes that European civil authorities were more concerned about creating regulations aimed at restricting the spread of epidemic cattle diseases like rinderpest than they were about periodic anthrax visitations. Mass slaughter of cattle, the most drastic exercise of state power, was first applied as control measure against rinderpest, and was irrelevant to anthrax. Anthrax was localized and periodic, unlike other diseases which could spread quickly over wide areas and required firmer measures to keep them from destroying the livestock of an entire region.

Anthrax, like other diseases, seemed to accompany the dislocations of people and animals associated with wars, because long-standing local precautions, prohibitions and vaccinations were abandoned and the invaders didn't know which fields were accursed. Karl-Friedrich Heuschinger's treatise on the historical-geographical-pathological nature of anthrax, published just before Koch's research, used separate outbreaks of anthrax to chart a pattern for European anthrax residing in specific places and rising with historic disruptions. The Walpole, Massachusetts, factory outbreak began in 1864, on the verge of the American Civil War; the *Hadernkrankheit* of Austria began to be noticed in 1870, as the Franco-Prussian War took place.

At the same time, in the 1840s to 1870s, average temperatures were rising, and records of rainfall and storm activity suggest a series of years that climatologists associate with the El Niño phenomenon. Worldwide climate changes, concentrations of livestock and warfare were creating an environment friendly to the germination and proliferation of anthrax spores just as Davaine and Koch arrived on the scene to study the causes. The anthrax ground was being created under them.

Where anthrax was localized and historical in Europe, it was transitional and momentary, becoming historical in America. It is possible that anthrax existed among the American bison and other ungulates prior to European settlement. Outbreaks in the twentieth century among concentrations of bison in Canada suggest that anthrax was not present in the indigenous bison but was transferred from domestic cattle early in the century.

That contact and the contamination of pastures by textile mill or tannery effluents contributed to creating an anthrax ground where one did not exist before. Fluid as well as airborne anthrax was created by human intervention in the transmission of spores. The pattern of wet followed by dry weather that generates anthrax infections in many places could then operate on the bison in the same way. Perhaps the spores always existed in the soil, and went through annual cycles; it required concentrations of cattle and a textile or tanning industry to make anthrax ground.

Spores may have been transported into Mexico and the American southwest with horses brought from Spain, a land of continuing anthrax outbreaks. The Native Americans acquired the horses and with them anthrax, which then spread to the buffalo. John Ewers' detailed study of the horse in Blackfoot Indian culture in the nineteenth century does not specifically list anthrax or anything like it among the diseases the Blackfoot treated in their mounts. According to picture chronicle of year signs created by Battiste Good, six famished Dakota Indians in a war party (1826–27) who consumed parts of the carcass of a buffalo all "ate-a-whistle" and died. It might have been ingestive anthrax, or any of the other diseases desperate people can get from rotting meat.

It is also possible that anthrax arrived in the Mississippi River Delta with French cargo ships coming from the Nile valley during French colonial settlement in the early 19th century, but the cargo ships also brought cattle that did not exist in the area before.

Early American records do give sparse evidence of animal or human anthrax. Hernando de Soto's expedition in the American southeast may have been troubled by the disease. Col. London Carter, owner of Sabine Hall in colonial Virginia, recorded "watery murrain" among his cattle in 1753 and again in 1757. This may be the first record of anthrax in America. The instances of carbuncles, including Washington's, are more obscure.

There were spores in American ground, only not enough cattle to magnify native or imported spores into an epidemic. If herds of indigenous ungulates suffered from anthrax it is not apparent from descriptions prior to the middle of the nineteenth century. Lewis F. Allen wrote in his 1878 treatise, *American Cattle*:

> The virgin soils of a new country are undoubtedly more free from diseasing influences, than regions tilled and pastured for many years … and in the two hundred and fifty years of their existence on American soil, taken altogether, our country has proved the healthiest cattle region in the world.

Allen reflects the general opinion that America was virgin land unsullied by Old World corruptions. He examined each of the breeds then prospering on American soil, and the imported diseases that attacked them.

Allen does not describe anything resembling anthrax in his extensive diseases and remedies section. Under "malignant epidemics" he refers to the "murrain" of Exodus and mentioned by a list of "profane" authors (before Christ), having existed in various countries of Asia and Europe down to the present day, "not continuously, but at different periods—and been attended with devastating fatality, sweeping at times, the countries which it ravages, of almost all their herds." Destruction of the animals is the only way to prevent the disease's spread.

The murrain, "as we understand it in America," is a casual disease, mitigated in force from its Biblical ravages, and certainly not as severe as bovine pleuropneumonia, or, even worse, rinderpest. This was a transfer of the vague but fearsome murrain idea of anthrax into America, where it became milder.

The United States Department of Agriculture (USDA) Special Report No. 34, *Contagious Diseases of Domesticated Animals,* published in 1881 just three years after Allen's book, has long, lavishly illustrated sections on swine plague, fowl cholera and contagious (bovine) pleuropneumonia, but it also has several papers in a miscellaneous section, on "charbon" or "anthrax." Earlier *Reports* of the Commissioner of Agriculture, for instance that for 1868, while they mentioned these other diseases as well as Texas fever, made no direct reference to anthrax or anything that resembled it. The 1881 *Report* introduced the disease. Spores may or may not have been imported into America from overseas, but during these few years "charbon" certainly was.

A paper titled "On the Etiology of Charbon" identifies *charbon* as a severe affection of domesticated animals in France, so serious and commonplace that farmers "consider themselves fortunate and give no further attention to the disease when the number of deaths do not exceed 2 or 3 percent, of the total number of animals in their flocks." The paper offers an extended translation of a report Pasteur read before the Academy of Sciences on his Eure-et-Loire experiment, followed by translations of remarks by Bouley, reports by Chauveau on the immunity of Algerian sheep to charbon, and by Toussaint on his experiments with preventive inoculations.

This sequence of papers is followed by a section on an "Outbreak of Anthrax in the Northwest" which said "a very malignant and fatal disease, resembling in its symptoms pleuro-pneumonia, was prevailing to an alarming extent among herds of calves imported into Illinois, Iowa and Missouri from some of the Eastern States." The alarm among cattle raisers that they were facing pleuro-pneumonia among their animals was allayed after Department of Agriculture veterinarians performed a thorough post-mortem investigation of the fallen calves and determined that it was anthrax fever (black leg), thus putting to rest rumors that contagious disease was spreading among the herds. Black leg was another phrase that was used to designate animal diseases by their visible effects, which might include anthrax as well as a number of other conditions caused by spore-producing bacteria.

Dr. James Law of Cornell University reported on an outbreak among cattle in western New York state. He wrote, "The fact that the tenant on the farm was a German who might have had visits from friends (immigrants or otherwise) carrying with them infected clothing, made it all-important that the case should be fully investigated." Dr. Law summarized the course of symptoms, the condition of the internal organs, and the composition of the blood of the cows that died, but he only reached a conclusion about the supposed causes of the outbreak when he considered the nature of the land. Loamy or gravelly surface underlain at some points by hardpan caused retention of moisture favorable to the "anthrax germ." He wrote that the disease was essentially local and unlikely to spread and recommended destruction of the diseased animals' carcasses to prevent further infection. He predicted there would be a few more cases in the coming years, but with due attention to the sick and the dead the disease would be extirpated.

The formation of the soil and the fluctuations of the weather were also the reasons given by L. McLean, a Department of Agriculture veterinarian traveling to New Mexico to study an outbreak of "supposed contagious disease" among cattle there. McLean found that J.S. Chisum, owner of the largest herd in the Pecos Valley, was at a loss to explain the sudden rise in mortality among his estimated 70,000 head of cattle.

McLean's examination of animals who had the disease and assessment of the symptoms reported was inconclusive. Learning that excitement seemed to bring the sickness, he had several hundred head rounded up and driven rapidly over several miles, but there was no marked effect. It was only when he found that a severe drought had been followed by heavy rains, and afflicted cattle had grazed on vegetation growing in marsh lands and drank only swamp water, that he had no doubt this was an outbreak of anthrax, "which was caused by miasmatic infection from decomposing organic matter contained in the soil and water of this region."

Anthrax was a destructive malady, yet it was a relief to ranchers that it wasn't a contagious disease; anthrax originated from infected foreigners' clothing and imported calves, or it was a miasma arising from moisture. At no point did veterinarians investigating outbreaks refer to anthrax as charbon, though their papers were positioned right after the most extensive presentation of contemporary French research on the disease published in America. Both bacteriological and environmental views alternated and coexisted, and there was one element their practitioners shared with each other and with someone like Allen: charbon or anthrax was a property of the land, brought forth by certain weather conditions.

The Commissioner of Agriculture sent specialists like Law and McLean to investigate possible cattle epidemics in the West for the same reason that national commissions were formed in France and Britain to study cattle plague. It was in the national interest to check the spread of contagious disease, which could devastate the industry and critically reduce the food supply to burgeoning cities and to workers. The farm with 5 cows in western New York might become the source of a wave of disease which, traveling westward, could even reach J.S. Chisum's 70,000 head if control measures were not in place. On the other hand the local anthrax occasionally suffered by cattle raised on the southern ranges could be carried elsewhere, though not by contagion.

In 1931 the Department of Agriculture issued Farmers Bulletin 784, entitled *Anthrax or Charbon.* During the fifty years between 1881 and 1931, as vaccination for anthrax became universal and cattle drives ceased, charbon and anthrax together continued to designate the mix of beliefs about the causes and origins of disease represented in the 1881 *Bulletin.* During this time anthrax or charbon advanced into many areas. Territories and states developed their own anthrax ground, formed by the realities of the disease among cattle and other livestock (horses and pigs as well) and by the word of the specialists and agricultural policy that applied to that particular region.

Mr. Norman Willis, writing to the Commissioner of Agriculture from Johnson County, Tennessee, in December 1880, tells of the anthrax fever causing his cattle to complain and drop. There was no disease among the cattle since the Civil War until this affection started. "We have no remedy," Mr. Willis wrote. "When one gets sick we drive it to a good place to skin, and it is not long thereafter before we get this job." He made mention of the consequences for the human skinners.

The beginnings of anthrax ground in Tennessee, Illinois, Iowa, Missouri, New York and New Mexico were the subject of early reports. In the intervening years there were accounts of anthrax in Maryland, well documented because Bethesda is the headquarters of the USDA and both tanneries and small cow herds were situated on the Maryland shore. Henry Washburn in his USDA Farmers Bulletin on anthrax quotes James Law. Since 1862 anthrax has prevailed along the banks of the Delaware River for a distance of 40 miles to New Jersey and Delaware, destroying some 70 to 80 percent of the farm stock. The great morocco industry on this river draws infected hides from India, China, Russia, Africa and South America, and the spores are carried and distributed by the tides. Louisiana, Arkansas, Florida and California also had formally described anthrax ground. Texas, which grew from a land of open range where vagrant herds of Spanish cattle wandered to a state of ranches producing beef for the rest of the country, has a long history of anthrax ground.

Some American cattle trails from Texas into the northern territories, the Chisholm and Goodnight-Loving trails for instance, became known as a source of disease in animals driven along their course. The cattle died, were left or were buried beside the trail and contributed a renewed mass of infection to the trail ground for the next steers to receive. The diaries of settlers on the westward migration routes occasionally mention the deaths of animals from "hollow-horn," a fever that was prevented by hollowing out cow horns and filling them with herbs. The migrants buried their cattle along the same trails.

Texas was rich in cattle in the years following the Civil War, and Texans found that they could obtain much higher prices for steers if they drove them north to more populated areas and eventually to railheads. Large numbers of longhorns moved along trails from the rangeland in Texas to the railroad depots in the north, where they were shipped to urban slaughterhouses and packing plants for shipment to burgeoning eastern cities. There were accursed trails and accursed fields, but given the economics of cattle raising it was still necessary to use them. The trails held a load of spores that continued to cause anthrax long after the great cattle drives of the late nineteenth century were over.

Some places acquired the reputation of disease before the discovery of spores as the cause of anthrax confirmed the danger. Cattle ranching in the American West was not the same as the generally settled condition of cattle raising in Europe and the American East, where relatively small herds remained in confined areas and accursed fields became known as accursed because there was nowhere else to pasture the cattle. In this way American anthrax ground was different from European anthrax ground and more like Australian and Argentinian anthrax ground.

It was distinctly anthrax ground. In 1868 an English veterinary journal published a piece on an invariably fatal disease that farmers in Illinois believed spread to their own cattle from longhorns driven north by South Texas ranchers. Allen also included a paragraph on the disease in his dismissive account of the "Spanish, or Texan cattle." Called "Texas fever," or "splenic fever" from the enlarged appearance of the dead animal's spleen, the disease did not affect humans, but its effects on livestock were so grave that authorities enforced laws routing Texas cattle away from settlements. In 1885 Kansas, the railway center, banned southern longhorns from entering the territory.

Koch's work discovering the bacterial cause of anthrax provided guidance for federal researchers. Dr. D.E. Salmon and later Dr. H.J. Detmers had associated Texas fever with splenic fever, and long-term persistence in the land, like anthrax. Their microscope examinations of blood and tissue from infected animals seemed to implicate *Bacillus termo* or *Bacillus subtilis*, which had appeared in Cohn's illustrations alongside Koch's in the same plate. A disease character similar to anthrax implied a similar causal bacterium. But Bureau of Animal Industry biologists Theobald Smith and Lucius Kilborne in 1893 announced that Texas fever was spread by ticks carrying a microorganism (later named Babesia), which infiltrated red blood cells. The cattle from the south had carried the Babesia-bearing ticks north with them and left the ticks on the grass where they pastured, ready to attach themselves to and infect any passing steer.

Babesosis was also of the ground like anthrax, but it was not spread by an agent within the ground but by ticks, which could be controlled by quarantining infected cattle and finally eradicated by dipping the cattle in pesticidal baths. Babesosis declined as cattle dipping became established but anthrax persisted wherever there were spores in quantity.

At the time of the anthrax attacks in October 2001, newspaper articles reported that ranchers in Texas were accustomed to living with anthrax, and recognized that the spore heritage of the trails could affect their herds. There was even an "anthrax triangle" identified between the towns of Uvalde, Rocksprings and Del Rio, where an apex touches the Rio Grande and the Mexican border. The area is flat ranchland where the roads follow cattle trails. A *New York Times* article on October 29, 2001, quoted a salesman at a farm and ranch supply business in Uvalde saying that anthrax had been around as long as people and animals, all the way back to the Bible.

In 2001 the Texas Natural Resources Conservation Commission fined Dr. Michael L. Vickers $9,000 for burning carcasses of animals dead from anthrax in an open pit. The existing law required that all animals to be disposed of had to be sent to a commercial incinerator or, if one was not available, placed in a landfill. Dr. Vickers, who had some prestige because he had isolated the Ames strain in 1981, took his case to the Texas legislature, and obtained a modification of the law to allow open pit burning in counties without animal crematories and with a population below 10,000. Anthrax could spread from buried corpses, explained M.E. Hugh-Jones of the University of Louisiana explained in support of Dr. Vickers' actions, but it is also true that terrorists could penetrate the burials in search of materials. The anthrax ground had changed a little.

Wherever cattle were buried there was anthrax. People who live in the area where the ground bears spores believe that anthrax is as universal and eternal as the earth itself. People elsewhere know about it only through its spread to their own ground. The geography of anthrax extends to the artificial ground of buildings, the Hart Senate Office Building and the postal annexes, where spore-bearing mail was handled. A figure like Larry Harris, who claims to have taken spore samples by probing buried cows, and who had plans to broadcast spores generally through sprayers, is transitional between the old rural ground and the new urban ground of anthrax, and between the ground and the air.

The year 2000 was notable for anthrax outbreaks worldwide, possibly the result of the intense El Niño weather that brought periods of drought and heavy rainfall either confined or alternating in many locales where this was not usual weather. The weather enhanced anthrax ground in many places, raising it to the level of ingestive or at least cutaneous anthrax in humans. The Roseau County, Minnesota, instances of ingestive anthrax from eating the meat of a "fallen" cow were in 2000.

The summer of 2001 in Texas was the worst for anthrax in over a decade, with over 1,600 cattle dead of the disease, one definite case of human cutaneous anthrax and one possible. The ranchers attributed the upsurge to a long drought followed by a rainy spring and again by drought. The spores in the ground had been raised by the action of the rain then were taken up by the cattle as they browsed the grasses nourished by the rain. As the drought returned the cattle browsed closer to the ground, taking up more spores with the dry, spiny leaves.

Most ranchers vaccinate their cattle, but they can't vaccinate the deer which roam in the wild, get anthrax and die, leaving more spores. The deer are an asset for ranchers in South Texas, because they draw sport hunters into the area where tourism is not a major source of revenue and ranching does not have great returns. As in South Africa, where tourist game parks hold animals susceptible to anthrax which can be communicated to domestic livestock, the ranchers try to manage the land to maximize benefits but they cannot escape the anthrax ground even through veterinary medicine.

Both Koch and Pasteur warned about spores remaining in the soil, though they disagreed about how they reached the cattle. They may have been responding to different kinds of anthrax ground. They were reflecting the knowledge of farmers that certain locations were prone to produce anthrax and certain weather conditions, wet followed by dry, magnified the outbreaks. Anthrax ground is modified by the climate and the weather which differ from place to place. The alkalinity or acidity of the soil and the presence of certain nutrients also have an effect on a place's hospitality to anthrax.

The "Siberian plague" named another type of anthrax ground governed by climate and weather. Koch criticized Pasteur's earthworm theory of anthrax spread by pointing to the frequency of anthrax in Siberia, where the ground is frozen most of the year.

In 1649 a Russian chronicle records that the ravages of *povetrie* (epidemic) were so severe among humans and animals that the tsar decreed the public squares should be closed and the streets scoured for dead animals, which should be buried deep lest they be taken and eaten. This sets two important themes of Russian anthrax ground, the exercise of absolute authority to counteract the spread of disease and the need to bury animals deep and securely to forestall hungry people.

*Siberskaia iazva*, "the Siberian plague," became better known when reformist aristocrats who had been exiled to Siberia after the Decembrist revolt (1825) communicated to their families and supporters the challenges they faced in their attempts to improve the livelihood of the peasants. The earliest treatise, *O Siberskoi iazve*, "On the Siberian Plague," was published in 1831. The disease referred to Siberia because visitors observed that its occurrence was regular and severe there, and whenever it broke out elsewhere in Russia it could be referred back to that faraway place, much as woolsorters disease could be referred to Pakistan.

The Primorski krai in the Russian Far East (not Siberia), with its cold winters and hot summers, was reported having episodes of *Siberskaia iazva* soon after settlement in the late 19th century, and a major outbreak in 1866 followed by periodic episodes of cattle and human disease. The increase of cattle breeding quickly followed by the development of a tannery industry constructed the anthrax ground, which regularly generated all forms of anthrax, including pulmonary cases.

Cattle that died of anthrax in that part of Russia could not be buried deep, and during the brief, concentrated thaw of spring the spores were released just as the grasses were growing. Cattle eating the grasses became infected and died. The soil passed through wet and dry periods each year, conditions favorable to building up a load of spores which would not be annihilated by the freeze. After investing a winter's feed in the cattle, the owners could only recover their losses by butchering and eating infected cattle and tanning their hides. Identifying the disease with Siberia was identifying a set of human-animal-soil-climate conditions that produced conspicuous afflictions.

The brief period of warmth is the opportunity for plants and animals that overwinter to breed. Mosquitoes and gnats are notoriously savage in the north, and so is anthrax, which is the Siberian plague because its form there is more virulent than elsewhere. It must kill animals in sufficient number to build a spore load for the winter. The chronicle of the building of the Trans-Siberian railway in the late nineteenth century tells of the anguish caused by the gnats attacking humans and *Siberskaia iazva* killing the animals.

The name *Siberskaia iazva*, translated into European languages as "Siberian plague" or "Siberian ulcer," was retained in Russian writings as a peculiar national designation for the disease, a Russian kind of anthrax ground, and it appears in medical writings, government planning reports and literature through the late Tsarist and Soviet period, only phasing into "anthrax" recently. There even was a 1723-entry bibliography of technical writings on *Siberskaia Iazua* published during the late Soviet period (1975), a demonstration of national interest that does not exist for any of the other anthrax grounds.

The association of *Siberskaia iazva* with "anthrax" in Russian writing is similar to the association of "charbon" with "anthrax" in American writing.

"And this Spring, on all sides, worms appeared in Stoudenets in incalculable multitudes," wrote Alexei Remizov in his 1911–12 novel *Piataia iazva (The Fifth Pestilence)*:

> And while they were crawling the weather was warm, but when they disappeared it became windy....
> But the creatures, though in outward appearance bearing a similitude to worms, still there was a *message* in 'their bodily composition and the dissection of their nature, 'all covered with little scattered hairs and some had little wriggling legs like teats on the belly, while the belly of others was quite smooth....

The appearance of the worms, which no one in the little rural village dares to touch but one woman puts on exhibit in her shop, does not lead to any plague effects among people or animals, though it does coincide with the Police Captain Alexander Ilitch sprouting a pair of ass' ears.

The sense of Linnaeus *Furia infernalis* worm that caused anthrax is preserved in Remizov's allusively symbolic story of village life.

The word most often used in reference to *Siberskaia iazva* is *borba*, struggle, the same word that in Lenin's writings and Soviet histories denotes the struggles of the workers against capital. The title of Sergei Bogoslavski's 1910 tract *Siberskai iazva i borba c neio* is repeated numerous times over the succeeding years in works that offer the same combination of exhortation and practical suggestions for holding back the disease.

F.A. Terentev's 1946 tract of the same title surveys the history and pathology before moving forward to the measures taken as it appears among herd animals, including detailed diagrams of the pits to be used to dispose of their bodies. In one it is recommended that the animals be

Construction of a cattle-burning pit "in the second style." Straw is placed in the bottom, the cattle are laid on the wooden cross-beams, doused with kerosene and covered with straw followed by a manure layer, leaving an airspace at both ends, then ignited. (Terentev 1946.)

stacked eleven deep in a hole only the width of one animal, and then covered with masses of gravel that cannot be moved. Only on the final page is there an etching of an upraised arm covered with carbuncles.

The Soviet government tried to blame the anthrax deaths in Sverdlovsk—which is on the eastern side of the Ural Mountains, toward but not in Siberia—on the consumption of infected black market meat. This was at least in keeping with the Siberian plague conception of the disease as it affected humans. There had been episodes of ingestive anthrax in the area before, the result of bachelors consuming the meat of diseased animals. American newspapers and magazines described the Sverdlovsk outbreak as "the Siberian ulcer," using an alternative translation of *Siberskaia iazva*. The spores in that case were not actually from the ground or dead cattle but from the air, which, official expediency aside, was as marvelous a source of anthrax as Remizov's worms.

The World Health Organization posts on the Internet a world map of anthrax distribution on which the countries with a large number of reported cases are shown in red. Clicking on, say, Mongolia or Argentina

Construction of a cattle-burning pit "in the American style." The cattle are covered with kerosene or other flammable liquid where they fall, then with a thick layer of straw topped with manure or peat. It is then ignited, kept burning until reduced to ashes and shoveled into the pit shown. (Terentev 1946.)

produces a chart of animal and human instances. This map reduces all kinds of anthrax ground around the world to uniform political divisions. Spores don't group themselves according to national boundaries, though the map does suggest that national veterinary and public health policies have an influence on the prevalence of anthrax illness within those boundaries.

The spread of national anthrax ground around the world can be traced in the publication and dissemination of manuals by agriculture authorities, often giving practical instructions on how to obtain vaccine and immunize animals. The Division de Ganaderia of Uruguay in 1910 issued a pamphlet entitled *Tristeza y carbuncle, indicaciones los hacendados sobre los principales sintomas, caracteres diferentes, y modo de preservacion de estas dos enfermedades*. It was urgent that ranchers learn to distinguish between babesosis (called *tristeza* or "sadness" from the depressed behavior of the cattle) and anthrax, and to know the different ways of preventing each. Anthrax ground was sometimes babesosis ground, and the dipping that controlled one would not prevent the other.

Argentina, Brazil and Mexico produced similar pamphlets around the same time.

Another world map of anthrax ground, suggestive rather than complete, is provided by the medical literature on gastrointestinal or ingestive anthrax. Need draws the spores up from the ground through the animals. This is the one variety of anthrax infection humans share with animals, which must be dying of the disease in an area for humans to be affected.

A survey of reports between 1970 and 2000 identifies 11 separate occurrences, all but one of them in developing countries, and all the result of eating raw or poorly prepared meat. These are articles describing individual cases of human disease, including treatment and prevention strategies. They therefore define moments in the emergence and control of anthrax ground.

An Ugandan occurrence involved 143 people and a Thai occurrence involved 74 in the same year (1984), all of them resulting from eating portions of the same cow distributed in a community. In Uganda the rapid resort to antibiotics limited the number of deaths to nine; it is not known what treatment was used to limit the number of dead to three in the Thai cases.

Most of the reports are of a single person, and even with antibiotics they did not all survive. The ground that led to these infections must have prevailed outside the published cases.

In the Bekaa Valley of Lebanon between 1960 and 1974 a surgeon named Antoine Ghossain treated and operated on victims of anthrax resulting from the consumption of raw meat. Often they were shepherds or their relatives who partook of meat from goats that had died of a sickness. The medical interventions led to the realization that certain pastures were more likely to cause the animals to become sick, and the practice of eating the meat of these animals was more likely to cause humans to become sick. As diagnosis and health care support improved, the resort to surgery also decreased. There never was enough experience developed in gastrointestinal anthrax surgery to be able to generalize about the best approach. All these factors were components of this particular anthrax ground.

Humans have even created anthrax nations in the form of the anthrax islands. As the result of weapons testing from before the Second World War to the Cold War, Gruinard Island off the coast of Scotland and then Grosse Ile in the Saint Lawrence River near Quebec City became anthrax ground. Gruinard Island became imbued with anthrax and remained anthrax ground for a long time before it was seared into lifelessness by decontamination, from which it is recovering.

Grosse Ile, a long term station for receiving immigrants and quarantine station, was used as an anthrax production site between 1942 and 1944, and probably afterward. Because of its significance to the many descendants of Irish immigrants who arrived there having fled famine, Grosse Ile became a national park after the buildings were razed or decontaminated. The large cemetery is more significant ground than anthrax, which never was in the ground there.

Vozhrozhdeniye Island in the Aral Sea had a history of bioweapons testing since the 1930s and in 1954 became a Soviet development facility where lethal anthrax spores were devised, tested and finally buried in quantity when treaty inspections were begun. According to one account barrels were filled with the pink powder, washed in bleach and buried two meters below the surface. After the island reverted to Uzbekistan and Kazakhstan in 1992, an Uzbek-American team came and carried off the records, but the spore load remains beneath while scavengers carry off from the surface ruins what metal they can sell. The island's ground is not anthrax but the possibility of antibiotic-resistant plague carried by surviving rodents.

Artificial anthrax ground is a passing formation, a massive concentration of spores for military purposes. It might be repeated by one power or another ambitious for that distinction, but for the most part it is the object of disavowal. Natural anthrax ground still exists with and without deliberate human assistance. The artificial ground, from the culture medium of the petri dish to the Gruinard Island concentration, is an outgrowth of the soil in which humans give one bacterium a competitive advantage for their own purposes. Soils throughout the world contain myriads of bacteria, most of them unidentified.

What life the bacilli actually live in the ground has long since been studied from their life in the artificial media of petri dishes, within the bodies and on the skin of animals and humans in which some can multiply.

Karl Wilhelm Nageli, a botanist contemporary of Robert Koch, believed that bacteria, which he referred to as *Pilze* (fungi), should not be divided into separate species. He cited his microscope examination of numerous bacteria to support his assertion that their morphology can't differentiate them. Classifying them as pathogenic and non-pathogenic was just using their effects on humans and animals to create illusory distinctions.

Nageli's follower Hans Buchner conducted experiments which he claimed transformed the "hay fungus" (*Heupilze, Bacillus subtilis)* into the anthrax contagion (*Milzbrandcontagium)*, which was in turn identical with all other contagions. Bacteria were so much alike that pathogens and non-pathogens could turn into each other with a little coaxing. There was a great prize in proving this: it could explain why animals with no apparent contact with anthrax-infected stock still developed the disease.

Koch published photographs of the *Heupilze* and the *Milzbrand-contagium,* and he pointed out how different they are from each other in shape and attributes. He was unable to repeat Buchner's experiment of transformation. Koch's identification of the anthrax bacillus as a sharply distinct natural entity became a standard for distinguishing bacteria. Those creating vaccines demonstrated that the virulent anthrax bacillus could be attenuated, and its character, if not its appearance, could be changed by temperature and chemical treatments. It was not the rigidly standardized bacterium Koch cultured and photographed.

Nageli and Buchner's bacteria form an ever-present cloud around Koch's bacteria. The growing discovery of biochemical attributes and genetic features specify bacteria and describe their mutability. Those multitudes of bacterial cells distributed throughout the world are not consistent even within a species. In a handful of soil they vary in many changing ways.

In microbiology textbooks it is not uncommon to find attribute charts comparing *Bacillus anthracis* with other bacilli. The differences between bacilli are related to the chemical environment, temperature, atmospheric pressure and other factors that stimulate or inhibit growth and decay. The attributes actually describe populations reaching a noticeable level rather than individual organisms, which would not be noticed if they were not multiplying prolifically. These population-multiplication attributes describe the milieu in which the bacilli exist.

The bacilli only come to notice in the degree and usefulness of toxicity to humans and animals. The ability of *Bacillus thuringensis* to obstruct the development of insect larvae has made it a pesticide substitute. Some bacilli, for instance *Bacillus globigii,* are known mainly as simulants of *Bacillus anthracis.* They multiply under the same conditions and produce spores but supposedly are not toxic to humans and animals.

It was *Bacillus globigii* that the American biowarfare production facility in Indiana was able to produce in quantity just as other weapons made the production of anthrax unnecessary. It was also *Bacillus globigii* that the U.S. Army in the 1950s sprayed over the Canal Zone and other populated areas in an attempt to simulate bacterial attacks.

*B. globigii* does, however, produce its own potentially toxic proteins, and can sicken people whose immune-systems are compromised by drugs or illness. When he first observed it in 1835 (long before *B. anthracis* was observed) Ehrenberg named it *Vibrio subtilis* because it moved about. As more comparisons were made *Vibrio subtilis* was seen to more strongly resemble the motionless *B. anthracis* than the active *Vibrio cholerae,* the active agent of cholera. Cohn designated it *B. subtilis* in 1872. The name

*B. globigii* was introduced in 1900. The nomenclature is as active as the bacilli themselves, changing between *B. globigii* and *B. subtilis*, and suggesting the transformational possibilities of all bacilli.

Comparing *B. anthracis* with *B. cereus* and *B. cereus* subsp. *mycoides* in 18 characteristics such as motility, catalase production, anaerobic growth, growth at 50 and 60 degrees Centigrade, and starch hydrolysis, has *B. anthracis* indistinguishable from *B. cereus* in all categories except motility, and not distinguishable from subspecies *mycoides* at all. A distinction from *mycoides* is in citrate utilization. Presence or absence of these characteristics distinguish *B. anthracis*, *B. thuringensis* and *B. subtilis* from each other and from many other bacilli known and unknown that resemble it morphologically. These characteristics define the conditions under which the bacilli proliferate: relatively warm or cold, salty, acidic or alkaline. The conditions make the bacilli and the bacilli make the conditions.

One literally overwhelming difference between *B. anthracis* and its otherwise similar compatriots in the soil is its toxicity to animal cells. *Bacillus anthracis* populations are unique among bacilli as far as anyone knows in the suite of proteins they produce that are toxic to animals if released in the proper combination, and they are unique in their combination of these proteins with a poly-D-glutamate capsule and spore formation. Other bacilli resembling *B. anthracis* in numerous ways produce toxins or have cell walls with that composition but *B. anthracis* is characterized by possessing them all together.

Vaccine history and biowarfare development have shown that *Bacillus anthracis* can lose and be made to lose these unique characteristics and come to resemble other bacilli. Or that the toxic properties can be engineered to poison humans or stimulate the immune system protectively against poisoning. *B. anthracis* seems to be a phase of a larger set of variations which remains stable under specific conditions in the wild and freely vary as key conditions change. Pasteur took advantage of this accidentally and Max Sterne did deliberately.

The population of bacilli in the soil has evolved to change identity. The names we give to individual types are tags which encompass a set of potentially changing features, which hold down a moment of an ever-changing mass. Using the same nomenclature implying relationships between bacteria like those between animals and plants is misleading. Horses don't metamorphose into donkeys with a change in the temperature and humidity.

Yet the nomenclature does describe the moment of the bacilli that impinges most upon human beings and domestic animals. With bacilli, as with other microbes, the name connotes the disease it causes as much as the microbe itself; it connotes the particular supportive ecology that exists in the human body when the microbe comes to notice there.

If it is only one moment in an enormous variety of potential bacilli, *B. anthracis* has evolved to hold on to that moment a little longer than other bacilli it might become or compete with in the soil. Even without the rich environment of the animal spleen or the human mediastinum, *B. anthracis* has outfitted itself to persist with less identity loss than the others. The proteins it produces can enter and break down other cells it encounters in the soil. Its spores form packages that help it persist until the conditions are right for it to multiply and there are other cells present for it to consume.

Bacteria change by exchanging the portions of the plasmids that contain their DNA with other bacteria. Even mutually dissimilar bacteria can conjugate, switch portions of plasmids with each other. Genes can also be carried from one bacterium to another or by infection with bacteriophages. The spore stage has preserved *B. anthracis* from these changes by locking it in a state that resists conjugation and bacteriophage invasion. The bacterium that germinates from a spore is the same as the one that produced the spore. Only that chemical and temperature conditions of germination can affect the attributes of the emerging bacterium. It is susceptible to invasion during that period, but the rapidity of multiplication and the toxins produced protect it from outside influences. Some may change but there always is a *B. anthracis* somewhere.

*B. anthracis* in turn is susceptible to other bacteria, and vanishes as a vegetative body as decay sets in. The proteins produced by bacteria of putrefaction dissolve *B. anthracis* cells. The cell wall attack of the fungal product penicillin renders it helpless unless it becomes spores, and bacteriophages readily enter and multiply within its cells. Its moment is one moment in the larger time of the soil, but it is a moment that repeats itself under the right conditions and has the unusual property of being able to transport itself to other likely sites.

The spores form when conditions change from those which favor reproduction and toxin production to those which favor dissemination. If the body of the dead animal is opened and the bacteria are exposed to the air; if the ground begins to dry after a period of warm rain, the cells generate small, hard bodies that enclose the DNA with instructions to make more of the same cells when conditions return to those favoring germination.

Where the vegetative cells grow in the wet and the warm, relatively anaerobic environment, breaking into other cells to liberate their nutrients, the spores persist in the dry, airy environment without reproducing themselves or competing with other cells. Or, they have successfully competed by being able to last where colonies of other bacteria die out or only persist in small relict populations.

*Bacillus anthracis* cells can enter the air in the company of other in spores, dust, on the leaves of plants, on the bodies of flies and in the hair and fur of animals.

*B. anthracis* and other sporulating bacteria have evolved not to evolve. The spore state calls off change and waits for threshold conditions under which reproduction and variation can begin again. Anthropomorphic language begins where humans enter. This is where humans have contributed to maintaining the identity of *B. anthracis* by giving it a lift and providing it with portable soil in the form of traveling mammalian bodies it can enter, ultimately enabling its spores to become more effectively airborne.

An elementary microbiology experiment probably not recommended any longer asks a student to pour boiling water over a handful of soil and culture the remains. This always yields bacilli, but seldom identifiable anthrax bacilli. The experiment demonstrates how unlikely it is that anthrax would enter the human realm spontaneously. It required the lens of human society to form its ground and become a disease.

The spores are waiting with many other spores and only very special conditions—warm weather following rain, cuts in the gums of a browsing cow, a microbiologist making a culture—will awaken them into bacilli. When certain conditions come about in the soil, the anthrax bacilli germinate together with all the other bacilli and other microbes whose requirements are met at that time. Those temperature and nutrient requirements are very narrow, reducing competition in the soil among the various bacteria and fungi increasing and decreasing in numbers, entering different physiological states.

Orchidists, for instance, struggle to germinate orchid cells by encouraging the growth of just the right bacteria and fungi in the vicinity. Brewers and breadmakers cultivate some bacteria and fungi while trying to exclude others. Anthrax bacilli are cultivated in the laboratory in a semblance of the soil conditions that nurture them.

Only a few microbes emerge into human consciousness, and there they occupy niches which we preserve parallel to their original media of growth. It is possible to breed and now even genetically to construct microbes that suit an intended purpose. The structures of disease among humans and animals draw upon specific origins at first unintentionally reproduced and extended among humans. Anthrax enters the body as if it were its own ground, and from there it enters the air.

Robert Koch, who first grew bacteria from animal blood in the laboratory, warned that anthrax bacilli grow naturally in swamps. He hadn't observed this growth, only its effects, but he was acquainted with farm practices to avoid infection in animals by keeping them away from certain swamps. He also wrote that no microscopist could ever look at a sample of soil and sort out the anthrax spores by sight. They would have to be cultured to know them.

The niche anthrax occupies in the human milieu parallels its competition with other microbes in the ground. The place where the anthrax bacillus multiplies is the same human and animal ground that plays host to other microbes. The unique features of anthrax make it able to occupy a niche described by comparing it with the diseases caused by the others. There is a general similarity between anthrax and other epidemic diseases affecting humans, projecting from their original niches into the peculiar accommodations humans have created. Like plague, tuberculosis and smallpox, anthrax has both respiratory and cutaneous forms. The big difference is that they can be transmitted directly from person to person while anthrax requires an intermediary.

Unlike syphilis and AIDS, anthrax is not transmitted through sexual activity, and unlike malaria it does not require direct injection into the bloodstream by an insect, though it may be transmitted that way. Mosquito transmission of anthrax has not been proven. It is mostly insects that feed on carrion that can transmit the disease. Blowflies have been known to pick up anthrax spores from the corpses of dead animals and inject the disease into wounds on living white-tail deer (in Texas) and kudu (in Kruger National Park, South Africa).

People who have no food other than infected meat can contract ingestive anthrax or any of a number of other diseases. An epidemic of Ebola in Gabon in early 2002 was traced to the meat of a dead gorilla eaten by desperately hungry refugees. HIV is thought to have entered the human population through consumption of the meat of monkeys or chimpanzees carrying a similar virus. And prionic spongiform encephalopathy is spread by eating the meat of cattle dead from the bovine version of the disease. It also can be spread through pituitary extracts of growth hormones taken from human cadavers and given to children whose parents feel they should be taller.

The fear that prionic disease might spread through animal products used in a great variety of manufactured goods, including soaps, gelatins and cosmetics, parallels the fear of anthrax spreading into the commodity stream through animal products. Anthrax as a disease of humans shares features with other afflictions but no one affliction has the versatility of anthrax: its ability to sicken and kill animals and people selectively, even after successful protective measures have been devised and there are vaccines.

This is probably due to the spore form of the bacteria which with expenditure of force and human devising can insinuate itself into many places and await the arrival of a medium. Smallpox, a virus, achieves a similar versatility by being able to travel in dust and on the surface of the skin and remain infective. Though they don't resemble each other physically, bacterial spores and virus crystals can travel the same air.

The difference between smallpox and anthrax as zoonotics is instructive. Animals get the same anthrax as humans who then can spread it to other humans. Cows and horses have been used as the source of anthrax vaccines. The poxes that cows (cowpox) and horses (grease) get serve to protect humans from smallpox by providing vaccination material. Some animal versions of smallpox are milder versions of the disease and protect the animal. For years doctors were using a form of what they thought was cowpox to make vaccines and they only realized with the advent of molecular biology that they were using a hybrid strain of the virus (vaccinia), of unknown origin.

Anthrax strains are not characteristic of any one animal, but can be communicated from animal to human and back. Mousepox, monkeypox, racoonpox and any number of other poxes control populations in the animals but do not afflict humans. Anthrax has been accidentally spread and deliberately engineered by humans to spread where it would not naturally reach; the poxes might also be engineered to be inescapably virulent and spread through the air, even on anthrax spores as a carrier.

There is an even more complex parallel between *Treponema pertenue*, the microbe causing syphilis in humans, and *Bacillus anthracis*. *Treponema* is behind a number of conditions that outwardly don't resemble each other. Analysts have been at a loss to determine how the *Treponema pertenue* that causes bejel, yaws and pinto, all skin diseases most visible in the tropics, is any different from the *Treponema pertenue* that causes syphilis. It may just be routes of infection, with the *Treponema* delivered to the genitals becoming most widely and mysteriously symptomatic. Syphilis of course has a range outside the tropics, but that may be because it has found an interior tropic in the human body, where temperature and humidity are ideal for its proliferation.

As bacteria *Treponema* are the opposite of *Bacilli*, at least as objects of human manipulation. They were only detected late in the period of microbial discovery, and even today are among the most difficult to distinguish in tissue specimens. They are also among the most difficult to culture in vitro, and in contrast with the fundamental success with anthrax, were not caused to reproduce in a medium until 1913. They were never seriously considered for germ warfare.

The complexity of syphilis is in the variety of surface effects the infection has once the bacteria become embedded in a body. They do their tissue damage over many years, giving appearances of a number of other infections, and they can be transferred from one generation to the next, doing such damage in the womb that a form of hereditary blindness can result. Anthrax infects tissue much faster than syphilis does, but the outward effects of infection are just as ambiguous and the underlying cause can only be detected with tests.

Mycobacteria, the bacteria that cause tuberculosis in humans, also have both respiratory and cutaneous manifestations, and they also have animal forms. They reside in tubercles often located in the wall of the lungs and can remain there without strong manifestations for long periods of time. They affect animals in a similar way, but don't spread from animals to humans. Unlike anthrax they are specific to their hosts.

The related mycobacteria that cause leprosy in humans produce an advanced infection similar to tuberculosis in its later stages, with erupting bone tissue and massive skin ulcers over a long period of time, more a state than a disease, creating a kind of person so long do they linger.

Sighting the gross effects of anthrax amid these other infections shows its distinctive effects upon humans. It starts by entering surfaces, causes an initial slight illness followed by a lull, and multiplies rapidly once it is in a cellular layer that supports it. If it is unchecked it can progressively enter other body surfaces, producing characteristic signs in lungs, spleen, intestine and brain. If checked it can linger in the lymph nodes and spleen, and proliferate whenever the immune system is compromised.

Until the anthrax toxin was isolated in 1954 it was believed that the bacteria were invasive rather than toxic. This was due to the sheer number of bacteria found in the blood of those killed by the disease. Though early students of anthrax pointed out that blood from a dead animal cleared of bacteria was still poisonous, the invasive appearance of the bacteria was used to explain its deadliness, comparing it to such proliferative invaders as the plague bacteria.

Diphtheria did not show such a high degree of proliferation in its victims, but instead has a very potent toxin, which was isolated in 1888. It then appeared that bacteria caused their damage by sheer number or by producing a powerful toxin. It slowly became clear that each bacterium produced proteins possibly toxic and the bacterial life cycle and the proteins served each other in specific environments.

The anthrax bacteria, like all the others, does its damage through the production of a toxin, and the physical multiplicity of the bacteria in lymph nodes and organs is secondary to and the result of the effects of the toxin. What we consider toxins are produced by bacteria as byproducts of their own metabolism which happen to affect the physiology of the host. Or they may help them compete with other bacteria, or with other cells, including the macrophages sent to engulf them. The more noticeable bacteria are those that produce toxins that allow them to invade the host more successfully. Viruses also produce—or cause the cells they invade to produce—interferon, a suppressant of both bacteria and other viruses.

*Bacillus anthracis* honed its invasive capsule and destructive toxins not in the animal body but in the soil. The clostridium bacteria that produce botulinus toxin, germ warfare standard and now cosmetic wonder, developed their toxin in airless spaces. Usually humans are affected, intoxicated, by toxins already produced by bacteria multiplying in airless environments such as canned food.

*Escherichia coli* developed its toxins in the digestive tracts of humans and animals, or under similar chemical conditions. *Clostridium tetani*, the producer of a strong toxin, one with a peculiar affinity for mammalian nerve endings, produces spores on exposure to air which then germinate when they enter the airless spaces beneath the skin. But tetanospasmin, the tetanus toxin, does not do anything for the bacteria, does not help them overcome immune resistance or compete with other bacteria. It's just a deadly byproduct of bacterial growth. The many other *Clostridia* that might enter the human skin through wounds then kept from air also have unpleasant but not particularly advantageous wastes, such as gas.

The anthrax bacteria, housed in their resistant capsules, ride their toxin to the opportune sectors of the body.

As Koch pointed out to the speculative Pasteur, it is very difficult to tell one bacterium from another just by inspecting soil samples. Culturing the bacteria and then testing the culture on animals discloses which bacteria are present. And culturing creates conditions favoring the multiplication of one type of bacteria by allowing that one type to outstrip others. In turn, culturing allows us to know what those conditions are. It follows that those occasions of the soil and body that most favor those conditions are host to the greatest concentrations of bacteria.

That those conditions may suddenly change in the soil made the spore state advantageous to sporifying bacteria, which survive changes in temperature and humidity encapsulated but take the risk of reproduction only when temperature, moisture and surrounding chemistry are favorable.

Other soil bacilli also produce toxins and enter a spore state. *Bacillus cereus*, genetically identical with *Bacillus anthracis* except for the toxin coding genes, may exchange genetic information with it. Under some conditions it can cause mild intestinal upsets in humans. *Bacillus thuringensis* has proven a boon because it produces a crystal that can damage the larvae of Lepidoptera insects (moths and butterflies) and can be made into an agricultural pest control powder not toxic to mammals. These bacilli most strongly resemble each other biochemically, and together can be distinguished from *Bacillus anthracis* only through careful tests.

*Bacillus anthracis* is distinct from these other bacilli and from most other bacteria in having a poly-D-glutamate capsule rather than a polysaccharide capsule. *Bacillus cereus* and other bacilli that reside as spores in the soil can cause upsets if they enter the stomach or intestines, but they can't ride the lymph system inside macrophages to multiply in the lymph nodes, spleen and brain.

The presence of anthrax bacilli is only established when it multiplies inside an animal body. Otherwise it hides itself in the soil, and is transmitted through contact with the soil, not from contact between animals as are the causative agents of tuberculosis, malaria, or trypanosomosis, to name just a few.

What cycles it goes through in the soil are subject to the conditions of vegetative life and encapsulation that Koch described. But we only know those conditions through the part of its arc that affects humans and animals, and which in turn has been modified by relations between humans and among animals. We know less about its relations with other bacteria and viruses in the soil and how that leads to emergences into human politics.

Do the bacteria form a part of biofilms or colonial masses? Do they multiply under the environmental conditions which are likely to bring the muzzle of an animal host close to the spores that are generated on contact with the air? How did the bacilli evolve this ability to emerge from the soil and into bodies as if they are soil, which they will become again?

Some of the bacterium's history can be traced in the different response of similar animals. Mice can be infected by as few as five spores, yet it takes a thousand units of toxin per kilogram to kill a mouse, and the lethal population of bacteria is 10 to the 7th power bacterial bodies per milliliter. Rats resist an initial infection very strongly—it takes 10 to the 6th power spores to infect them—but once infected they succumb to 15 units of toxin per kilogram and hold 10 to the 5th power bodies per milliliter. Monkeys, and humans, require 3,000 spores to infect, 2,500 units to kill, and show 10 to the 7th power bodies.

In October 2001 Harvard Medical School researchers announced that they had located the gene that in certain forms confers immunity to anthrax on strains of mice. The researchers thought that the protein the gene controls welcomes the lethal toxin of the bacilli, but experiments showed the opposite, that the protein promotes resistance. Some humans also carry this form of the protein, and resist the lethal factor, and the mice can serve as an experimental model for inducing the immunity in humans.

Both mice and rats have a strong commensal relationship with humans, and not with other animals that may carry anthrax bacteria, but their susceptibility to the bacteria is not mediated by humans. Koch's choice of mice as a source of anthrax bacteria was a wise one, because mice could easily be infected but would not die from the infection, and could survive while holding a more virulent strain that would affect other, more susceptible animals.

How mice evolved their susceptibility to infection and resistance to toxin may be the result of where and how they come into contact with anthrax. They do not live in the soil like rats, or find their food there, and they do not come into direct contact with masses of anthrax bacteria or spores, but more likely with concentrations of toxins in the human-raised and processed food they eat. Rats have direct contact with the bacteria and spores, and their germination and multiplication, and the toxins resulting.

Mice do not encounter anthrax spores in their habitat as often as rats do, and have no need to invest in an immunity to the bacterial capsules while rats do encounter the spores often enough to profit from an initial resistance to the proliferation of the bacteria. Mice do not resist the protective antigen but do resist the edema and lethal factors; rats do just the opposite. Rats are more likely to feed off the carrion of animals dead of anthrax and be exposed to intoxication; they also are more likely to dwell in the soil and encounter the spores.

Both mice and rats carry a dense bacterial load without being affected seriously. Why aren't they anthrax vectors for humans and other animals as they are for plague and some viruses? Because there is no intermediate vector, no flea that carries anthrax bacteria from mice and rats. Anthrax bacteria do not survive in rodent urine and feces to become spores and enter other animals through the lungs. Only large quantities of spores transmitted that way are effective. The small amounts that would be produced by mice and rats would not be enough to assure further establishment of bacterial colonies.

Mice and rats, like humans, are peripheral to anthrax transmission. They have been exposed enough for there to be selective pressure on their physiology fine enough to respond to the nature of the exposure. The main transmission cycle is with ungulates, but even ungulates are interrupting what goes on in the soil.

The virus that causes yellow fever in humans maintains itself in monkeys without causing death. But when humans clear the forest edge to plant crops and the monkeys raid the crops, mosquitos breeding in the water that collects in the fields and the creases of the plants bite monkeys and humans in close enough sequence to transmit the virus to humans, who cannot sustain the viral load the way monkeys do.

Mosquitoes and flies are not major carriers of anthrax bacteria. Nor are they of the bacteria that causes tularemia, *Franciella*, also a soil bacterium that travels between rodents and humans and has been a candidate for germ warfare.

The major difference between anthrax and these other pathogens is the size of the animals it affects. While other bacteria and viruses are carried around in small non-domesticated animals that live in the human periphery, anthrax bacteria invade and kill cattle. Anthrax bacteria invade and are carried by small rodents as well, but that is a dead end for them since there is no easy way for them to make the transition to other animals or back to the soil in a manner that allows them to sporulate in great numbers.

Anthrax bacteria invade large animals which remain susceptible to them because they usually do not survive a full blown infection to transmit their immunity to a particular strain. And conversely, any strain of anthrax that does not kill its host is rapidly selected out. Every life form that is known as a pathogen of humans and animals has what appears to be a strategy for including that animal's particular biomass in its growth pattern.

Anthrax projects a metaphor, that of soil. It simply extends its earthborne proliferation to the earth of the ungulate's interior, which it accesses through a number of portals. It is humid in there, nearly the right temperature. There is free iron.

Inside the animal there is internal transport to places where the exact conditions are met for multiplication. When the dead mass is opened up and exposed to air, spores quickly form and await transport and germination conditions. The soil where the conditions for proliferation are momentarily met because of a combination of rainfall and warmth is turned open and the spores are released.

The animal body is better soil. The precise conditions are met over a larger area, in a larger mass. The whole yard moves around.

Anthrax succeeds where tetanus fails and vice versa. The bacilli can make their way deeper into the body mass because of their unique capsule and penetrating toxins. As a result, however, they are highly localized. They perpetuate themselves only where the mass is buried. There have to be enough anthrax spores, a plague's worth or a cattle trail's worth, for it to last in a place.

Anthrax fails where plague succeeds. It can't easily make the jump from ground soil to walking medium because it does not have a guided missile, a flea or a mosquito, that is certain to move from one body to another. Those infected with plague walk around radiating bacteria through their fleas. Those infected with anthrax, much larger than the rats and fleas of plague, walk around till they drop and the anthrax spores seep out of their bodies into the soil, into their wool and hides.

*Yersinia pestis*, also a bacillus which forms an antigenic capsule, does not form spores, yet it manages to enter the air and human bodies. The seemingly improbable ground that *Yersinia pestis* multiplies in is the result of its changeable attributes and the collaboration of several animals in relations with each other.

The bacillus loses its capsule in the stomach of a flea, where it has come with the flea's blood meal on a rat carrying a population of the bacilli. When the rat dies and the flea leaves for a new, human host, the unencapsulated cells are regurgitated at the site of feeding and move into the human blood stream. There they are mostly consumed by leucocytes (white blood cells). The absence of the capsule causes the bacilli to be taken up by tissue macrophages, which unlike the leucocytes cannot digest them. The cells then develop capsules, break out of the macrophages and are free to multiply in the blood plasma and lymph indigestible by the leucocytes. In this latter phase *Y. pestis* uses the same strategy as *B. anthracis* to enter tissues and it has similar effects while there. The resulting bubos have long been mistaken for anthrax eruptions.

If *Y. pestis* multiplies in the lungs it can leap into the air with exhalations and enter other lungs in its encapsulated form and produce pneumonic plague. There is also a septicemic plague that results from direct skin contact with infected body fluids, somewhat in the manner of cutaneous anthrax.

*B. anthracis* has the expedient of the spores, which allow it to travel in goat hair sweaters, horsehair plaster, bone meal and bombs. If spores are ever recovered from other planets, *B. anthracis* may be among them. Or they may be evidence of panspermia or an alien invasion with highly unsophisticated interplanetary craft.

*Y. pestis* has its reservoir in rats and relies on fleas and dying breaths to travel the air. The two are unlike each other, yet they occupy a common ground in the human body. During the times when population and lack of sanitation permitted plague to spread, they probably also permitted anthrax to assume a plague aspect. When there is sufficient interconnectedness between masses of people and masses of animals the same disease effects arise.

In August 2001 twenty-three people who took part in the 4-H Barn Dance at the Lorain County Fair in Ohio came down with severe intestinal infections eventually found to be caused by the bacterium *Escherischia coli*, strain 0157 H:7. The bacteria were deposited on the barn floor in manure from animals judged in fair contests and remained in cracks in sufficient quantity to be raised into the air with dust by the dancing and contaminate the food and drink. The still viable bacteria in the flooring, the energy of the dance and the closeness of the space created an *E. coli* infectious environment where normally the bacteria are too heavy to be airborne. *E. coli* infections also broke out among children who had visited farms and petting zoos and a butter-making demonstration. Wherever animal intestinal products can enter the air, the bacteria receive the energetic boost, allowing them to enter the human digestive system.

An outbreak of anthrax among bison in Wild Buffalo Park, Alberta, Canada, was traced to inhalation of spores as the animals gave themselves dust baths. No anthrax-dead animals had been buried there; it was a dry summer after a comparatively warm, rainy spring.

People sweeping out summer cottages after a winter's infestation of rodents have developed hantavirus infections because the virus particles, shed by the animals, are light enough to be carried in the air along with the dust.

*Clostridium tetani* spores are found in soils throughout the world. Wherever the opportunity for entry exists in an enclosed, warmed animal space it increases and sends out its toxin. Its distribution exceeds the most extravagant projections of germ warfare planners, if their attack were upon infants. Annually it kills thousands of newborns in Bangladesh just because of the unsanitary circumstances of birthing. As sanitation improves, tetanus deaths decrease. But tetanus is as hidden in Bangladesh as it is within the soil.

Addicts in New York in 1983 developed malaria from sharing a needle used by a man who had come from Sierra Leone. Public health authorities traced a rash of internal anthrax infections among Scottish heroin addicts to a batch of Norwegian crystal that came originally from Afghanistan, where it picked up spores apparently during processing. The syringe accomplishes what the mosquito never could, and a new form of anthrax results.

Anthrax shares its ground with many other organisms provided with the means of traveling through it. Transmission of anthrax by mosquitos, which carry so many other organisms, has never been proven, but anthrax is transmitted by flies that feed on the carrion of animals that have died and remain exposed. This might have been an anthrax ground during serious epidemics, as in Zimbabwe in 1979–80, and during earlier periods when animals died faster than they could be buried, or they could not be buried deep enough to keep them from being exposed to the air. The German agents who plotted infecting reindeer and mules of the northern supply routes during the First World War had something like this in mind.

In the absence of such conditions anthrax remains in the ground, running through cycles there in competition with other life forms, and it only rises up with the help of energy on the surface—wind, the motions of humans and animals—and then only when the spores are in combination with other elements, such as dust particles, or silica, which buoy them aloft long enough and in sufficient quantity to be infectious. The imagination of anthrax is bound to the ground. They are suspended in the air only to live in the ground they enter.

Much effort has gone into calculating the concentration of spores required to kill a measure of the population. The U.S. Army tests with monkeys in their one-million-liter test chamber at Fort Detrick ascertained that the eight thousand spores per person would kill half the affected population (LD50). Other tests using different animals under a variety of conditions give a much wider range for the lethal dose (three thousand to fifty thousand). This is assuming that everyone affected breathes in the same quantity and all are immune-equal, which is never true.

Jeanne Guillemin concluded that the Sverdlovsk deaths were caused a much smaller quantity of anthrax spores released into the air than was estimated by U.S. defense analysts, at most a gram rather than kilograms. She pointed out that there were people in direct line of the spore release who did not even sicken, but only a few spores did kill some people. Only a tiny quantity of spores released would be enough to infect severely, perhaps irretrievably, the most vulnerable portion of the population. In heavily populated areas that number would be significant. Only some die; but some must die. Her conclusions were confirmed by the postal attacks of October 2001, where the spores were carried by the stream of the mails to many people unaffected by them but also to some of that small number of people most likely to die from inhaling one or two of them.

On the one-year anniversary of those attacks *The Washington Post* reported that many scientists and biowarfare experts were expressing doubts about the Federal Bureau of Investigation's persistent search for a single author of the anthrax attacks. They expressed the belief that to produce an aerosol that sophisticated would require more than one person and a large investment, "half a dozen … really smart people," as one specialist concluded. They would have to be able to coat the suitably lethal anthrax spores with a form of silica, neutral in itself but able to keep the spores from clumping together aloft, all the while containing them and avoiding injury to themselves.

The scientists were discouraging the FBI's one-person theory by pointing out that anthrax does not become airborne and humanly inhalable without careful technical design. The belief that anthrax is a powder that can be collected in the wild or concocted in a laboratory and then released into a population from a vial or an envelope had taken hold of the law enforcement imagination. Anthrax had become abstracted from its ground. The scientists were attempting to return it there.

After Dr. Larry C. Ford committed suicide on March 2, 2000, police began receiving telephone calls warning them that Ford had left behind a cache of weapons and anthrax. Ford was already a suspect in the attempted murder of his former business partner several days earlier.

Investigators searched his home and office and found a canister containing machine guns and plastic explosives next to the swimming pool, and vials containing pathogens in refrigerators at the home and office. They found salmonella, cholera, botulism and typhoid agents and a blowgun with darts, but no anthrax.

Police investigations uncovered Ford's consulting work with the South African Project Coast on chemical and biological weapons, and his alleged use of various biological agents to infect patients in his gynecology practice. Again following telephoned tips, this time that Ford had buried anthrax in a gold mine, police undertook searches in California. Documents found in a Nevada trash dump showed that Ford had been involved with anti-government groups trying to use bacteria to extract gold. The documents led them to an abandoned gold milling site outside Henderson, Nevada, where they found a separator funnel, a white liquid and instructions for making chemical and biological weapons, including anthrax, but nothing more. Only the word "anthrax" has been found.

During the ongoing cleanup at Fort Detrick, Maryland, crews have uncovered 200 glass vials, many containing live bacteria. In a few were a non-virulent strain of anthrax. That is the contemporary ground of anthrax, enclosed in vials among other bacteria within the ground.

The suspicion remains that there is something hidden, buried perhaps, like gold ore or treasure, enclosed by the earth but waiting for the right expertise to bring it into the air. Anthrax has always been that way, it seems.

# Appendix A: October 2001 in Manchester, New Hampshire

## Reports in *The Manchester Chronicle*

October 7—Recalling the city's "anthrax epidemic" of 1957, Antonio Jette's wife and daughter, interviewed by *Chronicle* reporter Nancy West, wondered if the recently reported death of a man in Florida from anthrax was due to "natural" anthrax, like that which killed Mr. Jette, or "terrorist" anthrax.

October 13—A dust-like substance reported, and a suspicious piece of mail.

October 14—Suspicious packages.

October 18—"Full circle:" The history of Garrett Phelan, who in 1917 emigrated from Fitchburg, Massachusetts, where anthrax was rampant in the textile industry, to Manchester, where he took a job in a tannery attached to shoe shop and contracted anthrax.

October 20—Man charged after sending letter labled "anthrax" to friend in Dover.

October 21—Representative John Sununu apologizes for handling of suspicious envelope. A woman who made the winning bid on a collector's postage stamp over the Internet received mail she thought might be contaminated. Tests came back negative. White powder coats a box and white granules fall out of a letter. The Manchester Fire Department sends samples to the state lab for testing.

October 25—Hooksett Middle School is closed and put in "lockdown" mode when a teacher reports a white powdery substance in a classroom.

October 27—A company in Hampton ensures that President Bush doesn't receive anthrax-tainted mail.

October 30—State laboratory workers are putting in 16-hour shifts testing samples sent from all over the state, but so far there has been no trace of anthrax.

# Appendix B:
# Warnings to Workers

1.

## WORKERS!
### Anthrax is a very serious disease.

Nevertheless, it can always be cured if it is treated *immediately*. It begins with a small pimple, *which must be cauterized within 24 hours. If not treated anthrax may produce death in a few days.* **Therefore, be warned in time!** *See the doctor at once,* if you have a pimple. *Have yourself bandaged at once,* if you have the smallest scratch. The scratch will allow dust to enter, *and an almost invisible grain of dust may contain the microbe which is capable of killing you. Beware of dusty goods,* and never carry them on your shoulders.

### Keep Yourself Scrupulously Clean.

*Wash before eating or drinking.* You may take anthrax by means of the digestive canal. *Wash before leaving the workplace,* or you may carry anthrax home with you.
N.B.—Doctor —— whose address is —— is responsible for the medical care of this establishment in all matters relating to prevention against and treatment of anthrax.

[Recommended in a French government circular promulgated to factory inspectors by the Minister of Labour, February 18, 1908. Reproduced with script intact from International Office of Labour 1908: 79.]

221

2.

Remember this photograph!
Don't let the blister shown here go too far!
Show it immediately to your foreman or to the doctor,
TOMORROW MAY BE TOO LATE!

[English translation of a warning in Greek, Polish, Russian, Croat and Italian on a poster originally published by the Liberty Mutual Insurance Company in a bulletin in the early 1900s. Accompanied by a series of photos of anthrax lesions on human skin, it was still to be seen on the walls of goat hair mills in the 1950s and 60s.]

# Appendix C:
# Some Novels with Anthrax

Brant, Kylie. 2001. *Born in Secret*. Silhouette. Spy Walker James has to infiltrate a terrorist compound to confiscate a deadly anthrax strain.

Brooks, Terry. 2002. *The Voyage of Jorio, Shannara, Book Two: Anthrax*. Earthlight.

Clark, Mary Jane. 2003. *Nowhere to Run*. New York: St. Martin's. During a broadcast, medical correspondent Dr. John Lee holds up a vial he claims contains weapons grade anthrax, precipitating an onslaught of investigators and doctors dispensing Cipro. News producer Annabelle Murphy is relieved to learn that the vial contains table sugar, but then has a mystery on her hands when a colleagure writing an exposé ends up dead of anthrax.

Coppel, Alfred. 1960. *Dark December*. Greenwich, Connecticut: Gold Medal. After a nuclear apocalypse, survivors must cope with anthrax, among other things.

De Prince, Elaine. 1997. *Cry Bloody Murder, a Tale of Tainted Blood*. New York: Random House.

Downey, Fairfax. 1942. *War Horse*. New York: Dodd-Mead. Life and times of a mare that escapes anthrax infection by German agents while awaiting shipment to war-torn France, where she survives the battlefields and returns home a veteran.

Gibson, Lloyd. 2000. *N*. Newcastle-upon-Tyne: Focus+. Titled after the code name given to anthrax for Second World War germ warfare experiments.

Hardy, Ronald. 1987. *The Wings of the Wind*. New York: G.P. Putnam's Sons. Dr. Lewis McKenna is the only survivor of a prison camp in Mao's China, burned by camp administrator John Chen Yucheng because a prisoner developed anthrax and a nearby herd might be endangered. McKenna flees Yucheng, attempting to reach the safety of Taiwan.

Hightower, Dwan D. 2002. *Anthrax: The Game*. New York: First Books Library.

Holmes, Chris. 2002. *The Medusa Strain*. Dallas: Durban House. Refers to the appearance of an anthrax colony on a gelatin plate.

Hoyt, Richard. 1995. *Snake Eyes: A John Denson Mystery*. New York: Tom Doherty Associates. Series detective John Denson uncovers a plot by a traveling preacher to dramatize his tent shows with anthrax infections. Biblical reference to plagues upon Egypt likely to be anthrax.

McCathern, Gerald. 1999. *Quarantine!* Hereford, Texas: Food for Thought. Terrorist spy cattleranch western.

Marcinko, Richard and John Weisman. 1995. *Rogue Warrior: Green Team*. New York: Pocket Books.

Robbins, Harold. 2001. *Man and Wife*. New York: Tom Doherty Associates. Same title as a book by Andrew Klavans, same year, same publisher, which does not mention anthrax. Several novels by Robbins have been published posthumously.

Shea, Robert and Robert Anton Wilson. 1975. *The Golden Apple*. New York: Dell.

Smith, Guy N. 1995. *The Plague Chronicles*. New York: Piatkus.

Thomas, Gordon. 1991. *Deadly Perfume*. London: Chapmans.

# Appendix D:
# The Chinese Source
# of Spores

[A letter from China printed in the *London Lancet,* quoted by Washburn 1911: 7.]

The disease which has been destroying cattle throughout this district continues its ravages, though with diminished virulence, probably because there is a scarcity of susceptible cattle. The mortality has varied from 50 to 75 percent of the infected animals. To determine the extent of the disease I made inquiry as to the number of hides exported during the first three months of this year. They say that more than 200,000 left Peking, and that half a million would not be too high an estimate for this whole district. As no cattle are being slaughtered, this represents, approximately, the loss of cattle from the plague.

The foreign firms that export hides, wool, bristles, and hair are in the hands of Chinese middlemen who roam about the interior buying here and there from the agricultural classes. I have been over some of the factories in Tientsin and have seen the steps they take to clean the stuff before its export. Bristles and hair are thoroughly well boiled in soda solution, wool is roughly carded and shaken free of as much dust as possible by machinery, and hides are sorted out and packed with naphthaline. The exporters claim that any further disinfection than is now given would spoil their goods and increase their expenses.

The real difficulty does not lie with *Bacillus anthracis* but with its spores, whose natural resistance is increased by their being embedded in the grease and dirt of the material while it is being dealt with in whole-

225

sale bulk in China. There can be little doubt that the passge home through the Indian Ocean and the Red Sea in the warm hold of a ship is all-conducive to their propagation and preservation, so that when the time comes for bristles and hair being carded and separated out by workers at home these spores are liberated to an active condition, ready for human infection to a much greater extent than is the case in China.

# Sources

## Chapter 1

Generations of George Washington's biographers have included accounts of his "anthrax," mostly as another demonstration of his firmness and fortitude. Guba and Chase (2002) reference Washington's own letter (to James McHenry, 3 July 1789) and the quotation of Dr. Bard's surgical instructions. Fenn (2001) tells of General Washington's initial hesitancy to have troops variolated (immunized with matter from active smallpox pustules) in the face of predicted British deliberate spreading of the scourge, and of his decision finally to organize a mass immunization campaign, since the Americans were less likely than the British to have been exposed to the disease. Marx's letter to Engels complaining about his carbuncles is in Engels and Marx (1981: 115). Marx's letter to Dr. Kugelmann is in Volume 17 of International Press English translation of Marx's works (Marx 1934: 58). The "suspected cutaneous anthrax in a laboratory worker" is evaluated in Centers for Disease Control and Prevention (2002).

## Chapter 2

Wilkinson (1994: 24) writes that Fournier recorded "for the first time, cases of industrial anthrax," and provides references to his writings. Macher (2002) summarizes Stone's reports. Ciannavei (2001) references local records on Walpole's anthrax epidemic. Alvin (1998), a history of medical services in nineteenth century Bradford, contains much on community response to the health of textile workers. Bartrip (2002: 237–42) examines Russell's report and the efforts of the Bradford Medico-Chirurgical Society. F. Marc Laforce (1978) and Cunningham (1976) contain references to primary materials on Bradford and on Bell and Eurich's work, and Bell's article on wool workers in Oliver (1902) is a source on his discoveries. In Allbutt and Rolleston's *The System of Medicine*, Bell and Legge defined woolsorters disease as a clinical entity, and John Spear (1880 and 1881) reports on the conclusions of the local government board investigating the

London skin and hide trade and wool industries. Wilkinson (1994: 163–80) describes the work of the Brown Sanatory Institute. Legge (1903) has detail on Eurich's work, but Eurich himself (1912) recapitulates his industrious examination of hair samples and the conclusions he reached. Eurich's daughter Margaret Bligh (1960) wrote a worshipful but informative account of her father's life work. Lipson (1953) and Wentworth (1947) provide historical background on the wool industry, and Hudson (1986) studies the economics of the developing wool industry in West Riding Yorkshire, where Bradford is located. Randall (1991) examines the social context of labor unrest in the textile industry in the period prior to the emergence of woolsorters disease. Engels does not mention Bradford or wool, but his book references many accounts of the health conditions in the cotton mills. The quotes from Dyer's *The Fleece*, from *The History of Sir John Winchcombe*, and the letter on woolsorters work conditions are from Lipson (1953). Dyer's poem is available in full on the Internet, together with Johnson's brief biography of Dyer. Derry and Williams (1960: 566–71) give a history of mechanical technology in the textile industries. Mortimer and Melling (2000) examine the history from 1880 to 1939 of government intervention to prevent industrial anthrax. Bartrip (2002: 233–66), after an overview of the investigations of and measures taken against industrial anthrax in late 19th century Britain, concludes that "the disease would have all but disappeared had the entire paraphernalia of inquiry, legislation and inspection never been." Romano (2001), the biography of Burdon Sanderson, does not mention his work on anthrax. Teleky (1948: 277), writing after another world war, explains that anthrax cases fall during wars because imports are cut off. Eppinger (1894) is the source of the information on *Hadernkrankheit* and the most comprehensive study of any occupational anthrax. The description of the ragsorters work is my translation of a passage on page 188.

# Chapter 3

International Labour Office (1908: 77–79) includes the French Ministry circular among many other recommendations and regulations. Lubin and Winslow (1990: 32, 33, 83, 326) examine the particular vulnerability of women workers to anthrax infections. Neale (1898) is a study of American anthrax legislation to that date. The 1919 Anthrax Prevention Recommendation of the International Labour Organisation is posted on their website. Wilson (1910: 863), the American edition of Salinger and a popular infectious disease reference of its time, refers to woolsorters and ragpickers disease. Donn and Hardy (1931: 150) refer to anthrax in their socialist history while Feldman (1937: 108) instances it as a "problem" of labor relations. On the Manchester outbreak, Plotkin, Brachman et al. (1960) and Brachman, Plotkin et al. (1960) provide the outward details, while Albarelli (2001) exposes the more recently obtained evidence of what went into the outbreak. Edward Hopper (1999: 555–59) in the course of his research into the testing of a polio vaccine in Africa, interviewed Stanley Plotkin, Brachman's co-investigator of the Manchester outbreak. Hopper wondered about the coincidence of the vaccination trials and the outbreak. Dalldorf, Kaufmann and Brachman (1971) report the woolsorters disease experiment in an *Archives of Pathology* article. Cold War politics that led to the biological and chemical weapons treaty are described by Cole (1998). Ivanovics (1938) is an early summary of research on the antigenic properties of the bacterial capsule. The North Carolina instance of cutaneous anthrax and the investigative response were briefly described in Centers of Disease Control and Prevention (1988). The most recent (cutaneous) anthrax infection in Bradford was reported in *BBC News* on Friday, 18 August 2000.

# Chapter 4

The sketches and calculations for the helium-powered balloon bomb filled with anthrax found in Kabul are described in "In the House of Anthrax," *The Economist* (November 24, 2001). The Inglesby article is available on the CDC's website. Cook's novel is lingering as a mass market paperback. Tierno (2001: 236–39) imagines a disgruntled USAMRIID technician using a rented crop duster to spray the spores. Furmanski's speculation is featured in an article on *NewScientist.com*, December 14, 2001, and Hatfill is profiled in a piece by Theodore Rozen in *Prospect*. The *Washington Times* article on Hatfill's speculations is by Fred Reed and was published on August 11, 1997. Aum Shinri Kyo's anthrax experiments were reported by Kaplan and Marshall (1996), and both the harmless nature of the bacteria and the success in generating them were noted. Takahashi, et al. (2000) outlines the investigation of Aum's anthrax release. Raider (2000: 259, fn. 96) in a long general study of Aum's "religious violence" does not even mention anthrax, but does comment that the sect was able to acquire and spray botulinum toxin without effect, that their problem was delivery. Had the book been published a year later, the author would have mentioned anthrax. Keim et al. (2001) gives the results of his team's molecular analysis of the anthrax released by the sect. The "Index Case of Fatal Inhalational Anthrax Due to Bioterrorism in the United States" (Bush et. al. 2001) was Bob Stevens, but Richard Preston (2002) renders him more than a case while giving a gruesome account of his death in the opening pages of his book. Fine (2001) is a brief report on tabloid consumers "flooding supermarkets with calls" out of fear that the papers might be contaminated. On November 1, 2001, the *Washington Post* published a list of 16 victims, excluding only Ottilie Lundgren, and giving type of anthrax infection, date confirmed, location and status. Of these, six are not named. Four had died. The CDC's October 31, 2001, update of its *Health Advisory* 45," Interim Recommendations for Protecting Workers from Exposure to *Bacillus anthracis* in Work Sites Where Mail Is Handled or Processed," lists four areas in which measures can be taken. The first, Engineering Controls, cites the ability of mail processing machines and their maintenance to aerosolize anthrax spores. Thompson (2003) is the most detailed account of the late 2001 anthrax attacks in America. Dr. Brachman was interviewed by Margaret Warner on PBS television network's *The Newshour* with Jim Lehrer, October 12, 2001. A transcript of the interview, in which Brachman gives some of the clearest information about anthrax presented during that period, is on the PBS website. A list of work-related respiratory conditions in an occupational medicine textbook, in addition to bagassosis (from moldy sugarcane millings) and suberosis (from cork dust), includes pituitary snuff–takers lung (from bovine and porcine pituitary snuff) and paprika-splitters lung, but not woolsorters disease. Hamilton and Hardy

(1974: 459–67) place organic dusts in a separate section from occupational infections, including woolsorters disease. North Carolina textile workers' respiratory disease concerns (brown lung) are a theme in the collection of workers' life stories in Conway (1979), but anthrax is not mentioned. The January 18, 2002, delay (Hsu 2002) and the January 22, 2002, reopening of the Hart Senate Office Building, the largest of three buildings housing the offices of U.S. senators, were widely reported in U.S. and international media.

# Chapter 5

The American Public Health Association survey, authored by Smyth (1939), undercuts a statement by Brachman in the interview cited above that there were a total of around 500 cases of anthrax of all varieties reported in the United States between 1900 and 2001.

Crowell (1919) reports on the quartermaster's caution about horsehair shaving brushes. In that same year the United States Government Printing Office issued a pamphlet on techniques for sterilizing shaving brushes. Harrison (2003) and Littlejohn (1994) tell of family shaving brush anthrax tragedies. Elspeth Huxley was not closely related to Aldous Huxley, though it is interesting that the two major British writers to mention anthrax bear the same name as Thomas Henry Huxley. Laessig (2003) mentions Stovall's paper. A piece on the anthrax-infected shaving brushes appeared in *Newsweek* as late as 1939. The spore on hair heat resistance experiments were by Schneiter and Kolb (1948). The gelatin rendering industry is the "most perilous" in Belgium from the standpoint of anthrax, according to "Occupational Diseases in Belgium" in the Foreign Letters section of the *Journal of the American Medical Association* 106 (1936: 1676). Pinkerton (1939) reports the case of the mink rancher, and Greener (1939) surveys mink farm outbreaks in Great Britain. Albrink (1965) reviews three "exotic" cases of inhalational anthrax, and Laforce (1994) adds several more recent ones. Briggs and Briggs (2003) analyzes the stories that spread to blame native people for a cholera epidemic in Venezuela. In a much broader way anthrax anecdotes may have a similar complexion. Gold (1935) gives clinical reports on 10 cases, the infected children and his attempts to reduce a lesion with antibiotic injections. Berton Roueché (1965: 3–34) in one of his collection of narratives of medical detection, originally published in the *New Yorker*, tells of "a man named Hoffman." Bales, Dannenberg and Brachman, et al. (2002) report on the survey of epidemiological investigations from 1950 to 2002, which includes a tabulation and references to the original reports. The CDC report on the Navy journalist-photographer's anthrax and the follow-up investigation is the subject of four reports in the Center for Disease Control's (before it became "Centers" and "Prevention" was added) *Morbidity and Mortality Weekly Report* (Center for Disease Control 1974a, 1974b, 1977, 1981). *News from CPSC* (Consumer Products Safety Commission), February 9, 1976, #76-011, reports on the product surveillance after the home handweaver's death. The two Philadelphia cases of inhalational anthrax, the secretary and the passing factory worker, are clinically described by Brachman, Pagano and Albrink (1961). The medical profile of Kathie Nguyen does not refer to her by name; nor does Barakat et al. (2002), on Ottilie Lundgren, published in the same issue of *Journal of the American Med-*

*ical Association,* refer to its subject by name. Nguyen is a "61-year-old woman in New York City" and Lundgren is a "94-year-old Connecticut woman" in keeping with the medical convention of not naming the victims; the same convention was followed even more strictly in officially reporting the Sverdlovsk outbreak of inhalational anthrax in 1979–80. Schwabe (1978: 48) notes his discussions with Maasai elders as part of a discussion of the relationship between animal and human health. Schwabe had previously published a guide to "unconventional foods" (insects, reptiles, and such). Majok and Schwabe (1996) contains more examples of local African response to anthrax in cattle. Wirtu et al. (1997) undertook their field research on "farmers' knowledge, attitudes and practices" in Ethiopia to help design an animal health and production improvement strategy. The paper was given at an international conference in Pune, India, that featured a number of other ethnoveterinary papers, none of which referred to anthrax. Evans-Pritchard (1940) is a "classic" ethnography of a cattle-herding people; Black-Michaud (1986) is a response to another "classic" ethnography on herders (Barth 1961). The Minnesota ingestive anthrax episode, such as it was, was reported by the Associated Press on September 8, 2001, though the CDC (2002) confidently declared that there had been no cases of ingestive anthrax in America during the twentieth century. The 2001 anthrax outbreaks in South Africa were reported by Adriana Stuijt, in the second part of a three part article for NewsMax.com, "Anthrax Set to Spread to the West." Stuijt begins the article stating that South Africa suffers from such poor governance that "veterinary and health care control standards have declined."

# Chapter 6

Blancou (2000: 83) lists five authors who believe the seventh Biblical plague of Egypt was anthrax. Later (86) Blancou notes that many of these early descriptions of conditions thought to be anthrax remain controversial and include symptoms that could be many other diseases. Scott gives a history of "the murrain now known as Rinderpest." Brown, Driver, Briggs and Gesenius is the Internet version of the Old Testament lexicon that traces occurrences of words in the Hebrew text and their corresponding translation(s) in the King James Bible. Ben-Noun (2002), an Israeli physician writing in Hebrew, states that the *sixth* plague of Egypt and the disease that afflicted Job (Shehin) match the clinical symptoms of anthrax. Blaisdell (1994) scans what is known (or suspected) about anthrax in Ancient Egypt. Homer's *Iliad* is available in many translations. Thucydides described the plague of Athens in his *History of the Peloponnesian War.* The original text of Hippocrates *On the Epidemics,* Book III, 3 and 7, faces a translation into English ("anthrakes" means "carbuncle") in Jones (1984), but Adams (1953) translates "anthrakes" as "anthrax." Juwanna (1999), in an extensive review of sources about and reputedly by Hippocrates, does not mention *anthrakes,* but does examine the Hippocratic rationalist conception of the plague of Athens as opposed to the religious beliefs of the ancient dramatists and Thucydides' positivism (206–9). Du Hamel's 1670 prescription for buboes and anthrax is in Thorndike (1958: 234). To trace the appearances of "anthrakes" and similar words in classical Greek literature I resorted to Liddell and Scott. The one New Testament instance of the word was identified by Thayer and Smith. Robert

Graves (1955: 193), drawing on a variety of classical sources, writes that Nessus told Deineira to mix his "seed" spilled on the ground as he died with blood and olive oil, and put it on the shirt, or soak wool in his blood and make a shirt from it, or to give Herakles Nessus' own shirt which he removed for her. Hansen and Freney (2001: 54) also cite the Herakles story as an classical anthrax visitation. The description of Hercules in the shirt of Nessus in Ovid's *Metamorphoses* has also been cited. Blancou (2000) is a major compilation of reports of animal disease instances and surveillance procedures. Boys who worked as tanners in Morocco (source of a famous leather) had to stand for long hours in a mixture of dog urine and feces (*British Archaeologist*, News Notes) which seems not to have destroyed the spores. While not requiring this extreme exposure, tanning was an industry whose workers were most prone to cutaneous anthrax (Leymann 1923). Brachman's 1955 test of the anthrax vaccine treated workers from four tanneries. Roueché (1965: 20) gives the story of the mackinaw-wearing grocery clerk, who also is tabulated in Bales, Dannenberg, Brachman, et al. 2002, as is the horsepad, game park outbreak, noticed in *News from CPSC* (November 1, 1974, Release # 74–073). Cocteau's journal (1999) gives anthrax a part in the pain of making great art, which in the case of film Cocteau describes as "dreaming while standing up."

# Chapter 7

I include the Latin to show which words Vergil uses where; for instance, he doesn't write "anthrax." The translation of Vergil's *Georgics* is MacKail (1950) and the passages quoted are MacKail (335, Book 3, lines 473–512) and MacKail (337, Book 3, lines 555–566). Eusebius (1932) is one of several conflicting translations. Guy de Chauliac's observations on anthraxes, buboes and their treatment are in de Chauliac (1971: v. 1, 287–89) a reprint of an early English translation of the *Grande Chirurgie*. Henry de Mondeville wrote a Latin surgical treatise (late 14th century) that was translated into French and published toward the end of the 19th century (Bos 1965) and John of Trevisa was a late 14th century translator into Middle English from Latin of a universal history and an encyclopedia (*De proprietatibus rerum*, On the Properties of Things), which contains among many other things advice on anthrax treatment. John is also thought to be the author of the Middle English poem "Piers the Ploughman." Rivetti (1592) has never been translated or reprinted. Slevogt, Fasch and Frischmuth (1681) is the dissertation. Hecker (1832) is available online in Babington's translation, followed by his equally interesting book on *The Dancing Mania*. Gottfried (1983) offers a wide-ranging, ecologically informed Black Death history, but does not consider the possibility of any cause but the plague bacillus. Freese (2003: 27) makes the buboes-coal-anthrax connection. Twigg's spatial and temporal study (1993) is a revision of his earlier position on the plague (1984) that emphasized anthrax. Herlihy (1997) is the culmination of a lifetime's work, beginning with the plague history of a single Italian town and ultimately reaching the conclusion that there were diseases in the Black Death in addition to the plague. Cantor (2001) cites Twigg (1984) and develops his own support for the conclusion that the Black Death was in part anthrax. One of the sources Cantor cites to support the role of anthrax is an unpublished paper delivered at a medieval studies conference by a graduate student, whom he calls Edward I. Thompson. According to a book review in the Canadian newspaper *Globe and Mail* (A Plague on the Black Death, Review of Books, July 14, 2001: D9), Edward Joel Thompson's paper ended out rejecting the thesis that the Black Death was caused by anthrax. The Black Death in Eyam and the genetic consequences were the subject of an American PBS documentary aired on *Nova*. Justin's history of the Saint-Domingue *pestis* is quoted in English translation by Morens (2002). Morens (2003) studies the veterinary and medical writings of the 1769–80 period which define anthrax as an epizootic and epidemic disease. Chabert's report is summarized by Wilkinson (1994: 125). More on the report is in Chapter 8. Kaufmann and Dannenberg (2002) offer information on the endemic nature of anthrax in Haiti as of 1973–74, and details on sporadic outbreaks are scattered in Haitian newspapers, for instance *Haiti Progres*. The "anthrax scare" surrounding the "potential plague ship" is reported by Lawlor (2003).

# Chapter 8

Blancou (2000: 86) quotes the Geneva medical society. Aristotle attributed the lesions, which may or may not have been anthrax, to the bites of lice, and he recommended treating them with lice that had been eviscerated. Enaux and Chaussier (1785) followed a treatise on the treatment of animal bites (including rabies), with one on malignant pustule. According to Geison (1995: 181), Louis Pasteur listed Enaux and Chaussier in 1876 as a "book to buy." Heuschinger (1850) gathered together geographical, historical and ethnological information on Milzbrand in the hope of detecting a distribution pattern, and was led to suspect a transmissible agent. The Spanish laws are mentioned in Blancou (2000: 95) preceding the dates of the adoption of regulations intended to reduce the spread of charbon. Scott (2000) is a brief history of rinderpest treatment and prevention strategies. Ford (1964: 79) refers to Brauell's crematory worker. Hurtel d'Arboval (1839: 220) is cited by Blancou (2000: 93). Bales et al. (2002) is the Centers for Disease Control and Prevention survey. The Texas sheepshearer's anthrax is reported by Taylor et al. (1993).

The origins of European veterinary schools are discussed by Wilkinson (1994: 65–85). Barberet's 1766 *Memorire sur les maladies epidemiques des bestiaux* is included in *Receuil* (1808). Fournier (1769) outlines his observations and experiments on the transmission of *charbon malin* in wool processing and butchery. Chabert's 1774 paper is summarized by Wilkinson (1994: 125–26), who on page 239, footnote 29 gives the reference to Linnaeus' (Carl von Linné's) *Amoenitates Academicae* (vol 3: 322) where the *Furia infernalis* is described. Baraillon (1787) is a 57 page pamphlet by a veterinarian on the animal diseases of the Moulins area of France, and the treatments locally applied. Gilbert (1796 "an III") is the account of research into *charbon* published under the revolutionary government. Herpin (1836) is an investigation of *sang de rate* in another locale of France. The word *Milzbrand* appears in German medical literature around the same time *charbon*, *fievre charbonneuse* and *sang de rate* appear in French. Theodorides (1968), a biography of Davaine, locates the beginnings of French experimental anthrax studies in the work of Barthélémy, and follows it to Rayer, Davaine and Delafond. Pollender (1855) pursues the microscopic and microchemical bases of *Milzbrand*. Brauell's discoveries are part of Saunders' (1980: 27–29) history of veterinary pathology in Russia 1860–1930. Schwab (1844), which contains the fullest descriptions of human anthrax zoonoses (contracted from diseased animals) has not been republished. Nocard and Laclainche (1903: 303–8) examine the early 19th century efforts to isolate the infectious matter of *fievre charbonneuse*. The sequence of discovery from Pollender, and Brauell to Delafond and Davaine is also the sequence of their becoming aware of each other's work and communicating their findings to scientific bodies. The sequence of discovery was recognized by Pasteur and Koch, who responded to it in different ways. Simonds' "splenic apoplexy" lecture is quoted by his biographer Pattison (1990: 102–4). Wilkinson (1994: 239 footnote 30) compares Theodorides' objective account of the discoveries with the "exaggerated and unbalanced statements" of a German author favoring his own compatriots. Wilkinson (1994: 124–30), referencing the original papers, follows the search for the anthrax particle with attention to the success or failure of individual researchers to make the correct discovery. Brauell's examinations of blood samples of anthrax victims are detailed in articles he published in the *Virchow Archiv* (1857 and 1858) and are referenced by Ford (1964: 79). Carter (1987) translates Koch's three main papers on anthrax, from the early exposition of the natural history of the bacilli to his polemic on the anthrax inoculation. Brock (1988) is a scientific biography of Koch and the source of many details here. Koch has not benefited and suffered from the posthumous mythification that has guided accounts of Pasteur's life and works, until the objective inevitable study (based on study of Pasteur's lab notes, by Geison 1995). Many of Pasteur's important papers on anthrax were co-authored with his students and colleagues, for instance Pasteur and Chamberland (1867). "You were born to sharpen pins and Pasteur was born to invent the anthrax inoculation, and the Revolution will leave you both to your respective employments," wrote the anarchist writer Peter Kropotkin in *The Conquest of Bread* (1968 [1913]: 249). Pasteur's son-in-law and biographer (English translation, 1906), René Valery-Radot, collected Pasteur's papers in the multi-volume *Oeuvres Completes*. A year by year chronological bibliography of Pasteur's scientific articles has been placed online by the Mediatheque of the Institut Pasteur, l, and there are links to the texts of some papers. A review of the papers shows Pasteur's general interest in the chemical properties of bacteria that enabled him to address anthrax as an agricultural problem. Schwartz (2003: 19–20) gives the example cited by one of Pasteur's colleagues of anthrax "spontaneously" arising among sheep from fields fertilized with processed animal remains, and equates it with the spread of mad cow disease in the twentieth century. Carter (1988) has written an account of Koch and Pasteur's controversy over the transmission of anthrax. The quote from Koch on the anthrax inoculation is in Carter (1987: 102), and the quote on Pasteur's vaccine is in Carter (1987: 111). Elzinger's letter in response to Pasteur's query on *la peste Siberienne* in cited by Frank and Wrotnowska (1968: 17) as is Pasteur's correspondence with the Director of the Studs (1968: 31). Thuillier's correspondence with Pasteur, is reprinted in the original with facsimiles of some of the letters in the same volume. It is the source of details on the Hungarian and German tests of the vaccine. Brock (1988: 140–68) has a chapter on the Egyptian cholera expeditions.

# Chapter 9

Simonds' description is quoted by Pattison (1990: 101). Ford (1964) is a history of bacteriological discoveries and techniques, and references papers by Pollender and Brauell. Wangensteen (1978: 60) references Davaine's bacterial multiplication calculations, the antiseptics studies of Davaine and Koch (406–7), and well as Schimmelbusch's mouse study (598 n 33). Hamilton (1985:40) recounts her medical school repetition of the Pasteur anthrax routine and Fulton (1946: 73) prints Cushing's letter.

Office Internationale des Epizooties (2000) contains instructions for anthrax diagnostics (Gram, McFadyean, Ascoli),and the United States Centers for Disease Control () lists approved tests for the detection of *Bacillus anthracis* in the Laboratory Response Network. Bibel and Chen (1976) is one of several studies of the Yersin-Kitasato controversy, and Marriott (2002) is a livelier account. Tauber and Chernyak (1991) wrote "the history of an idea" (immunology) as an intellectual biography of Metchnikoff. The evolution of the anthrax graphic began with drawings of the structure of the bacteria. Sargent (2002) writes of the limulus amoebocyte lysate test and the depletion of the horseshoe crabs harvested to provide the blood. The skin appearances of anthrax are frequently illustrated and are shown in dermatology atlases such as the one posted online by Johns Hopkins University. The United States Department of Labor displays photographs of them in a series of posters, warning workers to have these appearances treated (see Appendix B).

# Chapter 10

The "secret history of anthrax" during the First World War is reviewed by Albarelli (2001, Part 1) in an Internet article published soon after the October 2001 anthrax attacks. Albarelli's piece is also a recent example of information from "recently declassified documents," some of it hard to believe on examination. The Porton Down team of Redmon et al. (1998) published the key article in *Nature* on Baron von Rosen's luggage, its contents and the verification of anthrax spores in the glass vials. Bisher (2003) sees von Rosen as a "rebel leader" in the Finnish struggle for independence from imperial and then communist Russia. The History of Chemical and Biological Warfare: An American Perspective chapter of the *Medical Aspects of Chemical and Biological Warfare* section (Smart 1997) of the massive *Text of Military Medicine*, by an army of authors, contains some information on the First World War attacks (16), and a little more on the construction and deployment of chemical weapons, including the proposed snuff bomb (17). Witcover (1989) quotes passages from the records now stored in the United States National Archives of the post–World War I Mixed Claims Commission of the United States and Germany (1922–41) on the activities of Dilger, Hinsch and others. Landau (1934) was an important propagandistic disclosure of German germ warfare during the First World War and before the second one, and Rosebury (1949) shifts the blame to the Soviets. Furmanski (2000) cites both Landau and the Surgeon General's 1917 report. The history of Porton Down is a major part of the account of British biological weapons programs in Balmer (2001), and the later emerging American programs are seen through the history of Fort Detrick, Maryland (Covert 1993). Regis (1999: 22–32) tells of the early Porton Down anthrax bomb and bullet experiments and of the carry-over to the American germ warfare program. Bryden (1989) is the chief secondary source on the Canadian germ warfare programs during Second World War. As the grandson, son and brother of eminent biologists, Aldous Huxley was socially well situated to reflect contemporary scientific speculation on future war. He later moved to Hollywood and became an advocate of opening "the doors of perception" through the use of hallucinogens. Fox (1933) is the basic paper for twentieth century germ warfare because it declares its impossibility while stating how it might be done. Gruinard Island (Manchee et al. 1990 and Regis 1999: 27–31) briefly reentered the news after the October 2001 anthrax attacks. Operation Vegetarian is described by Rosie (2001). Albarelli (2001, Part 2) cites the *London Daily Telegraph* of July 1998 for the plan to send a Special Forces agent to infect Hitler's clothing. The grim history of Unit 731 came to light only slowly. Harris (1994), the basic study, describes Ishii's development and testing of anthrax bombs and other methods of delivery (umbrella points, leaflets and feathers), and the deal that Ishii and others made to give information in exchange for avoiding prosecution. The quote from Ishii is in Regis (1999: 110). Endicott and Hagerman (1998), denounced as a biased source, use Chinese and Soviet documents to report the alleged use of Japanese and German biowarfare techniques by the Americans in the Korean War. Morimura's book has not been translated into English, and the Japanese original is difficult to locate even in good collections of his many writings. I finally found it in the University of California Berkeley collection. An American novelist, Bill Warnock, wrote a thriller (*Frozen Secrets*, 1988) which drew upon Morimura's expose. Barenblatt (2001) reports on the Chinese survivors of Ishii's anthrax experiments. Sirisanthana and Brown (2002) relate Ishii's anthrax chocolates to Wouter Basson's and cite Harris (1994) for the statement that Ishii designed the chocolates to be given to children. On August 17, 2002 Tokyo District Court rejected claims for compensation by over 100 Chinese victims of Japanese germ warfare during World War II (*People's Daily Online*). The South African biowarfare program, Project Coast, like the Japanese program, was in the hands of one physician, Dr. Wouter Basson, who worked on a number of delivery methods for a number of different lethal agents. Gould and Burger (2002) provide a systematic review of each session in Basson's long trial. The references to anthrax are in Trial Reports 35 and 36, which contain testimony on the provision of anthrax spores, and Trial Report 63 relates Judge Willie Hartzenberg's April 11, 2002, pronouncement that Basson was not guilty on all counts. Unlike Ishii, Basson was charged, with 47 counts of murder and assault. His acquittal on the remaining counts on April 15, 2002, came after a two-year trial. Croddy (2002: 161–65) describes the development of an anthrax vaccine for humans. Nass (2000) reviews the same more technically without mentioning Cromartie and Watson's work. Harry Smith's team's discovery of anthrax toxin (Smith, Keppie and Stanley 1955) grew out of attempts to find a more convenient way to deliver the lethal essence of the bacillus, as had been done with botulinus. Regis (1999: 138–39) accounts the American turn from anthrax to Brucellosis, and the CIA holdback (203–14). Cole (1990) examines airborne spraying of bacterial simulants (*Serratia marcescens* and others) over American cities by the American military. Saddam Hussein's arsenal was the subject of an extensive report issued by the United Nations inspection team (UNSCOM) in 1999 (Pearson 2000). Carr and Renfrew (1957) describe a study of spores found in the respiratory passages of workers who showed no symptoms of anthrax. Boyer (2001) gives one account of the source of "the Ames strain," beginning his article with the destruction of the University of Iowa-Ames bacteria collection on October 12, 2001. Mangold and Goldberg (1999: 187) report Ken Alibek's statement, which is elaborated in Alibek's own book (2001).The information about the events in Sverdlovsk went through a number of transformations depending upon the purpose of the reporter. Even the name of the city was changed, to Yekaterinburg. Guillemin (1999) intends to give a human face to the anonymizing record, and supersedes the other sources. Nass (1992) makes the case for the political source of the Zimbabwe outbreak. The 1999–2000 anthrax eruptions in Zimbabwe were reported distantly in European and American news media, with a little more emphasis after the October 2001 anthrax episodes in America.

# Chapter 11

Romano (2002) describes Sanderson's learning Chauveau's technique of vaccine making and bringing it back to Britain, and notes his dismay at being marginalized by Pasteur. Wilkinson (1994: 172–75) chronicles the progress of contrasting vaccine approaches, and Greenfield's dismay at being marginalized by Pasteur. Carter (2001) examines Klebs' basic theoretical writings. Koch's views on Klebs' work are expressed continually in his writings, and the comment on the distinct properties of anthrax filtrates is in his 1881 article on the Etiology of Anthrax (Carter 1987: 62–3). Mann (1994: 124–25) views Pasteur's antibiosis and Sanderson's observations on mold-inhibiting bacteria as forerunners of antibiotics. Grison (1995) probes the secrets of Pasteur's development of the anthrax vaccine as revealed by his laboratory notebooks. Pasteur's attempt to prevent rabies with anthrax is noted with a footnote to Pasteur's notebooks in Grison (1995:188). Diachenko (1984) marks the 100th anniversary of Tsenkovskii's method. The anecdote about Metchnikoff's vaccine efforts is in the biography by his wife, Sonia. Dr. Shakespeare's account of bacteria therapy for anthrax is in Sajous, ed. (1888: 5, 506–10). A revision of this volume published the following year contains the first American publication of Koch's anthrax photographs. Sclavo's career is the subject of a volume celebrating the award of a gold medal by a scientific academy (Associazione 1925). Todd (1992) shows how Pasteur's vaccine was adapted to the Australian environment. Turnbull (1991), a Porton Down anthrax specialist, has written a thorough technical history of anthrax vaccines. Sterne (1939a) wrote his own history of saponin-added vaccine attempts. Sterne's papers (1939a and 1939b) are scattered in South African medical and veterinary journals while his vaccine is much more widely distributed. There is no one treatment of his work. Hambleton, Carman and Melling (1984) is one of the first systematic attempts to compose a vaccine history. Shlyakov and Rubinstein (1994) give an overview of Soviet vaccine development and Shlyakov, Blancou and Rubinstein (1996) summarize vaccine history's three stages: encapsulated spores, unencapsulated spores and subunits.

The Ames strain is the subject of Boyer (2001). Croddy (2002: 261–65) reviews the history of the American vaccine program, including Cromartie and Watson's work at Fort Dietrich, background of which is given by Covert (1993).Young and Collier (2002) provide an update of human vaccine development in the aftermath of October 2001. Becker (1911) tells of attempts to use salvarsan to destroy anthrax bacilli, and experiments with penicillin were reported both in the scientific literature and popular magazines during the 1950s. On the spectrum of antibiotics used to treat and prevent anthrax, see Barlam and Kasper (2001). Bayla (2001) reports on the vaccine developed by the Indian biotech researchers and Scientific American.com (2003) carries the announcement of the "bivalent" vaccine tests.

## Chapter 12

The report of white powder discovery at Latifiyah was carried by the Associated Press in many newspapers on April 4, 2003. The United States Federal Bureau of Investigation (FBI) has among the press releases on its website (www.fbi.gov/pressrel01) photographs of the envelopes and message sheets sent to Senators Daschle and Leahy, to Tom Brokaw and to the editor of *USA Today*. The envelopes and sheets were clearly enclosed in transparent plastic when photographed. Media reports of Cohen's December 16, 1997, executive order to vaccinate all military personnel against anthrax included a photograph of the secretary of defense holding up a yellow and white five-pound bag of sugar. On March 4, 1998, Cohen announced that service people in the Gulf would be the first to receive the vaccinations and on July 10, 2000, he said that the stockpiles of the vaccine were dwindling but the program would progress. He said that he and General Henry Shelton, army chief of staff, had been vaccinated. Randall Katz (2001) examines opposition to the military vaccination program, and there are numerous websites offering evidence of the program's problems. Heemstra (2002) "unmasks the deadly truth about the anthrax vaccine that prompted the Air Force to end his career." The U.S. Department of Defense brochure on the vaccination program answers frequently asked questions about the vaccine, including its role in Gulf War Syndrome. The CDC's *Mortality and Morbidity Weekly Report* for April 28, 2000 (49[16] 31–5), describes the surveillance for adverse events associated with anthrax vaccination, 1998–2000. The Scottish National Liberation Army anthrax bomb threat was reported in *The New York Times* on August 7, 2001. The Kings Cross station anthrax, both threatened and real, was reported by *BBC News*, April 5, 1998. Mikkelson (2001) commented on Ken Alibek's ironing advice. Larry Wayne Harris had been arrested in 1995 for possession of three vials of bubonic plague germs. His career and most recent arrest were reported by McCarthy (1998) and Edwards (1998). The CDC report, Neil Gallagher's statement and the B'nai B'rith hoax are brought together by Leonard Cole (1999). David Emery (2001), on his Urban Legends and Folklore site, reviews Klingerman virus stories.*BBC News*, October 15, 2001 surveys anthrax fears and precautions throughout the world as of that date. *The Times of India*, January 2, 2002 gives an account of the Mumbai post office scare. *BBC News*, October 18, 2001 confirmed that an "ordinary Kenyan" citizen was infected with anthrax from a letter sent from the United States. Siegel, Lefkovits and Shaviv (2001) report that a single Member of the Israeli Kenesset attended a briefing on anthrax amid the scares they describe. The anthrax spores allegedly in Deputy

Chief Minister Bhujbal's mail were reported by *rediff.com*, November 2, 2001, and Bhanumati's fainting spell is in *indiainfo.com*, October 20, 2001. *India Express*, October 1,2001 contains a brief account of the Vizhikkathode village post office scare. Hazou (2001) covers the Cyprus flour-tossing. Crowther (1983) gives a history of anthrax eradication in Cyprus. Pino-Marina (2002) tells of the closure of Friendship Post Office when white powder was found. *Arabic News*, October 23, 2001 is on the Morocco letters, and the threat against Prince William is noted by *Australian Broadcasting Corporation*, August 8, 2001. Talbot (2002) surveys the inexplicable itch of American schoolgirls in the fall of 2001. *Washington Post*, November 29, 2001, reports the Santiago, Chile, letter. Waageener's arrest is in *ABC News*, December 5, 2001. On August 15, 2002, expressing no remorse, he was sentenced to 19 years in prison. The powder spills were recorded in police blotter features and other brief local news in many newspapers around the world. Abrams (2002c) reports on Officer Pickett's joke. Associated Press (2002) is about the Wal-Mart employee's lawsuit and in O'Malley (2001) the deputy is hit with the white crystallized powder when he turns on his car's air vents. ABC Newsonline (2001) notes the Sydney airport white powder scare, Asher (2001) the Kroger grocery scare, and *Las Vegas Review-Journal* (2001), the Red Rock restroom scare. Cole (2002) is an expert assessment of the security impact of the scares, and Klein (2001) is a piece on elite police training that incorporates an anthrax scenario. Hendricks (2002) reports the powder-laced hate mail to San Francisco Bay area Latino leaders. Squatriglia and Stannard (2002) is on Dean Wilber's "threatening card packed with white powder," and Herel (2002) on "the first anthrax scare to hit San Francisco in months." News of the mailing to Al Gore's Nashville office was carried by wire services and Klien (2002) headlines the anthrax scare that closed "part of Marin General Hospital" on September 6, 2002. The Tacoma white powder incident was carried by the Associated Press on April 22, 2003, Rashbaum (2003) reported on the duct sniffing by the National Guard, and Warrick and Mintz (2003) on the South African vial offer. Tiffany (2000) begins with Johannes Kepler's examination of a snowflake and continues to other meteors (material manifestations of extramaterial influences).

# Chapter 13

The medical literature has regularly reported multiple cases of cutaneous and ingestive anthrax from sharing the meat of a single infected animal, for instance from Paraguay (at least 21 cutaneous cases, Harrison et al.,1989) and Korea (78 deaths from ingestive, Oh et al. 2001). Ravi Nessman (2001) quotes Dr. Huyseyin Caksen, an official in the Department of Pediatrics at Turkey's Yuzuncuyil University and a prominent specialist in treatment of anthrax. Salmon (1895) outlines the bacterial dimensions of meat inspection, which led to legislation and a national system in 1906. Thomassin (1780) is a specialized instance of a large literature on the health characteristics of particular places. Blancou (2000) reviews several others on the same subject. Cherkasskiy (1999) describes a Russian national registry of anthrax foci. On the possible role of anthrax in Hernando de Soto's expedition see Galloway (1992). Dragon, Elkins et al. (1999) review the history of anthrax in Canadian bison. Mallery (1893: 589) illustrates

Battiste Good's 1826–27 year of "ate-a-whistle." Williams (1932) speculates on the colonial introduction of anthrax into the Mississippi River Delta. Savitt (1978: 105 fn 56) includes anthrax among the diseases colonial masters treated in their slaves, citing Hanson (1959) and Greene (1965: I,148–49) for the Carter diary entry on watery murrain. Allen (1878: 22) proclaims the disease-free vigor of American soil, looks to the Bible and the Classics for the murrain (491) and refers to the actions the Missouri Legislature was planning to take against "the Texan Cattle Plague" (179). United States Department of Agriculture (1881: 298–310) announces the arrival of charbon into the New World, and (311–19) prints the reports of adventuresome veterinarians sent by the commissioner of agriculture to assist farmers and ranchers with mysteriously dying cattle. Bard (1886) is an early account of anthrax in California; Dinwiddie (1907) is on Arkansas. Milloy (2001) reports on anthrax in old Texas cattle trails, and the *Texas Handbook Online*, contains an entry on Texas Fever (babesosis) by Tamara Haygood which traces the effect of the disease on relations between Texas cattle trailers and their counterparts to the north. Diaries and letters of pioneers on America's mid–nineteenth century westward migrations are being published by the University of Nebraska Press. The diaries kept by "covered wagon women" in the collection edited by Moynihan, Duniway and Holmes (1997) contain a number of references to hollow horn or anthrax (pp. 15,16,197, 313, 316, 317). Stepan Khotovitskii (1831) wrote one of the earliest Russian treatises on the Siberian plague. Terentev (1946) is a pamphlet published after the Second World War on another struggle, that against *Sibirakaia iazva*, and is the source of the 1649 decree (3) as well as much information on suppression. Bakulov (1975) compiles a bibliography on *Siberskaia iazva* from 1859 onward. The history of anthrax in the Primorski region is the subject of a study poster by Turcutyuicov et al. (2003). Bratchikov (1895) is a review of the "Siberian plague" of horses in one specific Russian province over a period of twenty years. The quote from Remizov is from Alex Brown's 1927 (60–61) translation of the novel. Lopez y Lopez (1910) wrote the Uruguayan government pamphlet. Ghossain's Lebanon work is presented in Kalafani et al. (2003). Pala (2002) is on the history and present state of Vozhnorozhdeniye Island. Bryden (1989), on Canada's uneasy wartime relations with Britain and America, includes a portion on the anthrax production program and Grosse Ile. Koch's discussion of Buchner's views is in his 1881 *Etiology of Anthrax* paper (Carter, trans.: 1987: 72–76). Much of the information on microbes and the diseases they cause is from the online version of Baron (2001). Peter Turnbull's chapter on bacilli, has a table (15–1) of 18 different bacilli compared according to 17 attributes and a comparison of mouse, rat and human load tolerances of anthrax spores, bacilli and toxins. Landau (2001) and many others reported on the identification of an anthrax immunity gene in mice. Thomas (2002) reports on Dr. Larry Ford's "other life," his South African connection, and the search for his anthrax cache. Williamson (2003) writes on the Fort Detrick cleanup.

# Bibliography

ABC News.com. 2001. Suspect in Anthrax Hoaxes Caught. December 5.

ABC Newsonline. 2001. Powder proves harmless after Sydney anthrax scare. October 14.

Abrams, Jim. 2002 (April 5). Cop in Anthrax Hoax. www.chl.ca/CNEWSAttack 0204/05_anthrax-ap.html

Albarelli, H.P. 2001. *The Secret History of Anthrax,* Parts 1 and 2, Feds' Involvement in Anthrax Experiments, WorldNet Daily, November 21. www.world-netdaily.com/news/article.asp?ARTICLE_ID=25406

Albrink, W.S. and R.J. Goodlow. 1959. Experimental Inhalation Anthrax in the Chimpanzee, *American Journal of Pathology* 35: 1055–65.

Albrink, W.S., et al. 1960. Human Inhalation Anthrax: A Report of Three Fatal Cases. *American Journal of Pathology* 36: 457–71.

Alibek, Ken (with Stephen Handelman), 1999. *Biohazard: The Chilling Story.* New York: Dell Publishing.

Allen, Lewis F. 1878. *American Cattle: History, Breeding and Management.* New York. Orange Judd Company.

Alvin, Christine. 1998. *Medical Treatment and Care in Nineteenth Century Bradford: An Examination of Voluntary, Statutory and Private Medical Provision in a Nineteenth Century Urban Industrial Community.* Bradford: Bradford University (doctoral thesis).

Andrews, John B. 1917. Anthrax as an Occupational Disease. Washington, D.C.: Government Printing Office.

Arabicnews.com. 2001. Dozen suspect letters in Morocco, all tested anthrax free, official. October 23.

Asher, Ed. 2001. White powder sightings spur anthrax fears. *Houston Chronicle,* October 14.

Associated Press. 1999. FBI Takes Anthrax Hoaxes Seriously. March 5.

Associated Press. 2001. Thousands Infected with Natural Anthrax. November 11.

Associated Press. 2002a. Anthrax Struck N.C. in 1956 Outbreak. January 1.

Associated Press. 2002b. Pentagon Bars Pregnant Women from Taking Anthrax Vaccine. January 18.

Associated Press. 2002c. Wal-Mart Worker in West Palm Beach Sues over Anthrax Prank. March 13.

Associazione Italiana per Igene. 1925. *Medaglia d'oro offerta al Prof. Achille Sclavo nel III Congreso Nazionale dell'Associazione Italiana per Igene tenuto in Sardegna (Cagliari-Sassano) da le 5 al 14 giugno, 1925.*

BBC News. 1998. Anthrax found at rail station. April 5.

BBC News. 2001a. Anthrax fears shake world. October 15.

BBC News. 2001b. Kenya finds anthrax letter. October 18.

Bakulov, Igor Alekseevich. 1975. *Sibirskaia iazva zhivotnykh: ukazatel otechestvennoi literatury za 1883–1972* gg. *v kolichestve 1723 nazvanii.* Moscow: TSNSKhB VASKhNIL.

Bales, Michael E., Andrew L. Dannenberg, Philip S. Brachman, et al. 2002. Epidemiologic Response to Anthrax Outbreaks: Field Investigations, 1950–2001. *Emerging Infectious Diseases* 8, 10: 1163–1174.

Balmer, Brian. 2001. *Britain and Biological Warfare: Expert Advice and Science Policy.* London: Palgrave Macmillan.

Barakat, A.A., E. Sayour and A.A. Fayed. 1976. Investigation of an outbreak of anthrax in camels in the Western Desert. *Journal of the Egyptian Veterinary Medical Association.* 36: 183–86.

Barakat, Lydia A., et al. 2002. Fatal Inhalational Anthrax in a 94-Year-Old Connecticut Woman, *Journal of the American Medical Association* 287: 863–68.

Bard, Cephas.

Barlam, Tamar F. and Dennis L. Kasper. 2001. Antibiotic Treatment and Prevention of Anthrax. In www.harrisonsonline.com.

Baron, Samuel, ed. 2001. *Medical Microbiology.*gsbs.utmb.edu/microbook.

Barth, Fredrik. 1961. *Nomads of South Persia: The Basseri Tribe of the Khamseh Confederacy.* Boston: Little, Brown and Company.

Bartrip, J.W.P. 2002. *The Home Office and the Dangerous Trades: Regulating Occupational Disease in Victorian and Edwardian Britain* (Clio Medica 68). Amsterdam, New York: Rodopi.

Bayla, Pallava. 2001. New Anthrax Vaccine Developed in India. *National Geographic News,* November 6. news.nationalgeographic.com.

Becker, Georg. 1911. Die Bakteriologische Blutünterschung beim Milzbrand der Menschen. *Deutsche Zeitschrift Chirurgie* 112: 265–83 (reprint).

Bell, J.H and T.M. Legge. 1906. Woolsorters Disease, *The System of Medicine by Allbutt and Rolleston,* Vol. 2, pp. 227–57. London: Macmillan.

Ben-Noun, L. 2002. [Characteristics of anthrax: its description and Biblical name-Shehin]. *Harefuah* 141, Spec. No. 4–6, 124 (English abstract in PubMed).

Bernstein, Barton. 1987. Churchill's Secret Biological Weapons. *Bulletin of the Atomic Scientists,* January–February: 49–53.

Bibel, David H. and T.H. Chen. 1976. Diagnosis of Plague: An Analysis of the Yersin-Kitasato Controversy, *Bacteriological Review* 40: 633–51.

Bisher, Jamie. 2003. During World War I, terrorists schemed to use anthrax in the cause of Finnish independence. *Military History* 20: 18–22.

Black-Michaud, Jacob. 1986. *Sheep and Land: The Economics of Power in a Tribal Society.* Cambridge: Cambridge University Press.

Blaisdell, J.D. 1994. The curse of the pharaohs: anthrax in ancient Egypt. *Argos.* 10: 311–14.

Blancou, Jean. 2000. *Histoire de la surveillance et du controle des maladies animales transmissibles.* Paris: Office International des Epizooties.

Bligh, Margaret. 1960. *Dr. Eurich of Bradford.* London: Clarke.

Bos, Alphonse. 1965. *La chirurgie de maitre Henri de Mondeville: traduction contemporain de l'auteur.* New York: Johnson Reprint Corporation.

Brachman, Philip S., A.F. Kaufman, and F.G. Dalldorf 1966. Industrial inhalation anthrax. *Bacteriology Review*; 30: 646–659.

Brachman, P.S., J.S. Pagano, and W.S. Albrink. 1961. Two cases of fatal inhalational anthrax, one associated with sarcoidosis. *New England Journal of Medicine* 265: 203–8.

Brachman, P.S., S.A. Plotkin, et al. 1960. An Epidemic of Inhalational Anthrax: The First in the Twentieth Century, II: Epidemiology. *American Journal of Hygiene* 72: 6–23.

Brackbeck, M.K. 1995. The relationship of acute airway change to chronic (fixed) obstruction, *Thorax* 50: Supp. 1: S16–S21.

Bratchikov, I.L. 1895. Siberskaia iazva loshadei I krupnago rogatago v Viatskoi Gubernii za 20 let, 1876–1895. Moscow: Vyatka.

Briggs, Charles, with Clara Martini-Briggs. 2003. *Stories in the Time of Cholera: Racial Profiling during a Medical Nightmare.* Berkeley: University of California Press.

Broad, William J. 2002. Anthrax expert faces fines for burning infected carcasses. *The New York Times.* March 1: A16.

Broad, William J. and Judith Miller. 1998. How Iraq's Biological Weapons Program Came to Light. *The New York Times,* February 26: A20.

Brock, Thomas D. 1988. *Robert Koch: A Life in Medicine and Bacteriology.* New York: Springer-Verlag.

Brogden, Kim A., et al. eds. 2000. *Virulence Mechanisms of Bacterial Pathogens.* American Society of Microbiology.

Brown, Driver, Briggs and Gesenius, Hebrew Lexicon entry for Dbr. *The KJV Old Testament HebrewLexicon.* http:www.biblestudytools.net/Lexicons/Hebrewheb.cgi?number=1698&version=kjv.

Bryden, Wendy. 1989. *Deadly Allies: Canada's Secret War.* Toronto: McClelland and Stewart.

Budd, William. 1863. Observations on the occurrence of malignant pustule in England: illustrated by numerous fatal cases. *British Medical Journal* 1: 85–87; 110–13; 159–61; 237–41; 316–18.

Budd, William. 1864. Investigations of epidemic and epizootic diseases. *British Medical Journal* 2: 354–57.

Bush, Larry, Barry H. Abrams, Anne Beall and Caroline C. Johnson. 2001. Index Case of Fatal Inhalational Anthrax Due to Bioterrorism in the United States. *New England Journal of Medicine* 345: 1607–10.

Cantor, Norman. 2001. *In the Wake of the Plague: The Black Death and the World it Made.* New York: The Free Press.

Carr, E.A. and R.R. Renfrew. 1957. Recovery of Bacillus anthracis from the nose and throat of apparently healthy workers. *Journal of Infectious Diseases* 100: 169–71.

Carter, K. Codell, trans. 1987. *Essays of Robert Koch.* Greenwich, Connecticut: Greenwood Press.

Carter, K. Codell. 1988. The Koch-Pasteur Dispute on Establishing the Cause of Anthrax. *Bulletin of the History of Medicine* 62, no. 1: 87–95.

_____. 2001. Edwin Kleb's *Grundversuche. Bulletin of the History of Medicine* 75,4: 771–81.

Carus, W. 1998. *Bioterrorism and Biocrimes: The Illicit Use of Biological Agents in the Twentieth Century.* Washington, D.C.: Center for Nonproliferation Research, National Defense University.

Center for Disease Control.1974a. Cutaneous anthrax acquired from imported Haitian drums—Florida. *Mortality and Morbidity Weekly Report* 23: 142, 147.

_____. 1974b. Follow-up on cutaneous anthrax acquired from imported Haitian drums—Florida. *Mortality and Morbidity Weekly Report* 23: 149–50.

_____. 1977. Anthrax contamination of Haitian goatskin products. *Mortality and Morbidity Weekly Report* 26: 31.

_____. 1981. Anthrax contamination of Haitian goatskin products. *Mortality and Morbidity Weekly Report* 30: 338.

Centers for Disease Control and Prevention. 1988. Human Cutaneous Anthrax—North Carolina, 1987. *Epidemiologic Notes and Reports* 37 (26): 413–14.

_____. 2001. CDC Interim Recommendations for Protecting Workers from Exposure to Bacillus anthracis in Work Sites Where Mail Is Handled or Processed *Health Advisory 45* updated.

_____. 2001. Evaluation of *Bacillus anthracis* contamination inside the Brentwood Mail Processing and Distribution Center—District of Columbia, October 2001. *Mortality and Morbidity Weekly Report,* December 21, 50 (50).

_____. 2002. Suspected Cutaneous Anthrax in a Laboratory Worker. *Mortality and Morbidity Weekly Report,* April 5, 51 (13): 279–81.

Chamberland, Charles. 1883. *Le charbon et la vaccination charbonneuese d'apres les travaux recents de M. Pasteur.* Paris: B. Ronel.

Chambon de Montaux, M. (Nicolas). 1781. *Traité de l'anthrax, ou de la pustule maligne.* Neuchatel: chez Bolin.

de Chauliac, Guy. 1971. *The Cyrurgie of Guy de Chauliac, 2 v.* Oxford: Oxford University Press (Early English Text Society).

Cherkasskiy, B.I. 1999. A national register of historic and contemporary anthrax foci. *Journal of Applied Microbiology* 87, 2: 192–95.

Ciannavei, Guy J. 2001. Walpole's Anthrax Epidemic, 1867–1874. [website].

Clarke, I.F. 1992. *Voices Prophesying War: Future Wars 1763–3749.* Oxford: Oxford University Press.

Clifford, John. 1998. Bubonic plague or anthrax or measles. *Derbyshire Miscellany* 15, 2.

Cocteau, Jean. 1999. *La Belle et La Bete: Journal d'un Film.* New York: Editions du Rocher.

Cole, Leonard. 1990. *Clouds of Secrecy: The Army's Germ Warfare Tests Over Populated Areas.* Savage, Maryland: Rowman and Littlefield.

Cole, Leonard. 1997. *The Eleventh Plague: The Politics of Biological and Chemical Warfare.* New York: W.J. Freeman.

Cole, Leonard. 1999. Anthrax hoaxes: hot new hobby? *Bulletin of the Atomic Scientists* 55, 4: 7–13.

Cole, Leonard. 2002. *Antrax Letters.*

Cole, Monica. 1961. *South Africa.* New York: E.P. Dutton.

Collard, Patrick. 1976. *The Development of Microbiology.* Cambridge: Cambridge University Press.

Connolly, Ceci. 2002. Workers Exposed to Anthrax Shun Vaccine. *The Washington Post*, January 8.

Conway, Mini. 1979. *Rise Gonna Rise: A Portrait of Southern Textile Workers*. Garden City, New York: Anchor Press.

Cook, Robin. 1999. *Vector*. New York: G.P. Putnam's Sons.

Covert, N.M. 1993. *Cutting Edge: A History of Fort Detrick, Maryland, 1943–1993*. Fort Detrick, Maryland: Public Affairs Office.

Cox, Craig. 2002. Everyday Anthrax. *Utne Reader* 120 (March–April): 20.

Croddy, Eric, with Clarisa Perez-Armendariz and John Hart. 2002. *Chemical and Biological Warfare: What Every Concerned Citizen Should Know*. New York: Copernicus Books.

Crowell, Benedict. 1919. *America's Munitions 1917–1918*. Washington, D.C.: Government Printing Office.

Crowther, R.W. 1983. Anthrax eradication in Cyprus: an historical survey. *Tropical Animal Health and Production* 15: 103–05.

Cunningham, W. 1975. The control of woolsorters' disease. *Pharmaceutical Historian* 5: 4–5.

Cunningham, W. 1976. The work of two Scottish medical graduates in the control of woolsorters disease. *Medical History* 20: 169–73.

Dalldorf, Frederic, Arnold F. Kaufmann and Philip S. Brachman. 1971. Wool sorters' Disease: An Experimental Model. *Archives of Pathology* 92: 418–426.

Dauphin, Claudine. 1996. Brothels, Baths and Babes: Prostitution in the Byzantine Holy Land. *Classics Ireland* 3.

Davis, D.G. and R.W. Harvey. 1972. Anthrax infection in bone meal from various countries of origin. *Journal of Hygiene* 70 (3): 455–57.

Davis, Mike. 2002. *Dead Cities and Other Tales*. New York: The New Press.

Derry, T.K. and Trevor I. Williams. 1960. *A Short History of Technology*. Oxford: Oxford University Press.

Diachenko, S.S. 1984. (On the 100th anniversary of L.S. Tsenkovskii's development of the method of producing an attenuated vaccine against anthrax.) *Mikrobiologia Zhornal* 46 (6): 43–6.

Dinwiddie, R.R. 1907. Anthrax in Arkansas. *Bulletin of the Arkansas Agricultural Experiment Station*, no. 96.

Dirckx, J.H. 1981. Vergil on anthrax. *American Journal of Dermatopathology* 3: 191–95.

Donn, Robert W. and Jack Hardy. 1931. *Labor and Textiles: A Story of Wool Manufacturing*. New York: International Press.

Dragon, D.C., B.T. Elkins, et al. 1999. A review of anthrax in Canada and implications for research on the disease in northern bison. *Journal of Applied Microbiology* 87 (2): 208–13.

Dull, Peter, et al., 2002. *Bacillus anthracis* Aerosolization Associated with a Contaminated Mail Sorting Machine. *Emerging Infectious Diseases* [online journal], vol. 8, no. 10.

Durand, M. (veterinaire a Orbec). 1846. Memoire sur la maladie epizootique, dite fievre aphtheuse, cocotte, qui regna en Normandie en 1839. *Bulletin des travaux de la Societe d'Emulation de Lisieux* 1.

Echenberg, Myron. 2002. *Black Death, White Medicine: Bubonic Plague and the Politics of Public Health in Colonial Senegal, 1914–1945*. Portsmouth, New Hampshire: Heinemann.

Edwards, Tamala M. 1998. Catching a 48-Hour Bug. *Time* [online periodical], March 2, vol. 151, no. 8.

Emery, David. 2001. Return of the 'Deadly Blue Package,' *Urban Legends and Folklore* [online periodical], October 13.

Enaux, Joseph and Francois Chaussier. 1785. *Methode de traiter les morsures des animaux enrage y de la vipere, suivi d'un precis de la pustule maligne.* Dijon: Defay.

Endicott, Stephen and Edward Hagerman. 1998. *The United States and Biological Warfare: Secrets from the Early Cold War and Korea.* Bloomington: Indiana University Press.

Engels, Friedrich and Karl Marx. 1981. *Selected Letters: The Personal Correspondence.* ed. by Frederick D. Raddatz. Boston: Little, Brown.

Eppinger, H. 1894. *Die Hadernkrankheit* Jena: Gustav Fischer.

Eurich, Fritz. 1912. Anthrax in the woolen industry, with special reference to Bradford. *Proceedings of the Royal Academy of Medicine* 6: 219–33.

Eusebius. 1932. *The Ecclesiastical History,* vol. 2. J.K.A. Oulton, trans. Cambridge: Harvard University Press (Loeb Classical Library).

Evans-Pritchard, E.E. 1969 (1940). *The Nuer: A description of the modes of livelihood and political institutions of a Nilotic people.* New York: Oxford University Press.

Ezzell, J.W., et al. 1985. The genetic basis of Pasteur's attenuation of *Bacillus anthracis.* In: *World's Debt to Pasteur,* ed. by H. Koprowski and S.A. Plotkin. The Wistar Symposium Series, vol. 3, 107–16. New York: Alan R. Liss.

Feldman, Herman. 1937. *Problems in Labor Relations.* London: Macmillan.

Fenn, Elizabeth. 2001. *Pox Americana.* New York: Hill and Wang.

Fine, Jon. 2001. Anthrax Scare Spooks Tabloid Readers. *AdAge.com,* October 9.

Ford, W.W. 1964. *Bacteriology.* New York: Hafner Publishing Company.

Fournier, Jean. 1769. *Observations et experiences sur le Charbon Malin.* Dijon: Defay.

Fox, Leon. 1933. Bacterial Warfare: The Use of Biologic Agents in Warfare. *Military Surgeon* 72: 189–207 (reprinted 1942, 90: 563–79).

Frank, Robert and Denise Wrotnowska, trans. 1968. *The Correspondence of Pasteur and Thuillier concerning Anthrax and Swine Fever.* University, Alabama: University of Alabama Press.

Freese, Barbara. 2003. *Coal: A Human History.* Cambridge, Massachusetts: Perseus Publications.

Fuchs, Conrad Heinrich. 1843. *Phlogosen Entzündungen der Haut.* Leiden: Hazenburg & Co.

Fulton, John F. 1943. *Harvey Cushing-A Biography.* Springfield, Illinois: Charles C. Thomas.

Galloway, Patricia, ed. 1992. *The Hernando de Soto Expedition: History, Historiography and "Discovery" in the Southeast.* Lincoln: University of Nebraska Press.

Garcia del Real, Eduardo. 1908. *Atlas de Bacteriologia.* Madrid: Librería Académica.

Geison, Gerald. 1995. *The Private Science of Louis Pasteur.* Princeton: Princeton University Press.

Geissler, Erhard and John Van Courtland Moon, eds. 1999. *Biological and Toxin Warfare Development and Use from the Middle Ages to 1945* (SIPRI Chemical and Biological Warfare Series No. 18). Stockholm: Stockholm International Peace Research Institute.

Gibbons, William Futhey. 1902. *Those Black Diamond Men: A Tale of the Anthrax Valley.* New York: F.R. Revell.

Gilbert, F. 1796 (an III). *Recherches sur les causes des maladies charbonneuses dans les animaux, leurs caractères, les moyens de les combattre et de prevenir.* Paris: Imprimerie de la Republique.

Gold, Hermann. 1935. Studies on Anthrax: Clinical Report on 10 Human Cases. *Journal of Laboratory Clinical Medicine* 21: 134–52.

Gold, Hermann. 1942. Anthrax: A Review of 60 Cases with a Report on the Therapeutic Use of Sulfonamide Compounds. *Archives of Internal Medicine* 70: 785–821.

Gold, Hermann. 1955. Anthrax: A Report on 117 Cases. *Archives of Internal Medicine* 96: 387–96.

Gottfried, Robert S. 1983. *The Black Death: Natural and Human Disaster in Medieval Europe.* New York: The Free Press.

Gould, Chandre and Marlene Burger. 2002. South African Chemical and Biological Warfare Programme. http://ccrweb.ccr.uct.ac.za/cbw/cbw_index.html.

[Government Printing Office]. 1919. Anthrax and the sterilization of shaving brushes. Washington, D.C.: U.S. Government Printing Office.

Graves, Robert. 1955. *The Greek Myths.* 2 vols. New York: Penguin.

Greene, Jack, ed. 1965. *The Diary of Colonel London Carter of Sabine Hall, 1752–1778.* Charlottesville: University Press of Virginia.

Greener, A.W. 1939. Anthrax in mink (Mustela visonis). *Journal of Hygiene* 39: 149–53.

Guba, James E. and Philander D. Chase. 2002. Anthrax and the President, 1789. *The Papers of George Washington Newsletter* 5 (Spring): 4–6.

Gugliotta, Guy and Gary Matsumoto. 2002. U.S. Anthrax experts say FBI's wrong about letters. *The San Francisco Chronicle,* October 28, A4.

Guillemin, Jeanne. 2001. *Anthrax: Investigation of an Epidemic.* Berkeley: University of California Press.

Hambleton, P., J.A. Carman and J. Melling. 1984. Anthrax: the disease in relation to vaccines. *Vaccine* 2 (2): 125–32.

Hamilton, Alice. 1985. *Exploring the Dangerous Trades: The Autobiography of Alice Hamilton, M.D.* Boston: Northeastern University Press.

Hamilton, Alice and Harriet Hardy. 1974. *Industrial Toxicology.* Acton, Massachusetts: Publishing Sciences Group.

Hansen, Willy and Jean Freney. 2001. *La maladie du charbon: maladie d'hier, arme biologique d'aujourd'hui.* Toulouse: Editions Privat.

Hanson, Robert P. 1959. The earliest account of anthrax in man and animals in North America. *Journal of the American Medical Veterinary Association* 135: 463–65.

Harris, Sheldon. 1994. *Factories of Death: Japanese Biological Warfare 1932–1945 and the American Cover-up.* London.

Harrison, Laura Anne. 2003. Looking At The World Through Ancestor-Eyes. www.hickorygov.com/library/general/Columns/2003/01212003.htm.

Harrison, L.H., et al. 1989. Evaluation of serologic tests for diagnosis of anthrax after an outbreak of cutaneous anthrax in Paraguay. *Journal of Infectious Disease* 160 (4): 706–10.

Haygood, Tamara. 2002. Texas Fever. In *Texas Handbook Online.*

Hazou, Elias. 2001. Flour-tosser in Larnaca sparks anthrax scare. *Cyprus Mail.* October 13.

Heemstra, Thomas S. 2002. *Anthrax: A Deadly Shot in the Dark.* Lexington, Kentucky: Crystal Communications.

Herpin, Jean-Charles. 1836. *Memoire sur une apoplexie charbonneuse de la rate.* Paris: Huzard. 23 pages.

Heuschinger, Karl Friedrich. 1850. *Die Milzbrandkrankheiten der Thiere und des Menschen, Historisch-geographisch-pathologische Unterschungen.* Erlangen: Enke.

Hendricks, Tyche. 2002. Powder-laced hate letters provoke disgust. *San Francisco Chronicle.* March 13: A16.

Herlihy, David. 1997. *The Black Death and the Transformation of the West.* Cambridge: Harvard University Press.

Hopper, Edward. 1999. *The River: A Journey to the Source of HIV and AIDS.* Boston: Little, Brown.

Hort, Greta. 1957. The Plagues of Egypt. *Zeitschrift fur die Altestamentliche Wissenschaft* 69: 84–103 and 1958, 70: 48–59.

Hosack, David. 1812. *A case of anthrax.* New York: C.S. Van Winkle.

Hsu, Spencer. 2002. Hart Reopening Delayed After Discovery in Ceiling, First Tests on Hazmat Suit Are Negative. *The Washington Post,* January 18: A01.

Hudson, Pat. 1986. *The Genesis of Industrial Capital: A Study of the West Riding Wool Textile Industry c. 1750–1850.* Cambridge: Cambridge University Press.

Huxley, Aldous. 1925. *Brave New World.*

Huxley, Elspeth. 1962. *The Mottled Lizard.*

Indiaexpress.com. 2001. Anthrax fear has Kerala villagers running for 'cover.' October 16.

Indiainfo.com. 2001. White powder causes anthrax fear in Orissa village. October 20.

Inglesby, Thomas V. 2001. Anthrax: A Possible Case History. *Emerging Infectious Diseases* 5, 4 (July–August).

International Labour Office. 1908. *Bulletin of the International Labour Office,* vol. 3. London: The Labour Representation Printing and Publishing Company.

Ivanovics, G. 1938. Immunity against anthrax. *Zeitschrift fur Immunitatsforschungen und Experimentale Therapie.* 94: 367–532.

Jacobi, Eduard. 1904. *Portfolio of Dermochromes.* English adaptation by J.J. Pringle. 2 vol. London and New York: Rebman.

James, Michael S. 2001. Wild Anthrax: Rural Areas Have Lived With the Disease for Generations. *ABCNEWS.com,* November 2.

Jones, W.H.S., ed. and trans. 1984. *Hippocrates,* Vol. 1: The Epidemics Books 1 and 3. Cambridge: Harvard University Press.

Juwanna, Jacques. 1999. *Hippocrates,* trans. by M.B. DeBevoise. Baltimore: Johns Hopkins University Press.

Kalafani, Zeina A., et al. 2003. Endemic Gastrointestinal Anthrax in 1960s Lebanon: Clinical Manifestations and Surgical Findings. *Emerging Infectious Diseases* [serial online]. www.cdc.gov/ncidod/EID/vol9no/02-0388.htm

Karthikeyan, Kallaperumal, et al. 2001. Case report. *Indian Pediatrics* 38: 777–79.

Katz, Randall D. 2001. Friendly Fire: The Mandatory Military Anthrax Vaccination Program. *Duke Law Journal* 50: 1835–.

Kaufmann, A.F. 1990. Observations on the occurrence of anthrax as related to soil type and rainfall. *Salisbury Medical Bulletin Supplement* 68: 16–17.

Kaufmann, A.F. and A.L. Dannenberg. 2002. Age as a Risk Factor for Cutaneous Human Anthrax: Evidence from Haiti, 1973–74. *Emerging Infectious Diseases* [serial online]. www.cdc.gov/incidod/EID/vol8no8/020207.htm.

Keim, Paul et al. 2001. Molecular Investigation of the Aum Shinrikyo Anthrax Release in Kameido, Japan. *Journal of Clinical Microbiology* 39: 4566–67.

Klein, Joe. 2002. The Supercop Scenario. *The New Yorker,* March 18: 72.

Kristof, Nicholas. 1995. Japan Confesses Gruesome War Atrocity. *New York Times,* March 17.

Kropotkin, Peter. 1968. *The Conquest of Bread.* New York: Benjamin Blom.

Laessig, Ronald H. 2003. All in the (Public Health) Family. *Wisconsin State Laboratory of Hygiene Results,* Winter: 2.

Laforce, F. Marc. 1978. Woolsorters' Disease in England. *Bulletin of the New York Academy of Medicine,* vol. 54, no. 10 (November): 956–63.

Laforce, F. Marc. 1994. Anthrax. *Clinical Journal of Infectious Disease.* 19: 1009–14.

Lake, Ed. 2002. The Anthrax Cases, Analyzed by Ed Lake. www.anthraxinvestigation.com

Lamanna, Carl and M. Frank Mallette. 1965. *Basic Bacteriology: Its Biological and Chemical Background.* Baltimore: The Williams and Wilkins Company.

Landau, H. 1934. *The Enemy Within.* New York: G.P. Putnam's Sons.

*Las Vegas Review Journal.* 2001. White powder tests negative for anthrax. November 14.

Lascaratos, P. 1997. The "anthrax" of two Byzantine emperors, Constantine V and Leo X. *International Journal of Dermatology* 714–16.

Lawlor, Allison. 2003. Anthrax scare ends for potential plague ship. *The Globe and Mail,* April 29.

Lawrence, J.A., C.M. Foggin, and R.A. Norval. 1980. The effects of war on the control of diseases of livestock in Rhodesia (Zimbabwe). *Veterinary Record* 107:82–85.

Legge, T.M. 1903. Industrial Anthrax, 1899–1903. *Transactions of the Epidemiological Society of London,* n.s. 23: 153–83.

Leggett, William. 1947. *The Story of Wool.* Brooklyn, N.Y.: Chemical Publishing Company.

Lehmann, Karl Bernard and Rudolf Otto Neumann. 1896. *Atlas und Grundriss der Bacteriologie.* 2 vol. Munich: Lehmann.

Leymann, Hermann. 1923. *Anthrax in the Tannery Industry.* Geneva: A. Guary.

Lipson, E. 1953. *A Short History of Wool and Its Manufacture.* London: William Heinemann Ltd.

Littlejohn, LaNora. 1994. The History of Julia Alice (Tamplin) Littlejohn. www.geocities.com/lnlittlej/julia.htm.

Lopez y Lopez, Jesus. 1910. *Tristeza y carbunclo ...* Montevideo: Division de Ganderia.

Lubin, Carol and Anne Winslow. 1990. *Social Justice for Women: The ILO and Women.* Durham, North Carolina: Duke University Press.

McCarthy, John. 1998. Ex-anthrax suspect out of jail. *Las Vegas Review-Journal,* Saturday, March 7.

Macher, A. 2002. An industry-related outbreak of human anthrax, Massachusetts, 1868. *Emerging Infectious Diseases* [online journal] 8, 10: 8.

MacKail, J.W., trans. 1950. *Vergil's Works*. New York: The Modern Library.

Maguire, L.C. 1922. *Vaccine and Serum Therapy in Veterinary Practice*. London: Bailliere, Tindall and Cox.

Majok, Aggrey Ayon and Calvin W. Schwabe. 1996. *Development among Africa's Migratory Pastoralists*. Greenwich, Connecticut: Bergin and Garvey.

Mallery, Garrick. 1893. *Picture-Writing of the American Indians*. [2 volume replica published in New York by Dover Publications].

Manchee, R.J., et al. 1990. Out of Gruinard Island. *Salisbury Medical Bulletin* 68 (special supplement): 17–8.

Mann, John. 1994. *Murder, Magic and Medicine*. Oxford: Oxford University Press.

Marriott, Edward. 2002. *Plague: A Story of Science, Rivalry and the Scourge that Won't Go Away*. New York: Metropolitan Books.

Martel, Henri. 1902. *Recherches experimentales sur la variabilité de Bacillus anthracis*. Paris: Naud.

Marx, Karl. 1934. *The Works of Karl Marx, Vol. XVII: Letters to Dr. Kugelmann*. Moscow: International Press.

Masefield, John. 1940. *Basilissa: A Tale of the Empress Theodora*. London: Macmillan.

Massieu, Manuel Servín. 2000. *Microbiología, Vacunas y El Rezago Científico de México a Partir del Siglo XIX*. Mexico City: Plaza y Valdés.

Metchnikoff, Sonia. 1921. *The Life of Elie Metchnikoff*. Boston: Houghton-Mifflin.

Meyer, Hans. 1925. *Uber den Milzbrand beim Menschen* Inaugural Dissertation, Faculty of Medicine, University of Leipzig.

Mikkelson, Barbara and David P. 2001. Claim: Ironing your mail will kill off any lurking anthrax spores. *Snopes.com*, October 18.

Miller, Judith, Stephen Engelberg and William Broad. 2001. *Germs: Biological Weapons and America's Secret War*. New York: Simon and Schuster.

Milloy, Ross E. 2001. Anthrax Hides Along Cattle Trails of the Old West. *The New York Times*, October 29.

Mina, Bushra, et al. 2002. Fatal Inhalational Anthrax With Unknown Source of Exposure in a 61-Year-Old Woman in New York City. *Journal of the American Medical Association* 287: 858–862.

Mitchell, Richard G. 2002. *Dancing at Armageddon: Survivalism and Chaos in Modern Times*. Chicago: University of Chicago Press.

Mitzmain, M. Bruin. 1914. *Summary of experiments in the transmission of anthrax by biting flies*. Washington, D.C.: Government Printing Office.

Morens, David M. 2002. Epidemic Anthrax in the Eighteenth Century, the Americas. *Emerging Infectious Diseases* [serial online] 8. www.cdc/gov/incidod/EID/vol8no10/2-0173.htm.

Morens, David M. 2003. Characterizing a "new" disease: epizootic and epidemic anthrax, 1769–80. *American Journal of Public Health* 93 (6): 886–93.

Mortimer, Ian and Joseph Melling. 2000. The contest between commerce and trade on the one side, and humanity on the other: British Government policies and the regulation of anthrax infection in the wool textiles industries, 1880–1939. *Textile History* 31: 222–36.

Moynihan, Ruth B., David C. Duniway and Kenneth L. Holmes. 1997. *Covered Wagon Women: Diaries and Letters from the Western Trails, 1850*. Lincoln: University of Nebraska Press.

Nass, Meryl. 1992. Anthrax epizootic in Zimbabwe, 1978–80: Due to deliberate spread? *Physicians for Social Responsibility Quarterly*.

Nass, Meryl. 2000.The Anthrax Vaccination Saga: How Not to Develop a Vaccine Program, paper presented at the International Conference on Vaccination, 2000. www.mercola.com/2000/oct/29/anthrax.htm.

Neale, Arthur F. 1898. Anthrax: a study of national and of state legislation on this subject. *Bulletin/Delaware College Agricultural Experiment Station*, no. 37.

Nessman, Ravi. 2001. Natural anthrax infects thousands around the world every year, www.canoe.ca/Health0111/12_anthrax-ap.html.

Neumann, A.J. 2002. Doc, I'd like to know more about Anthrax. *The Draft Horse Journal* Winter 2001–02. www.drafthorsejournal.com/vetcolumns/winter 01_02/winter01_02.htm.

NewScientist.com. 2001. Wind may explain mystery anthrax cases. <www.newscientist.com/news/news.jsp?id=ns99991697.

[*Newsweek*]. 1939. Infected Shaving Brushes. 13 (February 6): 31.

Nocard, Evariste and Etienne Laclainche. 1903. *Les maladies microbiennes des animaux*. Tome I. Paris: E. Masson et Cie.

Office International des Epizooties. 2000. *Manual of standards for diagnostic tests and vaccines, Part 2, Section 2.2, Chapter 2.2.1, Anthrax*. Paris: Organisation mondiale de la sante animale.

Oh, H.B., et al. 2001. An outbreak of Cutaneous Anthrax in Changnyung, Korea in 2000.

Oliver, Thomas, ed. 1902. *Dangerous trades: the historical, social and legal aspects of occupations as affecting health, by a number of experts*. London: Murray.

O'Malley, Brigid. 2001. Collier deputy hit with blast of white powder after turning on car's air vents. *Naples* (Florida) *Daily News*, October 28.

Pala, Christopher. 2002. Anthrax Island. *The New York Times Magazine*, January 12: 36–39.

Pasteur, Louis. 1861. Animalcules infusoires vivant sans gaz oxygene libre et determinant des fermentation. *Comptes rendus de l'Academie des Sciences* 52: 344–47.

Pasteur, Louis. 1877. *Charbon et septicemie*. Paris: G. Masson.

Pasteur, Louis and Chamberland.

Pattison, Iain. 1990. *A Great British Veterinarian Forgotten: James Beart Simonds, 1810–1904*. London: J.H. Allen and Company.

Pearson, Graham. 2000. *The UNCOM Saga: Chemical and Biological Weapons Non-proliferation*. New York: Palgrave Macmillan.

Pinkerton, Henry. 1939. An outbreak of anthrax infection of minks with infection of a ranch owner. *Journal of the American Medical Association* 112: 1148–49.

Pino-Marina, Christina. 2002. Suspicious Substance Closes NW Post Office. *Washingtonpost.com*. February 14.

Plotkin, S.A., P.S. Brachman, et al. 1960. An Epidemic of Inhalational Anthrax: The First in the Twentieth Century, I: Clinical Observations. *American Journal of Medicine* 29: 992–1001.

Pollender, A. 1855. Mikroskopische und mikrochemische Unterschungen des Milzbrandblutes sowie uber Wesen und Kut des Milzbrandes. *Casper's Vierteljahrschriftliche gerichtliche ofentliche Medezin* 8: 103–14.

Preston, Richard. 2002. *The Demon in the Freezer: A True Story*. New York: Bantam Books.

Raider, Ian. 2000. *Religious Violence in Contemporary Japan: The Case of Aum Shinri Kyo*. Honolulu: The University of Hawai'i Press.

Randall, Adrian. 1991. *Before the Luddites: Custom, Community and Machinery in the English Woolen Industry, 1776–1809.* Cambridge: Cambridge University Press.

Rashbaum, William. 2003. Sniffing New York's Air Ducts for Signs of Terror. *The New York Times,* April 22.

_____. 1808. *Receuil de memoires et observations-pratiques sur l'epizootie.* Lyon: Reymann. rediff.com. 2001. Anthrax spores in Bhujba's mail. November 2.

Reding, Nick. 2001. *The Last Cowboys at the End of the World: The Story of the Gauchos of Patagonia.* New York: Crown Publishers. 104–5 el virus anda,111 hantavirus.

Redmon, Caroline, et al. 1998. Anthrax Sugar Cubes a War Relic. *Nature.*

Regis, Ed. 1999. *The Biology of Doom: The History of America's Secret Germ Warfare Project.* New York: Henry Holt.

Remizov, Alexei. 1927. *The Fifth Pestilence* and *the Tinkling Cymbal and Sounding Bass,* translated with a preface by Alec Brown. London: Wishart and Company.

Reuters. 2001. Prince William Death Threat Reports Dismissed. August 7.

Reynolds, Alice. 1927. *Unwanted.*

Rivetti, Giorgio. 1592. *Trattato sopra il mal delle pettichie, peste e giandussa: & il modo, che si ha da tener per curar le febri pestilentiali & altri simili mali. Con un capitolo de remedi contra il loglio.* Turin: Per Vittorio Benacci.

Romano, Terrie. 2002. *Making Medicine Scientific: John Burdon Sanderson and the Culture of Victorian Science.* Baltimore: Johns Hopkins University Press.

Rosebury, Theodor. 1949. *Peace or Pestilence?*

Rosie, George. 2001. UK planned to wipe out Germany with anthrax. *Sunday Herald,* October 15.

Rosner, David and Gerald Markowitz, eds. 1987. *Dying for Work: Workers' Safety and Health in Twentieth Century America.* Bloomington: Indiana University Press.

Ross, J.M. 1957. The Pathogenesis of Anthrax Following the Administration of Spores by the Respiratory Route. *Journal of Pathology and Bacteriology* 73: 485–95.

Roueché, Berton. 1965. *A Man Named Hoffman, and Other Narratives of Medical Detection.* Boston: Little, Brown.

Rozen, Theodore. 2002. Who is Steven Hatfill? *Prospect* www.prospect.org/webfeatures/2002/06/rozen-1-06-27.html.

Sajous, Charles, ed. 1888. *Annual of the Universal Medical Sciences, vol. V.* Philadelphia: F.A. Davis.

Salmon, D.E. 1895. The Federal Meat Inspection. *Yearbook of Agriculture* 1895: 67–83.

Sargent, William. 2002. *Crab Wars: A Tale of Horseshoe Crabs, Bioterrorism, and Human Health.* Lebanon, New Hampshire: University Press of New England.

Saunders, Leon. 1980. *Veterinary Pathology in Russia, 1860–1930.* Ithaca: Cornell University Press.

Savitt, Todd. 1978. *Medicine and Slavery: The diseases and health of Blacks in antebellum Virginia.* Urbana: University of Illinois Press.

Schmitt, Claire K., Karen C. Meysick and Alison D. O'Brien. 1999. Bacterial Toxins: Friends or Foes? *Emerging Infectious Diseases,* vol. 5, no. 2.

Schneiter, Roy and Robert W. Kolb. 1948. *Heat resistance studies with species of*

*Bacillus anthracis and related aerobic bacilli on hair and bristles.* Washington, D.C.: Federal Security Agency, Public Health Service.

Schwab, Konrad Ludwig. 1844. *Einige Fälle von Anthrax-Vergiftigung bei Schliessung des Schuljahres 1843/44 an der k. Central Veterinär-Schule mitgetheilt.* Munich: M. Pössenbacher.

Schwartz, Maxine. 2003. *When the Cows Turned Mad,* translated by Edward Schneider. Berkeley: University of California Press.

Scientificamerican.com. 2003. New Anthrax Vaccine Protects on Two Fronts. September 2.

Shlyakov, E.N., J. Blancou and E. Rubinstein. 1996. Vaccines against anthrax in animals from Louis Pasteur to our day. *Revue de Science et Technologie* 15 (3): 853–62.

Shlyakov, E.N. and E. Rubinstein. 1994. Human live anthrax vaccine in the former Soviet Union. *Vaccine* 12 (8): 727–30.

Shorter, Edward. 1997. *The History of Psychiatry: From the Era of the Asylum to the Age of Prozac.* New York: John Wiley and Sons.

Sidel, V., H.W. Cohen, and R.M. Gould. 2002. From woolsorters to mail sorters: anthrax past, present and future. *American Journal of Public Health* 92 (5): 705–6.

Siegel, Judy, Etgar Lefkovits and Miriam Shaviv. 2002. Only MK Ruz attends Knesset briefing. *The Jerusalem Post* [online edition], October 22.

Sinclair, Upton. 1906. *The Jungle.*

Sirisanthana, T., et al. 1984. Outbreak of Oral-Oralpharyngeal Anthrax: An Unusual Manner of Human Infection with *Bacillus anthracis. American Journal of Tropical Medicine and Hygiene* 33 (1): 144–50.

Sirisanthana, T. and A.E. Brown. 2002. Anthrax of the Gastrointestinal Tract, *Emerging Infectious Diseases* [online journal] 8 (7).

Slevogt, Johann Adrian, Augustin Heinrich Fasch and Johannes Frischmuth. 1681. *Anthrax pestilens, dissertatione inaugurii explicatus.* Jena: Typus Krebsianus.

Smith, H., J. Keppie and J.L. Stanley. 1955. The Chemical Basis of the Virulence of *Bacillus anthracis. Journal of Experimental Pathology* 36: 460–72.

Smyth, H.F. 1939. *A twenty-year survey of anthrax in the United States.* Pittsburgh, Pennsylvania: American Public Health Association, Industrial Hygiene Section.

Sparks, Brad. 2002. Did Anthrax Plague the Egyptians? *Biblical Archaeology.* http://www.christiananswers.com/abr/redtides.html.

Spear, John. 1880. *Tenth Annual Report of the Local Government Board.* London: H.M. Stationary Office.

Spear, John. 1881. The "woolsorters disease" or anthrax fever. *Transactions of the Epidemiological Society of London* (1875–81) 1: 317–23.

Squatriglia, Chuck and Matthew B. Stannard. 2002. Oaklander accused of anthrax mail threat. *San Francisco Chronicle.*

Sternberg, George. 1893. *Manual of Bacteriology.* New York: William Wood and Company.

Sterne, Max. 1939a. The use of anthrax vaccines from avirulent (unencapsulated) variants of Bacillus anthracis. *Onderstepoort Journal of Veterinary Science Annual Index* 13: 307–12.

_____. 1939b. Immunization of laboratory animals against anthrax. *Journal of the South African Veterinary Medical Association* 13: 53–7.

Stuijt, Adriana. 2001. Anthrax Set to Spread to the West. *NewsMax.com*. Friday, April 27.

Takahashi, H., et al. 2000. The Kameido Incident: Documentation of a Failed Bioterrorist Attack. *4th International Conference on Anthrax Programs and Abstracts Book*, June 10–13. Annapolis, Maryland, 27.

Talbot, Margaret. 2002. Hysteria Hysteria. *The New York Times Magazine*, July 2: 42+.

Tauber, Alfred I. and Leon Chernyak. 1991. *Metchnikoff and the Origins of Immunology: From Metaphor to Theory*. New York: Oxford University Press.

Taylor, J.P., D.C. Dimmit, J.W. Ezzell, and H. Whitford. 1993. Indigenous human cutaneous anthrax in Texas. *Southern Medical Journal* 86 (1): 1–4.

Teleky, Ludwig. 1948. *History of Factory and Mine Hygiene*. New York: Columbia University Press.

Terentev, F.A. 1946. *Sibirskaia iazva zhivotnykh I borba c nei*. Moscow: OGIZ, SOLCOGIZ.

Thayer and Smith, Greek Lexicon Entry for Anthrax, *The KJV New Testament Greek Lexicon*. http://www.biblestudytools.net/Lexicons/Greek/grk.cgi?number =4408&version=kjv

Theodorides, J. 1968. *Un grand medecin et biologiste Casimir-Joseph Davaine*. Oxford: Pergamon Press.

Theves,G. 1996. Le charbon: une maladie des animaux et de l'homme qui se cache dans la terre. *Actes du 13e Congres Benelux d'Histoire des Sciences. In L'homme et la terre*. Luxembourg: J. Massard, 19–40.

Thomas, Jo. 2002. California Doctor's Suicide Leaves Many Troubling Mysteries Unsolved. *The New York Times*, November 3: 18.

Thomassin, Jean Francois. 1780. *Dissertation sur le charbon malin de Bourgogne*. Dijon: A. Benoit.

Thompson, Marilyn W. 2003. *The Killer Strain: Anthrax and a Government Exposed*. New York: HarperCollins.

Thorndike, Lynn. 1958. *A History of Magic and Experimental Science, Vol. VII: The Seventeenth Century*. New York: Columbia University Press.

Tierno, Philip M. 2001. *The Secret Life of Germs: Observations and Lessons from a Microbe Hunter*. New York: Pocket Books.

Tiffany, Daniel. 2000. *Toy Medium: Materialism and Modern Lyric*. Berkeley: University of California Press.

*The Times of India*. 2002. Anthrax scare in Mumbai post office. January 2.

Todd, J.H. 1992. Adaptation to environment: the Pasteur anthrax vaccine in Australia. *Australian Veterinary Journal* 69, 12: 318–21.

Tizard, J.H. 1999. Grease, anthraxgate, and kennel cough: a revisionist history of early veterinary vaccines. *Advances in Veterinary Medicine* 41: 7–24.

Tucker, Jonathan B. 2001. *Scourge: The Once and Future Threat of Smallpox*. New York: Atlantic Monthly Press.

Turcutyuicov, V.B., et al. 2003. Anthrax in Primorskyi Region (Far East of Russia), poster presented at ASM Biodefense Research Meeting, March 11. www.asmbiodefense.org/tueabs.asp

Turnbull, Peter. 1991. Anthrax vaccines: past, present and future. *Vaccine* 9: 533–39.

Twigg, Graham. 1984. *The Black Death: A Biological Reappraisal*. London: Batsford.

_____. 1993. Plague in London: spatial and temporal aspects of mortality. In *Epidemic Disease in London*, ed. by J.A.I. Champion, Center for Metropolitan History Working Papers, 1: 1–17.

United States Department of Agriculture. 1881. *Contagious Diseases of Domesticated Animals*. Washington: Government Printing Office.

Valery-Radot, Rene. 1906. *The Life of Louis Pasteur*. London.

Van Ness, G.B., and C.D. Stein 1956. Soils of the United States favorable for anthrax. *Journal of the American Veterinary Medical Association*. January 1, 1956, 7–9. Van Ness, G.B. 1972. Ecology of anthrax. *Science*,172: 1303–1307.

Wangensteen, Owen and Sarah. 1978. *The Rise of Surgery: From Empirical Craft to Discipline*. Minneapolis: University of Minnesota Press.

Warner, Jack. 1999. Witnesses tell MARTA about man. *Atlanta Journal-Constitution*, February 14.

Warrick, Joby and John Mintz. 2003 (April 19). Vile Vials Live on in South Africa. *The Washington Post* as printed in *The San Francisco Chronicle*, April 20: A16.

Washburn, Henry. 1911. Anthrax, with Special Reference to its Suppression. *United States Department of Agriculture Farmers' Bulletin 439*. Washington, D.C.: Government Printing Office.

Watson, A. and D. Keir. 1994. Information on which to base assessment of risk from environments contaminated with anthrax spores. *Epidemiology of Infectious Disease* 113; 479–90.

Wentworth, William F. 1947. *The Story of Wool*. Brooklyn, New York: Chemical Publishing Company.

Wilkinson, Lise. 1994. *Animals and Disease: An Introduction to Comparative Medicine*. Cambridge: Cambridge University Press.

Williams, N.F. 1932. Anthrax. *Journal of the American Veterinary Medicine Association* 81: 9–25.

Williamson, Elizabeth. 2003. Ft. Detrick Unearths Hazardous Surprises. *The Washington Post*, May 27: B01.

Wilson, J.C., ed. 1910. *Modern Clinical Medicine: Infectious Diseases*. New York: D. Appleton and Company.

Wirtu, G., et al. 1997. Aspects of farmers' knowledge, attitudes and practices of animal health problems in central Ethiopia. In Evelyn Mathias, D.U. Rangnekar and Constance McCorkel, eds. *Ethnoveterinary Medicine: Alternatives for Livestock Development*, Proceedings of an International Conference Held in Pune, India, 4–6 November 1997. www.vetwork.org.uk/pune10.htm

Witcover, J. 1989. *Sabotage at Black Tom: Imperial Germany's Secret War in America, 1914–17*. Chapel Hill, North Carolina: Algonquin Books at Chapel Hill.

Wu, Tien-wei. 2001. A Preliminary Review of Studies of Japanese Biowarfare Unit 731 in the United States [online document].

Young, John T.A. and R. John Collier. 2002. Attacking Anthrax, *Scientific American* 286, 3 (March): 48–59.

# Index

257